THE MOSES LEGACY

THE MOSES LEGACY

In Search of the Origins of God

Graham Phillips

SIDGWICK & JACKSON

In loving memory of Jean Astle

First published 2002 by Sidgwick & Jackson
an imprint of Pan Macmillan Ltd
Pan Macmillan, 20 New Wharf Road, London N1 9RR
Basingstoke and Oxford
Associated companies throughout the world
www.panmacmillan.com

ISBN 0 283 07315 2 (HB)
ISBN 0 283 07350 0 (TPB)

1 3 5 7 9 8 6 4 2

A CIP catalogue record for this book is available from
the British Library.

Typeset by SetSystems Ltd, Saffron Walden, Essex
Printed and bound in Great Britain by
Mackays of Chatham plc, Chatham, Kent

CONTENTS

ACKNOWLEDGEMENTS

The author would like to thank the following people for their invaluable help:

Dr Samuel Colby, John Murrow, Karen Varbles and Robert Mason for agreeing to be interviewed. Translators: Dr David Deissman and Carole Snyder (Hebrew), Sarah Lloyd (ancient Egyptian) and Dr Toby Deler (Latin and French). Andrew Collins, Sally Morgan and Ron Wilson for historical research. Philosopher Deborah Benstead, research scientist Dr Yvan Cartwright and author Storm Constantine for sorting out a variety of problems. Caroline Wise and all at Atlantis for their hospitality. My researchers Louise Simkiss and Kellie Knights who have worked so efficiently. Hazel Orme, Liz Davis, Rafi Romaya and Charlie Mounter for all their hard work. Jodi Russell for her photographs and Graham Russell for his painstaking investigation. Lorraine Evans, whose groundbreaking research at the forefront of modern Egyptology helped inspire this book. Finally, a special thanks to Gordon Wise and Ingrid Connell at Pan Macmillan and Simon Trewin and Sarah Ballard at PFD.

AUTHOR'S NOTE

This book is an historical investigation into the birth of the ancient Israelite religion upon which today's monotheistic faiths are based. It is in no way intended to be a criticism of Judaism, Christianity or of any other modern faith or creed. Neither is it a theological debate concerning any religious practices or the actual existence of God.

Monotheism is arguably the single most influential concept in the history of humanity, but from the historian's perspective its origins in ancient Canaan around 3,500 years ago are still shrouded in mystery. By examining the work of eminent archae-ologists, historians and biblical scholars from various nationalities and persuasions, I have attempted to piece together the evidence for what really happened.

I began this work with no preconceptions and have tried to remain as objective as possible throughout. What I eventually concluded was that the Old Testament may be far closer to the truth than many historians have previously believed, and that biblical episodes which sceptics consider to be little more than myths were in fact a series of remarkable historical events.

Graham Phillips
London, 2001

1 THE ONE GOD

'And there arose not a prophet since in Israel like unto Moses, whom the Lord knew face to face.' (DEUTERONOMY 34:10)

If Moses existed he is arguably history's most influential figure. His words are the foundation of faith for over half the earth's population. The great monotheistic religions of the modern world derived from the holy laws he is said to have revealed to the ancient Israelites. Moses' God became not only the God of Judaism but of Christianity and Islam.

> Hear, O Israel: The Lord our God is one Lord: And thou shalt love the Lord thy God with all thine heart, and with all thy soul, and with all thy might. And these words, which I command thee this day, shall be in thine heart: And thou shalt teach them diligently unto thy children, and shalt talk of them when thou sittest in thine house, and when thou walkest by the way, and when thou liest down, and when thou risest up.

These are the words from the Jewish *Shema*, contained in chapter 6, verses 4 to 7 in the biblical Book of Deuteronomy, still considered Judaism's most important commandment. Christians, too, accept this passage as central to their faith. According to chapter 12, verses 28 to 30 in the New Testament gospel of Mark, when asked what was the most important commandment, Jesus replied:

> The first of all the commandments is, Hear, O Israel; The Lord our God is one Lord: And thou shalt love the Lord thy God with

ll thy heart, and with all thy soul, and with all thy mind, and with all thy strength: this is the first commandment.

The words are echoed in the *Adhán*, the Islamic call to prayer:

God is great. I bear witness that there is no deity but God.

Regardless of how each of these religions and their many different creeds interpret the scriptures, all believe that there is only one God and the acceptance of that fact is the most fundamental principle of their faith. According to the Bible, this commandment was revealed to Moses on Mount Sinai – the Mountain of God – nearly three and a half thousand years ago.

Before the apparent time of Moses there is no evidence that anyone in the world had ever considered worshipping just one god – not even the Israelites. Archaeology has revealed that the early Semites, the nomadic tribes who eventually became the Israelites, had many gods, as demonstrated by the numerous statuettes found in their graves. Even the Bible confirms that there was no such thing as the Israelite religion before Moses. Although God is portrayed as speaking directly to a few of Moses' forebears, such as Abraham and Jacob, there is no reference to the worship or acceptance of God by the Israelites as a whole. Even Moses has no idea who this God is when he first confronts him. According to the Old Testament Book of Exodus, Moses first discovers God on the Mountain of God when he speaks to him from a burning bush:

Now Moses kept the flock of Jethro his father-in-law, the priest of Midian: and he led the flock to the backside of the desert, and came to the Mountain of God, even to Horeb. And the angel of the Lord appeared unto him in a flame of fire out of the midst of a bush: and he looked, and, behold, the bush burned with fire, and the bush was not consumed. And Moses said, I will now turn aside, and see this great sight, why the bush is not burnt. And when the Lord saw that he turned aside to see, God called unto him out of the midst of the bush, and said, Moses, Moses. And he said, Here am I. (EXODUS 3:1–4)

From the biblical perspective this is where, when and how the Israelite religion first came into existence. For centuries after it was only the Israelites, also called the Hebrews, who followed this single-god religion. This God was a unique concept. Not only in that he was a single, universal deity, but that he had no name. Unlike other ancient gods, he was addressed as *Yhwh* or Yahweh, which later translators of the Bible rendered as Jehovah – a word that meant simply 'the Lord'. Acceptance of this same Lord as the only God is central to every modern culture of eastern and western Europe, the Middle East, North and South America, most of Africa and much of Asia. He had been the God of the late Roman Empire, the God of Byzantium, the God of the Arabs, the God of the crusaders, the God of the conquistadors and the God of the Victorian missionaries. Originally, however, he was only the God of the Israelites.

Until around 600 BCE the Israelites had maintained an insular existence along a fertile strip of land that is now the state of Israel, the West Bank and southern Jordan. Called Canaan by the Egyptians and Palestine by the Greeks and Romans, it stood at the crossroads of the great civilizations of Africa, Asia Minor and the Near East. According to the Bible, this had once been the united Hebrew kingdom of Israel, but by the time the area was opened up to the rest of the world only a small, autonomous Hebrew state remained – the kingdom of Judah around the city of Jerusalem. Later called Judea by the Romans, this was to be the kingdom of Herod, the province of Pontius Pilate and the land where Jesus was born and died.

In 597 BCE, Judah was invaded by the Babylonians and thereafter the culture and religion of the inhabitants – the Jews –

gradually became known to the rest of the world. Once the unique, monotheistic religion of the Jews became disseminated, its influence just continued to grow. When Alexander the Great annexed Palestine in 333 BCE many of the Greeks who settled in the area converted to the Hebrew God, and Judaism, as we now know it, began to evolve. Although the word Jew had once referred only to a citizen of Judah, the term was now applied to any convert to the Jewish God. Indeed, by the time of the Roman occupation of Palestine even the Jewish monarchy was Greek. In the first century CE, Christianity developed from Judaism and by the early fourth century it had become the state religion of the Roman Empire. When the Roman Empire collapsed and the new Arab empires arose throughout the Middle East, they, too, continued to venerate the same God.

Today there are so many different sects, denominations and cults following the one God that it is impossible to keep track of them all. The Roman Catholic Church is by far the largest Christian movement with almost a billion Catholics worldwide. The mainstream Protestants boast around 300 million members, which include the Anglicans, Episcopalians, Lutherans, Methodists and Presbyterians, with an additional 30 million Baptists. The Quakers, also known as the Society of Friends, have a world total of around 200,000 members; the Unitarians have a world total of around 500,000 members and the Pentecostals have an estimated 10 million following. Eastern Europe has its own Orthodox Church with over 130 million adherents. Then there are the rapidly growing offshoot Christian movements. The Jehovah's Witnesses have an estimated three million members, the Mormons, or Church of Jesus Christ and the Latterday Saints, have a worldwide membership of around 6 million; Seventh Day Adventist membership is around 200,000 and Christian Science has around 140,000 followers. Of the non-Christian movements, there are around 18 million Jews and well over a billion Moslems.

And all this began with a small nation in Palestine that seems to have been virtually unknown to the world until 597 BCE.

The only history we have of the Hebrews before this time is contained in the Jewish *Tanak* – what Christians call the Old Testament of the Bible. Although it covers the history of the Hebrews for over a millennium before the Babylonian invasion, it does not appear to have been written until around 550 BCE.

The events the Old Testament describes surrounding the inception of the Hebrew religion scarcely sound credible to modern thinking. Going by biblical chronology, it begins somewhere around 1300 BCE. It starts with Moses speaking to God in a burning bush, and is furthered when the Israelites escape bondage in Egypt after being helped by a series of divine plagues. Following the escape, when God divides the waters of the Red Sea, the Israelites are guided through the wilderness by an enormous pillar of fire. They are able to conquer Canaan after the impregnable walls of Jericho miraculously fall down. There follows the age of heroes, such as the mighty Samson, who single-handedly pulls down the Philistine temple of Dagon, and King David, who kills the giant Goliath in single combat. Then, around 1000 BCE, there comes the golden age of Solomon, when the wise king becomes the wealthiest man and Jerusalem the richest city in the world. Finally, there is the age of prophets whose lives are surrounded by wondrous events, such as Elijah, who ascends to heaven in a flaming chariot, and Ezekiel, who is visited by God on a flying throne.

Despite these biblical claims, there is no contemporary record of any of these figures. Neither is there a single contemporary account of any of these miracles. Even the Egyptian records, of which many survive, say nothing of the plagues of Exodus, which apparently included events that could hardly be ignored, such as day turning to night and the Nile turning to blood. Archaeology has excavated nothing in Jerusalem from the supposed time of

Solomon to reveal anything but a relatively low level of culture. As for the surrounding empires, if their records are any indication, they do not seem to have even noticed that Jerusalem was there.

When Moses was apparently revealing the laws of God to the Israelites, the kingdom of Egypt had been in existence for over two thousand years and the pyramids of Giza had been standing for almost as long. Egypt was at the height of its power and the eighteenth-dynasty pharaohs, who included the famous Tutankhamun and the heretic Akhenaten, were on the throne. In Mesopotamia the Babylonian Empire stretched through Iran and Iraq, and the Hittites of Turkey were establishing their own empire throughout Asia Minor. In the Mediterranean the Minoans of Crete had created an empire based on sea power that covered the Aegean. Britain was seeing the building of Stonehenge, and in India Hinduism was established and the hymns of the Rig-Veda were being composed.

By the time Solomon was on the throne, the Egyptian and Hittite empires had collapsed, the Minoans had been overrun by the Mycenaeans from mainland Greece, and the seafaring Phoenicians of Lebanon had taken control of the Mediterranean. By the time of the Babylonian invasion of Judah, the Assyrian Empire had risen and fallen, the Tarquin dynasty had been founded in Rome, and the Hellenic city states had risen to prominence in Greece. The Persian Empire was established in what is now Iran, and the Iron Age Celts had spread throughout much of northern Europe and the British Isles. At the very time the Old Testament seems to have been written Lao-Tse was founding Taoism in China, Zen Buddhism was evolving in Japan and the first oracle of Delphi was installed in Thessaly. If the Bible is to be believed, throughout all this time, and with all these changes going on in the world, the one-God religion of the Hebrews survived and thrived.

Modern thinking is somewhat polarized concerning how this religion really developed. On the one hand there are the fundamentalists, who accept every word of Old Testament account as historical fact, and on the other there are the sceptics, who maintain that it was not until late in their history that the Israelites conceived of monotheism. To the former, it is blasphemous to question the biblical account, and to the latter it is just too preposterous to contemplate. In the middle are the historians, whose consensus tends to be that, although monotheism may have developed well before the Babylonian invasion, the story of how it originated did not take shape until this time. They reason that many of these biblical stories were inspired by the Jews' captivity in Babylon. After Judah was invaded, the Babylonians returned with the majority of Jerusalem's citizens as slaves and it was amongst them, during this so-called Babylonian Exile, that the accounts were compiled. It is argued that the story of Moses and the Exodus was an allegory, perhaps based on the visions of a religious leader concerning how God had long ago delivered his people from bondage and would soon do so again. Likewise, the golden age of Solomon is considered nothing more than a fable of a time of past glory that would one day return. The Jerusalem of Solomon was merely a copy of Babylon, at the time of the Exile the most splendid city in the world. As for the exploits of ancient Israelite heroes and the lives of the prophets, these were little more than folklore such as exists in every ancient culture. Finally, there are the archaeologists, who generally regard the ancient Hebrews as a loose alliance of unsophisticated Bronze Age tribes, fighting for a precarious existence in a no man's land, hemmed in between the mighty empires of the Middle East and Asia Minor.

One thing that is certain is that by the time of the Babylonian invasion in 597 BCE the Jews had a single God known as

Yahweh. The Babylonian king Nebuchadnezzar actually records the destruction of the Jews' chief centre of worship – the Jerusalem Temple. Besides the Old Testament, however, there is little to go on as to how this religion came about. From the historical perspective it is certainly one of the world's greatest enigmas.

At one time I tended to agree with the popular consensus that much of the Old Testament history was little more than mythology. That was until I examined the biblical account of the plagues of the Exodus. In the mid-1990s I was working on my book *Act of God*, which concerned the 3000-year-old mystery of an Egyptian tomb. The period of Egyptian history I was investigating included the period in which the Exodus story seems to have been set. Astonishingly, I discovered that a natural catastrophe had occurred in Egypt around this time that closely matched the plagues of the Exodus as described in the Old Testament.

According to the Old Testament account in the Book of Exodus, when the pharaoh refused Moses' demands to let the Israelite slaves leave Egypt, God punished the Egyptians by a series of what the Bible calls plagues: darkness over the land, the Nile turning to blood, fiery hailstorms, cattle deaths, a plague of boils and infestations of frogs, lice, flies and locusts. To the modern mind it sounds like myth and legend. However, such events might have been the result of a natural catastrophe – a gigantic volcanic eruption.

First of all, there was the plague of darkness. This might have been the result of a massive cloud of fallout ash. One of the largest eruptions in recent years was the Mount St Helen's eruption in Washington state, USA, in 1980. After the eruption the sun was obscured for hours 800 kilometres from the volcano, and after the even larger eruption on the island of Krakatau near Sumatra in 1883 the skies were darkened to a much greater distance – it was actually as dark as night for days on end over a thousand kilometres away. According to Exodus 10:21–23:

> And the Lord said unto Moses, Stretch out thine hand towards heaven, that there may be darkness over the land of Egypt, even darkness that may be felt. And Moses stretched forth his hand towards heaven; and there was thick darkness in all the land of Egypt three days: They saw not one another, neither rose any from his place for three days: but all the children of Israel had light in their dwellings.

If just one of the ten plagues matched the effects of a volcanic eruption it would be interesting enough: the fact is, they all do. In Exodus 9:23–26, we are told that Egypt is afflicted by a terrible fiery hailstorm:

> And Moses stretched forth his rod toward heaven: and the Lord sent thunder and hail, and fire ran along upon the ground; and the Lord rained hail upon the land of Egypt. So there was hail and fire mingled with the hail, very grievous, such as there was none like it in all the land of Egypt since it became a nation. And the hail smote all throughout the land of Egypt, all that was in the field, both man and beast, and brake every tree in the field.

This would be an accurate description of the dreadful ordeal suffered by the people on the Sumatra coast after the eruption of Krakatau – pellet-sized volcanic debris falling like hail; fiery pumice setting fires on the ground and destroying trees and houses; lightning flashing, generated by the tremendous turbulence inside the volcanic cloud. Even after the lesser eruption of Mount St Helen's, volcanic debris fell like hailstones, flattening crops hundreds of kilometres away.

The Exodus account of another of the plagues could easily be a report given by someone living in the states of Washington, Idaho and Montana, over which the volcanic fallout cloud was blown after the 1980 Mount St Helen's eruption:

And it shall become small dust in all the land of Egypt, and shall
be a boil breaking forth with blains upon man, and upon beast . . .
(EXODUS 9:9)

Fine dust causing boils and blains! Hundreds of people were
taken to hospital with skin sores and rashes after the Mount St
Helen's eruption, due to exposure to the acidic fallout ash, and
livestock perished or had to be destroyed, due to prolonged
inhalation of the volcanic dust. According to Exodus 9:6: 'And all
the cattle of Egypt died.'

After the Mount St Helen's eruption, fish also died and were
found floating on the surface of hundreds of kilometres of waterways. The pungent odour of pumice permeated everything, and
water supplies had to be cut off until the impurities could be
filtered from reservoirs. According to Exodus 7:21: 'And the fish
that was in the river died: and the river stank, and the Egyptians
could not drink of the river, and there was blood throughout all
the land of Egypt.'

As well as the grey pumice ash volcanoes blast skywards, many
volcanoes, such as Krakatau, have another, more corrosive toxin
in their bedrock: iron oxide. (This is the same red material that
covers the surface of Mars.) At Krakatau thousands of tonnes of
iron oxide were discharged killing fish for miles around. It would
certainly explain the Exodus reference to the Nile turning to
blood, as iron oxide would turn the river red: 'And all the waters
that were in the river turned to blood'(EXODUS 7:20).

The remaining plagues do not immediately suggest themselves
as having had anything to do with a volcanic eruption – frogs,
flies, lice and locusts. However, they can be linked as closely
with volcanic activity as the fallout cloud itself. Those who have
not suffered the dreadful effects of a volcanic eruption might
imagine that once the eruption has subsided, the dead have been
buried, the injured tended, and the immediate damage repaired,

the survivors can begin the task of putting their lives back together, free from further volcanic horrors. This is often far from true, as the entire ecosystem has been affected. Most forms of life suffer from volcanic devastation but, remarkably, some thrive.

After the blanketing of the countryside with fallout ash, crawling invertebrates and insects in their larval, pupal or egg stage would be safe underground, as would burrowing snakes and rodents; so also would frog-spawn, protected under submerged ledges. Insects have a short life cycle and accordingly reproduce at a frightening rate. After such a cataclysm, therefore, they have plenty of time to establish a head start on their larger predators and competitors. Moreover, compared to bigger animals, they reproduce in vast numbers. Swarming insects are therefore commonly associated with the aftermath of volcanic eruptions. Having survived the calamity, the ash-cover forces them to seek out new habitations and food supplies – and heaven help anyone who gets in the way.

An excellent example is the flesh-crawling aftermath of the Mount Pelée eruption on the island of Martinique in the West Indies in 1902. Volcanic debris covered the nearby port of St Pierre, killing over thirty thousand people, but the horrors did not end there. The survivors endured a terrifying episode when huge swarms of flying ants descended upon the sugar plantations and attacked the workers. As they fled for their lives, the vicious creatures seared their flesh with dreadful acid stings. It was no fluke that the insect assaults had followed the eruption: the creatures had attacked before when Mount Pelée had erupted in 1851. On this occasion they not only drove away workers and devoured entire plantations, they were even reported to have attacked and killed defenceless babies while they were still in their cots. Three types of insect infested Egypt, according to the Exodus account: lice, flies and locusts.

Aaron stretched out his hand with his rod, and smote the dust of the earth, and it became lice in man, and in beast; all the dust of the land became lice throughout all of the land of Egypt. (EXODUS 8:17)

Behold I will send swarms of flies upon thee, and upon thy servants, and upon thy people, and into thy houses: and the houses of the Egyptians shall be full of swarms of flies, and also the ground whereon they are ... And the Lord did so and there came a grievous swarm of flies ... and the land was corrupted by reason of the swarm of flies. (EXODUS 8:21–24)

And the locusts went up over all the land of Egypt, and rested in all the coasts of Egypt: very grievous were they; before them there were no such locusts as they, neither after them shall be such. For they covered the face of the whole earth, so that the land was darkened; and they did eat every herb of the land and all the fruit of the trees which the hail had left: and there remained not any green thing in the trees, or in the herbs of the field, through all the land of Egypt. (EXODUS 10: 14–15)

Frogs are perhaps the most prepared of all the vertebrates for such a cataclysm: like insects, they produce vast numbers of offspring. Each frog lays literally thousands of eggs. Under normal conditions this is a biological necessity, as the tiny tadpoles emerge from the eggs almost completely defenceless. The only chance the species has for survival is in numbers. When frogspawn hatches, the local fish are in for a banquet and only one or two of the tadpoles ever survive to become frogs. However, after the Mount St Helen's eruption the predatory fish were decimated. The tiny would-be frogs, on the other hand, were kept safe inside their spawn. By the time they emerged, the hazardous chemicals had washed away down-river, but the fish had not yet returned. The result was a plague of frogs throughout much of Washington State. In their thousands, they littered the countryside – so many were squashed on the roads that driving conditions were hazardous: they clogged waterways, covered gardens, and infested houses. According to Exodus 8:2–8, this is exactly what happened to the ancient Egyptians:

> Behold, I will smite all thy boarders with frogs. And the river shall bring forth frogs abundantly, which shall come up and come into thine house, and into thy bedchamber, and upon thy bed, and into the house of thy servants, and upon thy people, and into thine ovens, and into thy kneading troughs ... And Aaron stretched out his hand over the waters of Egypt; and the frogs came up, and covered the land of Egypt.

Over the years, various scholars have individually attributed these plagues to different natural phenomena. The darkness might have been due to a particularly violent sandstorm, the hail the result of freak weather conditions. The boils were caused, perhaps, by an epidemic, and the bloodied river by some seismic activity far to the south, near the Nile's source. Swarms of locusts, flies and infestations of lice would not have been uncommon. However, the likelihood of them all happening at the same time seems just too remote. A volcanic eruption, however, would account for them all.

The only real problem with attributing the plagues of Egypt to a volcanic eruption is that they do not appear in Exodus in the order in which they would have occurred after such an event. The darkness and fiery hail would have come first, followed by the sores, the bloodied river, dead cattle and fish, and some time later the frogs and insects. In Exodus blood comes first then fish, frogs, lice, flies, cattle deaths, boils, hail, locusts and darkness. However, Exodus seems to have been written many centuries after the events being described. The account of the plagues might have been handed down orally for many generations and certain details moved around.

When we realize just how similar the plagues of Egypt are to

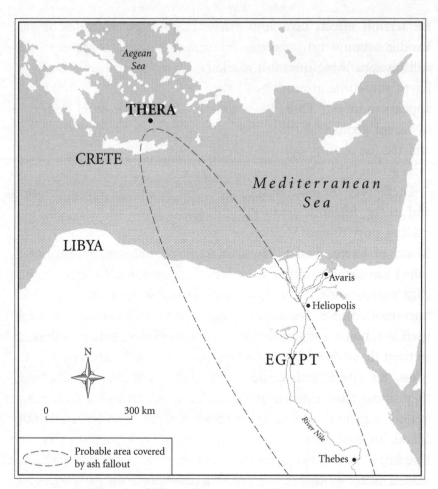

Volcanic fallout from the Thera eruption

the terrible effects of a volcanic eruption, these episodes of the Exodus account no longer seem so implausible. However, there still remains a big question mark. Did a volcanic eruption affect Egypt sometime around 1300 BCE, when the story of the Exodus appears to be set? There have been no known volcanoes in Egypt in recent geological times, but a large enough eruption to have afflicted the country occurred on the Aegean island of Thera some-time around the period in question.

Thera was the southernmost of the Greek Cyclades islands, and in the fifteenth century BCE it had supported an important trading port of the Minoan civilization, centred on the nearby island of Crete. Today Thera is a crescent-shaped island, now called Santorini, forming a bay almost ten kilometres across. The cliffs surrounding it are ribbed with layers of volcanic debris and once-molten rock, testifying to the island's violent past. The bay itself is actually a crater formed by the ancient eruption, and it is so deep that it is said no ship's anchor reaches the bottom. In the 1930s, the Greek archaeologist Spyridon Marinatos was the first to propose that at some point towards the end of the Minoan period a gigantic volcanic eruption had all but destroyed the island. In 1956 two geologists, Dragoslav Ninkovich and Bruce Heezen, of Columbia University, USA, conducted a survey of the seabed to try to determine precisely how large the eruption had been. From their survey ship, the *Vema*, they were able to ascertain the exact size of the volcanic crater – fifty-one square kilometres – and from this, they estimated the incredible magnitude of the event.

There are various types of volcanic eruption: some spew forth rivers of molten lava, others produce searing mud slides, but by far the most devastating is when the pressure of the magma causes the volcano literally to blow its top. Going by the resultant crater size, that is what happened at Thera almost three and a half thousand years ago. It was similar, in fact, to the Mount St

Helen's eruption when the explosion blasted away the mountain-side with the power of a fifty-megatonne bomb.

In an instant, on the morning of 18 May 1980, a mass of searing volcanic material blasted outwards, killing every living thing within 251 square kilometres. Thousands of acres of forest were flattened and molten debris covered everything like the surface of the moon. What had once been a bustling tourist resort over sixteen kilometres from the volcano was covered entirely with pumice. Within a few hours, a cloud of ash some eight kilometres high, containing billions of tonnes of volcanic material, had rolled 800 kilometres east. In three states – Washington, Idaho and Montana – the massive volcanic cloud covered the sky and day was turned to night. Throughout the area ash fell like rain, clogging motor engines, halting trains and blocking roads. Seven million hectares of lush farmland looked like a grey desert, and millions of dollars' worth of crops were flattened and destroyed.

Mount St Helen's was one of the most destructive volcanic eruptions in recent years, yet compared with the explosion of Thera it was tiny. When Ninkovich and Heezen published their findings on the Thera explosion, they used the Krakatau eruption as a comparison. In August 1883 Krakatau exploded with a force twenty times that of Mount Saint Helen's. The eruption was heard over 4800 kilometres away in Melbourne in southern Australia, a volcanic cloud rose eighty kilometres into the air, fallout ash covered thousands of square kilometres. Over thirty-six thousand people perished. It has been estimated by the size of the resultant crater, that nine cubic kilometres of volcanic material blasted skywards from Krakatau – yet Thera's crater is almost six times bigger. Accordingly, the explosion would have been heard half-way around the world, volcanic debris would have been hurled over a hundred kilometres high, and the ash fallout would have covered well over a million square kilometres.

The last nuclear weapon mankind used in warfare was the atom bomb that destroyed half of the Japanese city of Nagasaki in 1945. It was a 20-kilotonne explosion (the equivalent of twenty thousand tonnes of conventional explosives). Mount St Helen's exploded with a far greater force of 50,000 kilotonnes; Krakatau reached an incredible 1 million kilotonnes; yet Thera dwarfs them both with a staggering 6 million kilotonnes. It would take six thousand of the most destructive modern nuclear warheads – each with the power to wipe out an entire city – to equal the explosive magnitude of Thera. It is estimated by adding the mass of the original volcano to the size of the crater that 114 cubic kilometres of debris was ejected skywards. It would have formed a massive fallout cloud that was blown in the direction of Egypt.

The ancient samples of pumice taken from the seabed during the *Vema* survey showed that the fallout cloud was carried on the wind towards Egypt. The Egyptian coast is only 800 kilometres from Thera. Judging by the effects of the smaller Mount St Helen's and Krakatau eruptions at such a distance from the volcanoes, it is fairly certain that Egypt would have suffered the full horrors of the fallout cloud. At the time the Hebrews, or later the Jews, might well have interpreted the event as the divine intervention of God.

Why such an event is not recorded in surviving Egyptian records is something I will return to later. The important point is that the biblical plagues no longer seemed as mythological as they once had, which begged the question: how many more episodes in the Old Testament might have been based on historical events? This is how my current investigation began. As the story of the Exodus plagues no longer seems so fantastic, perhaps the biblical story of the origins of the Hebrew religion warranted serious investigation. I decided to research not only the Bible but also historical records and archaeological discoveries to see if I could find any evidence as to how it really came about. As the concept of the one God has been so influential in the world, and its inception is still an enigma to historians, it seemed to me that this was one of the world's greatest unsolved mysteries. What were the true origins of God?

Summary

- The words of Moses are the foundation of faith for over half the world's population. The great monotheistic religions of the modern world derived from the holy laws he revealed to the Israelites nearly three and a half thousand years ago. Moses' God became not only the God of Judaism but of Christianity and Islam. Regardless of how each of these great religions and their many different creeds interpret the scriptures, all believe that there is only one God and the acceptance of that fact is the most fundamental principle of their faith. According to the Bible, this commandment was revealed to Moses on Mount Sinai – the Mountain of God – over three thousand years ago, and it was his followers, the Hebrews, who alone kept the faith alive before others adopted it over a thousand years later.

- The only history we have of the Hebrews before the sixth century BCE is contained in the Jewish *Tanak* – what Christians call the Old Testament of the Bible. Although it covers the history of the Hebrews for over a millennium, it does not appear to have been written until around 550 BCE. The events the Old Testament describes surrounding the inception of the Hebrew religion scarcely sound credible to modern thinking. Going by biblical chronology, the Hebrew religion begins somewhere around 1300 BCE. It starts with Moses speaking to God in a burning bush, and is furthered when the Israelites escape bondage in Egypt after being helped by a series of divine plagues. Following the escape, when God divides the waters of the Red Sea, the Israelites are guided through the wilderness by an enormous pillar of fire.

• Modern historical thinking is that such stories were inspired by the Jews' captivity in Babylon. After Judah was invaded in the early sixth century BCE, the Babylonians returned with the majority of Jerusalem's citizens as slaves, and it was amongst them, during this so-called Babylonian Exile, that the accounts are thought to have been compiled. The story of Moses and the Exodus, it is proposed, was an allegory, perhaps based on the visions of a religious leader concerning how God had once delivered his people and would do so again. However, there is compelling evidence that one of the most unlikely events in the Old Testament might have taken place: the plagues of the Exodus.

• According to the Exodus account, when the pharaoh refuses to let the Israelites leave Egypt, God punishes the Egyptians by a series of what the Bible calls plagues, including darkness over the land, fiery hailstorms, the Nile turning to blood. Such events may have been the result of a natural catastrophe: the gigantic volcanic eruption on the island of Thera that occurred around the time the story is set. Within a day of the Thera eruption a fallout cloud of volcanic debris would have drifted high over Egypt, the skies would have darkened and pellet-sized volcanic debris fallen like hail. As well as the grey pumice ash the volcano blasted skywards, Thera released iron oxide that would have stained the water of the Nile red.

• One thing that is certain is that by the time of the Babylonian invasion in 597 BCE the Jews had a single God known as Yahweh. The Babylonian king Nebuchadnezzar actually records the destruction of the Jews' chief centre of worship, the

Jerusalem Temple. From the historical perspective it is certainly one of the world's greatest enigmas as to how this religion came about. As the story of the Exodus plagues no longer seems so fantastic, perhaps the biblical story of the origins of the Hebrew religion needs serious investigation.

2 THE HEBREW BIBLE

Before we can begin any investigation into the true origins of the Hebrew religion, we need to answer certain essential questions regarding the primary source for Israelite history: the Hebrew Bible, also known as the Old Testament. In fact, it is the only surviving history of the Israelites to pre-date the Roman Empire. Although it purports to explain the Israelites' origins and to outline their history for a period of well over a thousand years before Roman times, the narrative is also filled with religious annotations that are, by their nature, far from objective. Needless to say, it also contains numerous accounts of miraculous episodes that hardly seem credible to the modern mind. Just how accurate is the Old Testament as an historical text? To begin with: what exactly is the Old Testament and when was it written?

The Bible, coming from the Greek word *biblia*, meaning books, is divided into two sections, the Old and the New Testaments. The New Testament is a purely Christian collection of manuscripts, brought together in one volume during the early fourth century CE when the Roman Empire adopted Christianity as the state religion. It is comprised of four separate accounts of Christ's life and teachings – the gospels of Matthew, Mark, Luke and John – together with an anonymously compiled account concerning the ministry of his disciples: the Acts of the Apostles. These are followed by the letters of St Paul, an early, and arguably the most important, Christian convert, and the brief writings, or epistles, of a number of other Christian leaders of the first century CE. It ends with the Book of Revelation, a transcript of prophetic visions experienced by an enigmatic figure known as St John the Divine sometime during the second half of the first century CE.

For many centuries before the birth of Christ various Hebrew prophets had foretold the coming of a priest-king, a holy warrior called the Messiah who would unify all the Hebrews into a strong new kingdom. Around CE 30, after Jesus's crucifixion, a small Jewish sect, centred on Jerusalem, came to believe that Jesus had been the Messiah. However, this sect differed from others in their interpretation of the nature of the Messiah. Called the Nazarenes by other Jews, they believed that the Messiah would unite Israel, not by war but through a message of love and peace. For them, it was Jesus's teachings concerning God's new Covenant with the Jews that would ultimately unify the Hebrew world. Primarily due to the ministry of St Paul, a new sect sprang from the Nazarenes: non-Jewish Greeks and Romans who came to interpret Jesus's teachings as having relevance for all mankind. Jesus was now called by the Greek term for Messiah, *Kristos*, 'anointed one' – the Christ. Although Christianity sprang from Judaism, it soon became a markedly different religion. Nevertheless, it continued not only to venerate the God of Israel, it helped to preserve the history of the ancient Hebrews and make it known throughout the world. To establish Jesus's place against a religious and historical framework, it was important for the early Christians who collated the Bible to include the Jewish texts they called the Old Testament.

The Old Testament is a Hebrew collection of historical and religious manuscripts that together outline the history of the ancient Israelites, concentrating on their faith and relationship with God. It is comprised of thirty-nine Hebrew texts or scriptures. Although they are now referred to as books, they were originally scrolls that first came together in one collection around 500 BCE. This composite text was known as the *Tanak*, but for convenience' sake it is often referred to as the Hebrew Bible, as opposed to the Christian Bible with its appended New Testament.

The present Old Testament comes from a Greek translation known as the Septuagint, compiled by Greek-speaking Jewish scholars during the third century BCE. The original books of which it is comprised were evidently composed by many different scribes and at different periods of time. No specific dates are given in the narrative, but it begins with the creation of the world and ends with the Persian occupation of Palestine, known from other sources to have occurred during the sixth century BCE.

The New Testament is set in a period when history is comparatively well documented in Greek and Roman works. The Old Testament, however, is set in a time from which far fewer records have survived, almost none from the land of Canaan where the people of Israel made their home. In fact, the Hebrew Bible is the only near-contemporary history of the early Israelites to survive. The reason why so few ancient Hebrew manuscripts now exist to complement the Old Testament is that nearly all were destroyed following two Jewish revolts against Rome.

The Romans generally allowed an occupied nation to continue with their religious practices so long as they paid tribute to the gods of Rome. Elsewhere, this created few problems as the occupied states simply venerated the Roman gods alongside their own. The Greeks, for example, in the city of Ephesus, had a huge cultic centre to the fertility goddess Artemis. The Romans permitted this cult to continue unhindered so long as the Greeks also consecrated the temple to the Roman fertility goddess Diana. The Greeks agreed, and Diana and Artemis were thereafter considered merely different names for the same deity.

All this was alien to Jewish thought. The Jews could live begrudgingly with Roman administration, but Roman gods were heresy. Their God was the only god and had no equivalent elsewhere. During the earlier Greek occupation of Palestine, an attempt to force the Jews to accept Zeus as the Greek equivalent to the God of Israel ended in bloody insurrection. Alexander the Great had annexed Palestine in 333 BCE and for two and a half centuries the Jewish state remained a Greek province. Alexander's successors, the Ptolemy dynasty, who ruled Palestine from Egypt, were tolerant towards Judaism and allowed it to continue unhindered. In fact, many Greeks who moved into the area converted to Judaism and the religion spread throughout much of the eastern Mediterranean. By the second century BCE, all this changed when the Greek Seleucid kings of Syria took control of Palestine.

Fearing the spread of Judaism, in 169 BCE the Seleucid king Antiochus IV, decided to reverse the trend and tried to Hellenize the Jews. Jewish practices were forbidden and scriptures were destroyed. Worst of all, Antiochus plundered the Jerusalem Temple – the Jews' holiest sanctuary – and erected a giant statue of the Greek god Zeus over the high altar. This act of sacrilege so angered the Jews that in 167 BCE Judas Maccabaeus, the son of the high priest, led a mass uprising against Seleucid rule. After a lengthy guerrilla campaign, the Seleucids were forced to reverse their policy and a new, tolerant administration was established in Palestine. The Greeks even established a Jewish dynasty, the Hasmoneans, to rule as client kings.

Aware of the Maccabaean revolt, and fearing a repetition of events, when the Romans annexed Palestine in 63 BCE they not only tolerated Judaism, they even allowed the Sanhedrin, the priesthood of the Jerusalem Temple, to retain considerable political power. They also agreed to the continued rule of the Hasmonean kings. Roman toleration went so far that in 19 BCE they even granted the Jewish king Herod the Great permission to rebuild the dilapidated Jerusalem Temple as one of the grandest structures in the Roman world.

Trouble began shortly after Herod's death, around the time of the birth of Christ. As there was much dispute concerning Herod's successor, the emperor Augustus decreed that Jewish Palestine should be divided into four separate provinces – Galilee, Gaulanitis, Perea and Judea – to be governed individually by Herod's four sons. The old kingdom of Judah around Jerusalem, now called Judea by the Romans, went to Archelaus. In 6 CE, however, when Archelaus proved incompetent, Augustus removed him from office and appointed a Roman governor in his place.

This meant that for the first time since the Maccabaean revolt a Gentile, a non-Jew, was directly ruling the holy city of Jerusalem. This, more than anything else, is why there was such anti-Roman feeling amongst the Jews at the time of Jesus's ministry during the governorship of Pontius Pilate. Rebellion finally erupted during the despotic rule of the emperor Nero in CE 66 and, because of trouble elsewhere in the empire, the rebels held the city of Jerusalem for almost four years. However, after Vespasian became emperor, and Rome had solved its internal troubles, his son Titus was sent to retake the city. This he did with ruthless efficiency, and thousands of innocent men, women and children were butchered in the streets.

In CE 70 Herod's magnificent new temple was reduced to rubble when the Romans looted it of its treasures and burnt it to the ground. The emperor even ordered the entire complex to be demolished stone by stone. The precious temple treasures were carted off to Rome, while countless scrolls containing the official records of Jewish history perished in the flames.

It was another half-century before the Jewish state was finally dissolved. In CE 131 the emperor Hadrian decided to build a pagan shrine on the site of the demolished Jerusalem Temple, and rioting broke out in the streets. It soon became full-scale rebellion, led by a mysterious figure called Simeon Bar Kokhba. It seems that he started off as a minor resistance leader, waging a feckless guerrilla campaign from a base-camp somewhere in the Judean hills. Seizing the opportunity, Bar Kokhba rallied the mob and took control of Jerusalem. So outnumbered were the Roman forces that the governor, Tinus Rufus, had no alternative but to order an evacuation of the city and the Roman forces retreated to Caesarea, some ninety kilometres to the north-west. The Jews once again had control of their ancient capital and, in the euphoria, thousands hailed Bar Kokhba as the Messiah. Even the previously pro-Roman Sanhedrin were caught up in the excitement and officially sanctioned his claim.

The emperor immediately sent a new legion to Palestine, but Bar Kokhba's frenzied rebels wiped them out before they got anywhere near Jerusalem. After this, the emperor played safe and assembled a full-scale invasion force, drawing men and equipment from units stationed as far apart as Syria, Arabia, Mysia and Egypt. Led by the veteran general Julius Severus, this new army progressively reconquered Palestine, destroying whole towns and massacring entire populations as they went. In CE 135 Bar Kokhba was finally surrounded at the fortress of Bethther, some twelve kilometres south-west of Jerusalem and, after a lengthy siege, the Romans breached the walls and slaughtered the surviving defenders, including Bar Kokhba.

After Bar Kokhba's defeat, the recriminations were dreadful: far worse than anything that followed the first revolt. The emperor decided to make an example of the Jews and an estimated half-million lost their lives. It did not stop there, and for years a succession of emperors persecuted the Jews. The ongoing oppression resulted in the virtual annihilation of Jewish Palestine and the dispersal of the Jewish people for almost two millennia. In all, 455 towns were destroyed during the reprisals and along with them virtually all the manuscripts containing the Jews' own accounts of their history. Only a handful of manuscripts has ever been retrieved, such as the Dead Sea Scrolls, which were hidden in caves in the Judean wilderness to the east of Jerusalem following the first revolt. The exception were the books that now make up the Old Testament, which survived as religious texts of Jews outside Palestine and with the Christians. (Although they had suffered under the Roman emperor Nero in the sixth decade of the first century, by the time of the second Jewish revolt the Christians had separated sufficiently from their Jewish origins to escape the persecution of the Jews.) Because so little documented Jewish history survived this Roman holocaust, verifying Old Testament history is a matter of historical detective work.

Jerusalem and its surrounding Jewish state had once been independent of foreign rule. It remained free from foreign occu-pation for some four hundred years until the Babylonians invaded the area around 597 BCE. In turn, when the Persians conquered Babylon in 539 BCE they took control of Jerusalem and after them the Greeks annexed Palestine in 333 BCE. Consequently, from the early sixth century BCE, Jewish history is increasingly recorded in the external records of the Babylonians, Persians, Greeks and Romans. Unfortunately, from these records alone it is impossible to tell the exact nature of Jewish religious belief as it existed prior to this time, or how the Jews saw and interpreted their own history. Certainly by the Greek occupation in 333 BCE the Old Testament as we now know it was in existence. The Greeks not only verify the existence of the Hebrew Bible, they actually translated it into Greek to be housed in the great library of Alexandria in Greek-occupied Egypt. From then on we know that the Jewish religion, as outlined in the Old Testament, had crystallized and that the Jews saw their history as it is now portrayed in the Bible. Ironically, however, reliable Jewish history only begins around the time that the Old Testament leaves off, during the Persian period around 500 BCE.

What about the all-important period when the Israelites still existed as an independent people? Only one complete extra-biblical history of the ancient Hebrews still survives, which predates the second Jewish revolt and the dispersal of the Jews. This was the work of Flavius Josephus, a Jewish historian who wrote a history of his people around the end of the first century CE. He had been a priest in Jerusalem at the time of the first revolt, but survived because he surrendered to the Romans and joined the Roman headquarters as an interpreter. Presumably, as a priest, he had had access to Jewish historical records. His works included *Jewish Antiquities* and *History of the Jewish Wars*, and for the period 175 BCE–CE 74 he is considered of incomparable value, providing a useful historical background to the New Testament. Although his *Jewish Antiquities* provides some interesting extra-biblical commentary for the Old Testament period, Josephus' work was written seven centuries after the end of Jewish independence and cannot on its own be taken as verification of the events outlined in the Hebrew Bible.

The most important question to address concerning the books of the Hebrew Bible is, when and by whom were they written? As many are named after the leading contemporary religious figures, the impression the reader has is that eyewitnesses to the events compiled them over many centuries. Traditionally, the first five books were written by Moses and the rest by a variety of Hebrew scribes and prophets. However, although many of the books of the Old Testament refer to a time many centuries earlier, most biblical scholars now believe that they were not committed to writing in their present form until after the sixth century BCE.

Comparative studies of other contemporary civilizations suggest that many episodes in the Old Testament narrative could not have been written during the period they purport to cover as the text contains anachronisms. In the 1970s, for example, the Egyptologist Professor Donald Redford, of Toronto University, drew attention to numerous Egyptian terms and references found throughout the Old Testament that were not current before the seventh century BCE at the earliest. There are many, for instance, in the story of the patriarch Joseph and his time in Egypt, which the Bible portrays as having been well over a millennium before the Babylonian period – around 1700 BCE. According to Genesis 37:25, Joseph and his brothers encountered a company of Ishmaelite traders, 'who came from Gilead with their camels bearing spicery and balm and myrrh, going to carry it down to Egypt'. The Egyptians depicted every type of animal in their art, but never once showed camels as a means of transport until the seventh century BCE. Like other contemporary works from the Asiatic, they showed asses carrying goods. The oldest literary reference to domesticated camels is by the people of the Arabian Gulf around 850 BCE, and not by Egyptians for another two centuries.

Other Egyptian elements in the story reflect the seventh century BCE at the earliest. For instance, in Genesis 42:16, Joseph uses the oath 'by the life of the pharaoh', which did not exist in that form until the seventh century BCE. Another example is Potiphar, in whose home Joseph becomes a servant. Potiphar only occurs as an Egyptian name at the same late date. Money in the form of coins is referenced repeatedly, although the oldest known form of coinage was that used by the Lydians around 650 BCE.

On linguistic grounds too, many of the Old Testament texts show evidence of having been composed long after the events they portray. None of them could have been committed to writing in their present form until at least the ninth century BCE as before this time there was no written Hebrew. The early Hebrews might have written on Papyrus, as the Egyptians did, or on clay tablets, as did the Babylonians, but they would not have used the Hebrew alphabet as this did not develop until after 1000 BCE. Around this time the Hebrews began to trade

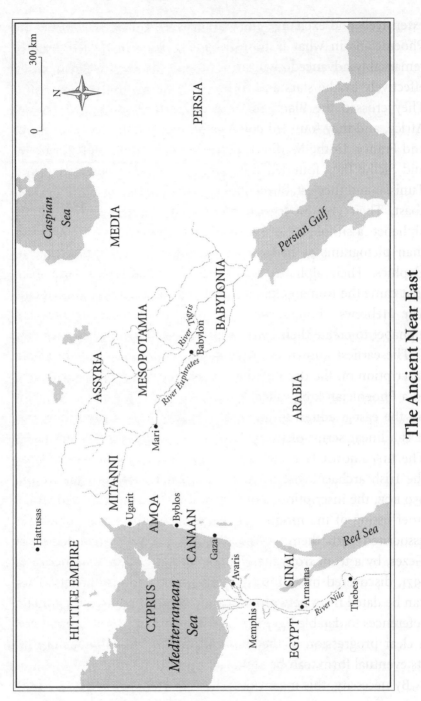

The Ancient Near East

extensively and exchange cultural ideas with their neighbours the Phoenicians in what is now Lebanon. The Phoenicians were a remarkably advanced civilization: they were the first to navigate effectively by the stars and to keep their bearings in open water. They crossed the Black Sea, they were the first to sail around Africa, and they founded colonies on the Atlantic coasts of Spain and France. In the Mediterranean they colonised Cyprus, Rhodes and Sicily; they founded the great port of Carthage in modern Tunisia; and they established a kingdom at Thrace on the Turkish coast. Their greatest legacy, however, was the invention of the alphabet, a simple set of symbols that represented sounds rather than pictograms as had earlier writing such as Egyptian hieroglyphics. Their alphabet was adopted by the Greeks and from that came the Roman alphabet that we still use in the West today. The Hebrews, though, were the first to adopt the Phoenician alphabet to create their own twenty-two-letter alphabet.

The earliest known example of the Phoenician alphabet is an inscription on the decorated lid of a stone sarcophagus belonging to a Phoenician king called Ahiram, found at the ruins of Byblos on the east Mediterranean coast. Dating from around 1000 BCE, it is a linear script of twenty-two letters similar to later Hebrew. The first known Hebrew variant was found at Gezer in 1909 by the Irish archaeologist R. A. S. Macalister. Dating from around 950 BCE, the inscription is on a limestone fragment incised with a brief listing of the months of the year and the agricultural tasks associated with them. A more recent excavation conducted at Gezer, by a team from the Hebrew Union College of America in 1971, discovered more inscribed limestone and clay tablets. They can be dated from between 900 and 800 BCE because they contain references to datable Egyptian and Babylonian events. From these, a clear progression of the Hebrew alphabet, from Phoenician to its eventual form, can be seen.

By necessity, this meant that the entire written language of the

Hebrews developed to accommodate these changes. Written mnemonic forms occurred that linguist Dr David Benedek, of the Hebrew University in Jerusalem, sees as evidence of a late composition of the Old Testament texts. In 1982 he proposed that many verses in various books of the Old Testament would make no sense if written in the earlier form of the Hebrew alphabet as it existed prior to 800 BCE. Moreover, he argued that the texts could not have been written until after the Assyrians occupied Palestine around 725 BCE.

Although the Assyrians allowed a Jewish king to remain in office in Jerusalem, he was a puppet and the country was subject to considerable Assyrian influence. The lasting legacy, even after the Assyrians left around a century later, was the development of a hybrid Hebrew-Assyrian language. In much the same way as Middle English developed from Saxon and French after the Norman Conquest of 1066, so a new form of spoken Hebrew developed in Palestine, known as Mishnaic Hebrew. Dr Benedek drew attention to many passages in the Old Testament that only flowed lyrically, or even made sense, if they had been written in Mishnaic Hebrew. In English literature an example of Dr Benedek's logic could be applied, for instance, to Wordsworth's famous line, 'I wandered lonely as a cloud'. If its date was unknown, a linguist could tell that it was written after the Middle Ages because otherwise Wordsworth's poetic use of the word 'wandered' would have been meaningless. In Wordsworth's day, as today, the word meant both 'to drift', as does a cloud, as well as 'to walk aimlessly', as the poet is doing. In Middle English 'wander' meant to walk with a 'wand' – a staff or walking-stick. If the poet had written before the development of modern English he would not have chosen such a word to compare his own meanderings with the motions of a cloud. A typical example cited by Dr Benedek is the word *beth*, which in Mishnaic Hebrew means both a house and a family. It is used to describe a building, such as *beth-el*, the house of God, and a family, such as *beth-Yudah*, the family (or descendants) of Judah. In earlier archaic Hebrew two different words were used: the word for house was *bayi*, the word for family was *mispeth*. Terms such as 'the house of David', which the Old Testament often uses when referring to David's descendants, would have been meaningless unless the text was committed to its present form after the late eighth century BCE.

Some elements in the Old Testament narrative, such as the early Genesis story, were almost certainly interpolated into the Old Testament during an even later period, following the Babylonian occupation. There are mythological elements in the Genesis story that were clearly taken from Babylonian sources.

Founded around 2000 BCE, Babylon – eighty-eight kilometres south of Baghdad – was one of the greatest cities of the ancient world. It was the capital of Babylonia, in what is now Iraq. During the seventh century BCE Babylonia was annexed by its northern neighbour Assyria, although it rose to prominence again after 640 BCE when the Assyrian Empire collapsed. From both the biblical account and Babylon's own records, we know that in the year 587 the Babylonian king Nebuchadnezzar sacked Jerusalem and returned with many thousands of Jews in chains. For the next half-century many endured slavery in Babylon – a period to which Jews refer as the Babylonian Exile. Nevertheless, the Jews in captivity continued to practise their religion, under the guidance of such prophets as Ezekiel. Eventually, around 539 BCE, the Babylonian Empire was conquered by the Persians and their king, Cyrus II, allowed the Hebrews to return to Jerusalem. Here, Cyrus appointed a Jewish king, Sheshbazzar, to rule as governor on his behalf, and allowed the Jews to rebuild the Jerusalem Temple. It was during the Babylonian Exile that Babylonian mythology appears to have influenced the Jews, who incorporated it into their own account of the world's beginnings, found in Genesis, the first Book of the Old Testament.

Much of what is known of Babylonian mythology comes from discoveries made during archaeological excavations of the Assyrian city of Nimrud, some thirty kilometres south of Mosul in northern Iraq. In 1845, the British archaeologist Sir Austen Henry Layard excavated the ruins of the royal palace built for the king Ashurnasirpal II around 880 BCE. Amongst the treasures discovered were artefacts accumulated from all over the Middle East, including Babylonian tablets dating from the period of the Assyrian occupation of Babylon. Now in the British Museum, in these texts we discover the tale of Dilmun, the mythical garden of delight. Said to be somewhere along the river Euphrates, the Garden of Dilmun was where Babylonians believed that mankind was created. The similarities between the Dilmun epic and the Garden of Eden story found in the Book of Genesis are too similar to be ignored.

In the Genesis account, after God has created the world in seven days, he plants the Garden of Eden and there puts the first man, Adam, and, from one of Adam's ribs, creates the first woman, Eve. In the middle of the garden there are two forbidden trees: the Tree of Life, whose fruit bestows eternal life, and the Tree of Knowledge, whose fruit imparts knowledge of good and evil. God, who appears personally to Adam and Eve, tells them that they can eat any fruit in the garden except from these two trees. However, before long, they are tempted to eat the fruit from the Tree of Knowledge by an evil serpent and, to prevent them also eating the fruit from the Tree of Life, God expels Adam and Eve into the harsh, wide world. We are not told where the Garden of Eden is but, since one of its rivers is called the Euphrates, it seems to have been somewhere in Mesopotamia, around modern Iraq.

In the Babylonian Dilmun story, the first man is also created in a garden paradise beside the Euphrates and, like Eve, the first woman is created from one of his ribs. Although there is no forbidden fruit, the couple are eventually expelled from the garden by the god Marduk after they have disobeyed him. Although it is possible that both stories evolved from an earlier source, the Genesis account itself implies that the ancient Hebrews originally had a different version of the creation of mankind story, and that the Garden of Eden motif was added later. The Genesis narrative contradicts itself. Some verses before he creates Adam and Eve, God has already created man and woman.

> So God created man in his own image, in the image of God created he him; male and female created he them. And God blessed them and said unto them, Be fruitful and multiply, and replenish the earth, and subdue it: and have dominion of the fish of the sea, and over the fowl of the air, and over every living thing that moveth upon the earth. (GENESIS 1: 27–8)

According to Genesis 1:31, this occurred on the sixth day of creation. It is only after he rests on the seventh day that God creates Adam:

> And the Lord God formed man of the dust of the ground, and breathed into his nostrils the breath of life; and man became a living soul. (GENESIS 2:7)

It would seem clear from this that the Babylonian myth of creation has been appended to the account at some later time. Indeed, the entire Adam and Eve story appears to make no sense in the narrative as it now exists. If all mankind were descended from Adam and Eve, as the Garden of Eden story asserts, then where did their son Cain find a wife?

And Cain knew his wife; and she conceived, and bare Enoch: and he builded a city, and called the name of the city, after the name of his son, Enoch. (GENESIS 4:17)

Moreover, where did he find the labour to build an entire city? Surely, in order for any of this to make sense, the former account of mankind's creation was the original Hebrew version and the Garden of Eden story a later interpolation.

The story of Noah's flood also appears to have been taken from Babylonian mythology. In the Genesis account, the entire human race is said to descend from Adam and Eve, and nine generations later Noah is born. By this time God has decided that mankind has become corrupt and wicked and tells Noah that he has decided to cleanse the world. This he will do by means of a great flood – the Deluge – that will cover all the earth. Noah must build a boat, the ark, and fill it with two of every living creature so that they, together with Noah and his family, will be saved. For forty days and nights it rains and the whole world is flooded. Eventually the flood-waters recede enough for the ark to come to rest on top of a mountain. Here, Noah builds an altar to the Lord, and God vows that he will never again do such a terrible thing. As a sign of this promise he creates the rainbow.

An almost identical legend, the Epic of Gilgamesh, survives from ancient Babylon. Dating to around 1600 BCE, it includes the story of Uta-napishtim, a man directed by a god to prepare for the flooding of the world. Uta-napishtim, his family and a variety of animals are saved from the deluge in an ark that eventually comes to rest on a high mountain. Just like Noah, the hero knows that the world will never be flooded again when a rainbow appears in the sky.

Another Genesis story that appears to have originated in Babylon after the mid-seventh century BCE is that of the Tower of Babel. According to the narrative, many generations after

Noah's time his descendants have settled in Shinar, in the land of Babylonia, where they have become great in number. Here, in an attempt to reach heaven, the people decide to build a tower – the Tower of Babel. To prevent its completion, God gives each group of workers a separate language so that they can no longer communicate and scatters them throughout the world to stop them coming together again for such an enterprise.

Babel, meaning Gate of God, was the Hebrew name for the city of Babylon. The Tower of Babel is therefore a tower in Babylon. According to Genesis 11:4, this is how mankind decided to build the tower:

> And they said to one another, Go to, let us build us a city and a tower, whose top may reach unto heaven.

Reference is made to just such a building in Babylon by the Assyrian king Esarhaddron, around 681–665 BCE, when he occupied the city. Esarhaddron was responsible for rebuilding a tower sacred to the god Marduk that had been in ruins for centuries. Directly translated, the name the king gave to the tower was 'the building of the foundation platform of heaven and earth whose top reaches heaven'. It was a series of platforms, each some eighteen metres high by modern reckoning. However, the tower reached only five tiers before being abandoned after a series of accidents attributed to the anger of Marduk. Its similarities to the Tower of Babel are too close to be coincidence – its name, the divine intervention to prevent its completion and its location. All but the most fundamentalist biblical scholars now accept that the story was inspired by this historical event. As it did not occur until Esarhaddron's reign in the seventh century BCE, the account could not have been written before this time.

It is not only the parallels with Babylonian mythology that lead modern scholars to consider that elements in the early Genesis narrative were taken from Babylonian sources. There are also the polytheistic elements: indirect biblical references to the existence of other gods. According to Genesis 3:5, the serpent in the Garden of Eden tells Eve: 'Your eyes shall be open and ye shall be as gods' – plural not singular. There are even divine sons of God as there are sons of the gods in Babylonian mythology. According to Genesis 6:2, just before the time of Noah, 'the sons of God saw the daughters of men that they were fair; and they took them wives'. Even God himself makes reference to other gods. In Genesis 3:22, when he discovers that Adam has eaten the forbidden fruit, we are told: 'And the Lord God said, Behold, the man is become as one of us.'

From such considerations, modern biblical thinking is that much of the early Genesis account was added to Jewish scriptures during or after the Babylonian Exile. This early section of Genesis is concerned with mankind as a whole and is of a markedly different ambience to the rest of the Old Testament. It talks of a time when mankind in general – before the Israelites – had sinned repeatedly against God and that God had punished them repeatedly. Babylonian mythology, and episodes from Babylonian history, would have ideally suited the purpose. According to the Old Testament, Ezekiel, the religious leader of the Jewish exiles in Babylon, saw the captivity of the Jews and the destruction of the Jerusalem Temple as God's punishment for their sins. Ezekiel prophesied that if the exiles renewed their faith in God then they would be returned to Jerusalem and the temple would be rebuilt. When this eventually happened under the Persians, it was seen as a fulfilment of Ezekiel's prophesy and his reforms of Judaism were introduced. In all probability, the reworked Genesis account was also accepted at this time.

From such assorted evidence most modern biblical scholars and historians alike now consider that the books of the Old Testament acquired their present form sometime between 650 and 500 BCE. Nevertheless, it is highly unlikely that the entire Old Testament was composed during this time, only that this was when it was finally committed to the texts as they still survive. There were probably earlier texts and oral accounts from which the books were transcribed. The important point is that the Old Testament is unlikely to be a contemporary record of the earlier Hebrews. As there were certainly religious and probably political reasons for compiling the Hebrew Bible, it is reasonable to assume that alterations to the earlier version of events might have occurred. Considering the miraculous events it portrays, the sceptic can be forgiven for thinking that the entire narrative is no more historical than the mythology of ancient Greece. Was the Ark of the Covenant any more real than the Golden Fleece? Is the might of Samson any more credible than the strength of Hercules? Is the story of the destruction of the walls of Jericho any more believable than the legend of the Trojan horse? To determine just how reliable the books of the Old Testament are as historical texts, and to arrive at a chronology, it is best to work backwards, beginning with the earliest foreign records of any detail against which they may be compared.

Summary

- The Old Testament is a collection of Jewish historical and religious manuscripts, which tell the story of the ancient Hebrews, concentrating on their faith and relationship with God. It is comprised of thirty-nine Hebrew texts that first came together in one collection around 500 BCE. Its narrative is set in a time from which few records still exist. In fact, the Hebrew Bible is the only near-contemporary history of the early Israelites to survive. The reason why so few ancient Hebrew manuscripts now exist to complement the Old Testament is that nearly all were destroyed following two Jewish revolts against Rome that occurred in the late first and early second centuries CE.

- On the face of it, the books of the Old Testament were compiled over a period of many centuries and were derived from day-to-day contemporary records. Traditionally, the first five books were written by Moses himself and the rest by a variety of Hebrew scribes and prophets. However, regardless of who the original authors might have been, many biblical scholars now believe that they were not committed to writing in their present form until the late seventh or early sixth centuries BCE.

- The Old Testament appears to cover a period of many centuries before the seventh century BCE. However, comparative studies of other contemporary civilizations suggest that many of these biblical episodes could not have been written during the period they purport to cover as the text contains anachronisms. Camels, for instance, are described in Egypt during the narrative which is set around the eighteenth century BCE, whereas the oldest literary reference to domesticated camels is by the people of the Arabian Gulf around 850 BCE, and not by Egyptians for another two centuries. Many such anachronisms are found throughout the Old Testament. Money, for instance, in the form of coins, is referenced repeatedly, although the oldest known form of coinage was that used by the Lydians around 650 BCE.

- On linguistic grounds many of the Old Testament texts show evidence of having been composed long after the events they portray. Mishnaic Hebrew, in which most of the texts were written, did not evolve until the eighth century BCE. Although these might have been translations from older texts, written mnemonic forms occur in the narrative that linguist Dr David Benedek, of the Hebrew University in Jerusalem, sees as evidence of late composition of the Old Testament texts. Many verses in various books of the Old Testament would make no sense if written in the form of Hebrew that existed prior to the Assyrian occupation of Palestine around 725 BCE.

- Some elements in the Old Testament narrative, such as the early Genesis story, were almost certainly interpolated into the Old Testament during an even later period, following the Babylonian occupation of the sixth century BCE. There are mythological elements in the Genesis story that were clearly taken from Babylonian sources, such as the Garden of Eden, which is remarkably similar to the Babylonian Garden of Dilmun legend, and Noah's flood, which is almost identical to the Babylonian Epic of Gilgamesh.

3 THE ISRAELITES

The Old Testament history of the Israelites before the Babylonian Exile can be divided into seven distinct periods:

- The Age of the Patriarchs – an ancient time when the Hebrew ancestors were chosen by God.

- The Sojourn in Egypt – when the Israelites were enslaved by the pharaohs.

- The Exodus – when the Israelites left Egypt and wandered in the wilderness for forty years.

- The Conquest of Canaan – when the Israelites first settled in Palestine.

- The Age of Judges – when the Israelites existed in Canaan as twelve separate tribes.

- The Unified Monarchy – when the kingdom of Israel existed as a single state.

- The Divided Monarchy – when the Hebrews existed as two separate kingdoms.

To begin with, what does the Hebrew Bible tell us about the last era, the period of the Divided Monarchy?

The history of the independent Jewish kingship in Palestine is covered by four books of the Old Testament: the first and second Book of Kings and the first and second Book of Chronicles.

According to these texts, for many generations the Hebrews had been divided into two separate kingdoms. In some unspecified period in the past the Hebrews had been united as the kingdom of Israel under two great kings: David and his son Solomon. After Solomon's death there arose a dispute between two rival successors: Solomon's choice, his son Rehoboam, and the religious leader, the prophet Ahijah's choice, the wealthy landowner Jeroboam. Two separate monarchies were thus created. As the majority of the Hebrew people sided with Jeroboam, his kingdom continued to be called Israel, although its previous capital, Jerusalem, was in the hands of Rehoboam and his supporters. Rehoboam's kingdom, centred on Jerusalem, became known as Judah, named after the Hebrew tribe of Judah of which the kingdom was chiefly comprised. Although Israel, with its new capital in the north of the country at Samaria, was by far the largest of the two kingdoms, the fortifications of Jerusalem, coupled with the quarrelsome nature of Israel's tribes, guaranteed Judah's survival as an independent state.

According to the Bible, the Hebrews continued to exist as two separate kingdoms until Israel was conquered by the Assyrians, whose new empire expanded south and west from northern Mesopotamia. According to various passages in Kings and Chronicles, this happened because a state of war existed between Israel and Judah, and the Judean king, Ahaz, appealed to the Assyrians for help. The Assyrian king, Tiglath-pileser III, agreed to assist in return for allegiance from the kingdom of Judah, in effect making the country an Assyrian vassal state. When the Assyrian army moved into his country, Pekah, the king of Israel, was forced to withdraw from besieging Jerusalem, deposed in a mass uprising and replaced by Hoshea, Israel's last king. All that then remained of the country was a small hilly enclave around the capital of Samaria, surrounded on all sides by the Assyrians. Hoshea managed to hang to power for a short while by offering

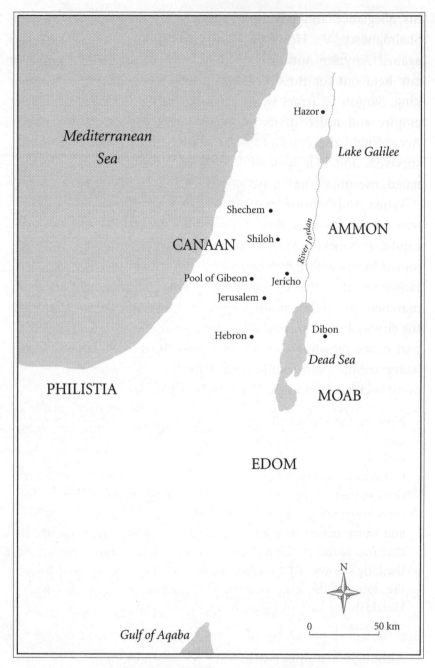

Canaan at the time of David

his allegiance and paying tribute to the new king of Assyria, Shalmaneser V. However, when Hoshea eventually rebelled against Assyrian authority, Samaria was besieged. Although the city held out for three years, it finally fell to the new Assyrian king, Sargon II. Israel was then fully absorbed into the Assyrian empire and much of its population was deported into slavery. Accordingly the country of Israel ceased to exist. Only Judah survived, and it is from this kingdom that the term Jew originated, meaning a native of Judah.

When Ahaz's son Hezekiah became king of Judah the country was under Assyrian domination, controlled from the empire's capital at Nineveh. When King Sargon of Assyria died, Hezekiah joined forces with Egypt in a rebellion against Assyrian authority. However, after the Egyptian army was defeated, the Assyrians marched into Judah and besieged the city of Jerusalem. Although the city walls held and the capital survived, the price for Hezekiah's part in the rebellion was the seizure of much of Judah's land and heavy tribute paid to the new Assyrian king Sennacherib. This event is chronicled in the Old Testament in II Kings 18:13–16:

> Now in the fourteenth year of king Hezekiah did Sennacherib king of Assyria come up against all the fenced cities of Judah, and took them. And Hezekiah king of Judah sent to the king of Assyria to Lachish, saying, I have offended: return from me: that which thou puttest on me will I bear. And the king of Assyria appointed unto Hezekiah the king of Judah three hundred talents of silver and thirty talents of gold. And Hezekiah gave him all the silver that was found in the house of the Lord, and in the treasures of the king's house. At the time did Hezekiah cut off the gold from the doors of the temple of the Lord, and from the pillars which Hezekiah the king of Judah had overlaid, and gave it to the king of Assyria.

Although a number of earlier inscriptions have been found referring to events chronicled in the Old Testament, this is the oldest biblical event to be found in the official court archives of a foreign country. Inscriptions unearthed in the ruins of the Assyrian city of Ninevah, at Mosul in northern Iraq, have confirmed that Judah was a vassal state of Assyria and that Hezekiah and Sennacherib were historical figures. In 1840, before he excavated Nimrud, Sir Austen Henry Layard excavated the ruins of the royal palace beneath a mound now called Nabi Yunus. Here he discovered Sennacherib's own account of his campaign against Hezekiah preserved on a magnificent series of carved wall reliefs that are now on display in the British Museum. It follows the biblical narrative closely:

> As to Hezekiah the Jew, he did not submit to my yoke, I laid siege to 46 of his strong cities, walled forts and to the countless small villages in their vicinity, and conquered them by means of well-stamped ramps, and battering-rams brought near the attack by foot soldiers . . . I drove out 200,150 people, young and old, male and female . . . Hezekiah himself, I made a prisoner in Jerusalem, his royal residence, like a bird in a cage . . . Hezekiah himself did send me, later, to Nineveh, my lordly city, together with 30 talents of gold, 800 talents of silver, precious stones, antiomy, large cuts of red stone, couches inlaid with ivory . . . and all kinds of valuable treasures, his own daughters, concubines and female musicians.

Moreover, the event can be dated. Sennacherib records this siege of Jerusalem in 701 BCE, according to our modern calendar. Furthermore, when this is coupled with the Bible's own chronology of Hezekiah's and his father's reign, it can be determined that the kingdom of Israel had previously been eradicated in 722 BCE.

An even earlier foreign inscription concerning a campaign against the kingdom of Israel comes from the kingdom of Moab, situated to the immediate east of the Dead Sea. It includes reference to a rebellion against Israel by the Moabite king Mesha. Called the Moabite Stone, it was discovered at Dhiban in southern Jordan in 1868 by a Prussian clergyman named F. A. Klein. Found amongst the ruins of the city of Dibon, the capital of ancient Moab, it is a black basalt slab some ninety centimetres high and sixty centimetres wide, and inscribed with thirty-four lines of text in a language similar to Hebrew. Within a few weeks a row broke out over ownership of the artefact and it was smashed by the local Bedouin before it could be removed. Luckily, most of the pieces were recovered and these, along with an impression made before the stone was broken, allowed all but the last line to be reconstructed. The restored stone is now in the Louvre in Paris and a cast of it may be seen in the British Museum. The Moabite Stone proved of immense importance to biblical historians. It not only confirmed an episode in the Bible, previously thought by sceptics to have been fictitious, but it enabled an approximate dating for the foundation of the ancient Israelite monarchy.

According to the Old Testament Jeroboam became the first king of lesser Israel after it divided from Judah, and his reign saw a period of relative stability in the kingdom. However, after his death the country endured a turbulent period beset with coups, counter-coups and civil war that lasted until a strong army commander called Omri seized the throne. By the end of his reign Omri had not only defeated the Syrian army to the north and made peace with Judah he had also moved his army into Moab, subjugating its people. This is confirmed by the inscription on the Moabite Stone:

> I am Mesha, son of [the god] Chemosh, king of Moab ... My father reigned over Moab for thirty years, and I reigned after my father who made this temple for Chemosh in Qarhoh ... As for Omri, king of Israel, he humbled Moab for many years and Chemosh was angry at his land.

According to the second Book of Kings, Omri was succeeded first by his son Ahab, who reigned for twenty years, and eventually by his grandson Jehoram. On Ahab's death, we are told, Mesha rebelled:

And Mesha king of Moab was a sheepmaster, and rendered unto the king of Israel an hundred thousand lambs, and an hundred thousand rams, with the wool. And it came to pass, when Ahab was dead, that the king of Moab rebelled against the king of Israel. (II KINGS 3: 4–5)

Again, the Moabite Stone confirms that just such a rebellion occurred:

And his [Ahab's] son followed him and he also said, 'I will humble Moab' ... But I have triumphed over him and over his house, while Israel has perished.

In the Kings' account Jehoram calls upon the help of his new ally, Jehoshaphat the king of Judah.

And the king Jehoram went out of Samaria the same time, and numbered all Israel. And he went and sent to Jehoshaphat the king of Judah, saying, The king of Moab hath rebelled against me: wilt thou go with me against Moab in battle ... (II KINGS 3:6–7)

The Moabite Stone confirms this too:

And the house of Judah dwelt in Horanaim and Chemosh said to me, 'Go down and fight against Horanaim.' And I went down and fought against the town and took it ...

Although it contains only a short passage relating to a minor event in biblical terms, the Moabite Stone tells us much. It confirms the existence of Omri, one of Israel's most important kings, and shows the extent of the country's influence in the area in pre-Assyrian times. It also confirms the existence of two separate Hebrew kingdoms. Most importantly, it makes dating possible not only for Omri's reign but for the establishment of the Israelite monarchy and the unification of Israel.

The stone appears to have been erected to commemorate the building of the royal palace of Qarhoh at Dibon, about twenty kilometres east of the Dead Sea, where the stone was found:

It was I [Mesha] who built Qarhoh . . . and the wall of the citadel; also I built its gates and I built its towers and I built its palace . . . And I cut beams for Qarhoh with Israelite captives . . .

The site of Dibon was excavated in the early 1950s and again in 1965. During these excavations sections of a city wall and gateway were found, which seem to have been those to which Mesha referred. Recent radiocarbon dating of the timbers of the gate by the British Institute at Amman for Archaeology and History suggests that it was erected sometime in the mid-ninth century BCE. A more precise date can be gained from contemporary inscribed clay tablets unearthed in Babylon by the Scottish archaeologist Robert Cleave of Edinburgh University in 1931. Now in the British Museum, they make reference to the construction of a fort at Dibon in 853 BCE. This presumably occurred immediately after the successful rebellion to prevent the Israelites from retaking the city. Consequently, we have a pivotal date that can be coupled with the Books of Kings own chronology. According to the Old Testament the rebellion took place in the eighteenth year of Jehoshaphat of Judah's reign:

Now Jehoram the son of Ahab began to reign over Israel in Samaria the eighteenth year of Jehoshaphat king of Judah . . . (II KINGS 3:1)

If the stone dating is correct, then Jehosahphat must have come to the throne of Judah in 871 BCE. From this we can determine approximately when the kingdom of Israel was founded. I Kings 22:41 tells us that Jehoshaphat's father Asa ruled immediately before him; I Kings 15:10 tells us that Asa had reigned for forty-one years; and I Kings 15:9 tells us that Asa's reign began in the twentieth year of Jeroboam of Israel's reign. By this reckoning, Solomon's death and the schism of the country occurred in 932 BCE. As I Kings 11:42 says Solomon reigned for forty years and I Kings 2:11 tells us that David reigned for seven years in Jerusalem, then the original kingdom of Israel was established in 979 BCE.

Of even greater importance for any historical investigation into the origins of Hebrew religion and the one God of Israel, the Moabite Stone confirms that Israel was worshipping Yahweh at least as early as the mid-ninth century BCE:

> And Chemosh said to me, 'Go, take Nebo from Israel.' So I went by night and fought against it from the break of dawn until noon, taking it and slaying all, seven thousand men, boys, women, girls and maidservants, for I had devoted them to Chemosh. And I took from there the altar stones of Yahweh, dragging them before Chemosh.

Leaving aside, for the time being, the religious aspects of the Old Testament narrative, such as miracles and prophets communing with God, there seems no serious reason to doubt that the Books of Kings and Chronicles do describe historical events during the period of the divided monarchy. The period immediately preceding the schism, the golden years of the unified monarchy under David and Solomon, however, is more obscure. No contemporary texts or inscriptions outside the Bible make reference to either of these figures. Sceptics see this as detrimental to the case for their historical existence, especially considering that not only is the Hebrew nation being depicted as at the height of its power but that both of these kings are portrayed as influential on the foreign scene.

According to the Old Testament, Saul was the first of the tribal leaders chosen by God to be the king of all the Israelites. However, he failed to hold the kingdom together and his son-in-law

David was chosen to replace him. David eventually became the first king accepted by all of the Hebrews, and after seizing Jerusalem from the Jebusites, made the city his capital and the kingdom of Israel was established. His son Solomon succeeded him and a golden age continued for forty years.

After acquiring great wealth, in the fourth year of his reign Solomon built the first Hebrew temple in Jerusalem. It is described in I Kings 6–7 and II Chronicles 3–4. It was around fifteen metres high, some thirty metres long and ten metres wide; its walls were flanked by columns and its roof was surrounded by gilded spikes. Two towering, free-standing columns stood before the entrance, which itself was flanked by two gigantic golden statues of angels. Inside, there was an outer sanctuary, housing braziers for the animal sacrifices and the high altar, bearing the *menorah*, the golden seven-branched candlestick that symbolized the presence of God. Finally, beyond this, in the innermost sanctuary, the 'holy of holies', rested the Ark of the Covenant. Next to the temple, Solomon constructed two magnificent palaces, one for himself and another for his chief wife, an Egyptian princess (I KINGS 7:1–12). She was just one of seven hundred wives.

The Kings' and Chronicles' accounts portray Solomon as extraordinarily wise and extremely wealthy:

> So king Solomon exceeded all the kings of the earth for riches and for wisdom. And all the earth sought to Solomon, to hear his wisdom, which God had put in his heart. (I KINGS 10:23–24)

This is typified in the story of the Queen of Sheba, who travelled from some distant country with a caravan of camels laden with precious gifts, to satisfy her curiosity about the fabled wealth and wisdom of her fellow monarch (I KINGS 10:1–13). Solomon answered all her 'hard questions' and dazzled her with the splendour of his court. She heaped upon him four and a half tons of gold, spices and sacks of precious stones, and he, not to be outdone, returned the gifts many times over.

Unfortunately, the story of Solomon fails to withstand historical scrutiny. Although the legend of Solomon's vast copper or, in some versions, diamond mines has existed from some indeterminate time, and was popularized in 1886 in Rider Haggard's *King Solomon's Mines*, the Bible does not tell us how Solomon accumulated this vast wealth. The archaeological record shows nothing in Palestine of this period to suggest the wealth attributed to Solomon's court. Indeed, the available archaeological evidence indicates a distinctly low material culture. Everything about Solomon in the Bible sounds wildly exaggerated – his wisdom, his wealth, his wives and his concubines. The same applies to the building of the Jerusalem Temple. It was a relatively small structure, yet it apparently required a workforce of thirty thousand men to hew the timbers, eighty thousand to quarry the stone and seventy thousand to haul them home.

There is not a single contemporary reference to Solomon in the many neighbouring countries that were keeping written records during the tenth century BCE. At the time when the Bible tells us that Solomon created a major empire in the Middle East, none of his contemporaries seem to have noticed it, not even the Phoenicians, with whom he apparently traded, worked closely and forged an alliance. The Egyptian pharaoh was supposedly his father-in-law, yet no Egyptian records of the period, of which many survive, make any reference to him. As for Sheba, whose queen was so impressed by Solomon, there is no historical evidence that the country even existed. Without the biblical accounts, we would be unaware of Solomon's existence.

Only an archaeological excavation of the site of Solomon's temple and his palaces would settle the issue. Unfortunately, the site is now beneath the Dome of the Rock complex. This magnificent mosque is one of the most sacred sites in the Islamic world because it is said to mark the spot where the Prophet Muhammad ascended to heaven. Religious feelings run so high that it is unlikely ever to be excavated – certainly not in the foreseeable future.

If Solomon existed, it is far more likely that his reign, which surviving annals or oral accounts might have portrayed as a brief period of unity and internal stability for Israel, was transmuted by later generations into the royal splendour of the Babylon of the Jewish Exile. Solomon had been the only king of a united Israel to have lived and died a king: his father had spent much of his life in hiding, fighting to bring the country together, and his son lost most of the kingdom the moment he came to power. To the Jews in Babylonian captivity, the age of Solomon probably came to be regarded as the Camelot years for Israel.

Although there is no near-contemporary record to confirm Solomon's father David's existence, his reign, as outlined in the Old Testament, seems more feasible. Indeed, at least two important events concerning it have been supported by archaeological finds. The rise of King David is chronicled in the Hebrew Bible in the Book of Samuel, attributed to the prophet of that name. (In the Christian Bible the Book of Samuel is now two books: the translators of the Septuagint divided it into two parts.) Samuel is portrayed as God's chosen spokesman, who unites the twelve Hebrew tribes. According to the first Book of Samuel, the prophet is instructed to unite the tribes of Israel under one king. First he chooses Saul, who ultimately fails to keep the country together. Samuel then proclaims Saul's son-in-law David king. Saul ignores the prophet and refuses to accept David, even though he has distinguished himself as the people's hero after slaying the Philistine champion Goliath in single combat. Instead, David is forced to flee into the countryside where he raises a guerrilla army. When Saul dies, his son Eshbaal becomes king at the capital of Mahanaim in northern Israel, but the powerful tribe of Judah proclaims David king at the city of Hebron in the south of the country. David's army, led by his commander Joab, march north and meet with the forces of Eshbaal, led by his commander Abner, about half-way between the two capitals. The place where the two armies converge is described as the Pool of Gibeon. At first the two leaders agree to a conference:

> And they met them at the pool of Gibeon; and they sat down, the one on the one side of the pool, and the other on the other side of the pool. (II SAMUEL 2:13)

However, the conference ends in disarray and a battle ensues:

> And there was a very sore battle that day; and Abner was beaten, and the men of Israel, before the servants of David.
> (II SAMUEL 2:17)

Although the war continues for some time, the death of Abner and the defeat of his army ultimately results in the collapse of the Saul dynasty and Eshbaal is murdered by two of his officers. Until the death of Eshbaal, David is accepted as king of all Israel.

The pool of Gibeon is where the fate of Israel is said to have been decided. If the account is true then it is one of the most important military sites in biblical Palestine. From the Samuel description, the Pool of Gibeon was situated where the Arab village of El-Jib now stands, some twelve kilometres north of Jerusalem. However, until the 1950s historians doubted this story, as there was no evidence that the place had ever been called Gibeon, and archaeologists took the same view as geological surveys indicated that there could not have been a pool in the area of sufficient size to be noted as a prominent landmark. When the site was excavated in the 1950s the American archaeologist Dr James Pritchard, of Pennsylvania University, astounded all the sceptics when he uncovered what could well have been described as a pool – a great stone water-shaft sunk into the bedrock, some twelve metres in diameter and eleven metres deep. It was part of an elaborate system to supply water to an adjoining vineyard. It had a spiral stone stairway winding down to the bottom, where a tunnel continued another fifteen metres down to a natural reservoir that lay twenty-seven metres below the surface.

That all this was found at the site was fascinating, but many still doubted that it had ever been called Gibeon. However, a jar handle was soon uncovered, inscribed in Hebrew 'Vineyard of Gibeon'. For an archaeologist to find the name of an ancient site on the site itself is almost too good to be true, and at first Pritchard suspected a hoax. Ultimately, however, no fewer than fifty-six of these jar handles were found, all marked in the same way. The inscriptions were dated to the seventh century BCE, around four hundred years after David's time, but radiocarbon dating carried out in the 1980s on organic deposits found during an excavation of adjacent wine-cellars showed that the site had been in use at least three hundred years earlier. Although it is currently impossible to say for certain that the 'pool' was there at the time the Samuel account says, the discovery adds credence to a previously doubted biblical episode.

David's capture of Jerusalem is another event that was once considered fanciful. According to the account that appears in both the second Book of Samuel and the first Book of Chronicles, when David became king the Jebusite stronghold of Jerusalem still remained, right in the middle of Israelite-held territory. As it was such an easily defended and prosperous city, David was determined to make it the capital of Israel. According to the account, he discovered a secret method of entry into the walled city, through a water-shaft or underground gutter that the Jebusites had dug from inside their city down to a spring outside their walls. David offered a big reward to the first man who could climb up this shaft and lead an attack on the Jebusite defenders from the inside. This, it seems, is how the city was taken (II SAMUEL 5:6–8).

In the Kidron Valley, at the bottom of Ophel Hill in the south-eastern quarter of Jerusalem, a rock-cut passage leads down to small cave containing a fresh-water spring known as the Spring of Gihon. It is also known as the Virgin's Spring: an early Christian legend held that the Virgin Mary washed the swaddling clothes of the infant Jesus there. In 1876, a British engineer, Charles Warren, visited the spring and noticed that in the roof of the cavern above it an opening led up into darkness. As it was large enough for a man to climb into he decided to investigate. An experienced mountaineer and potholer, he returned the next day with climbing tackle and made his way up into the opening. It took him a long time to worm his way up a vertical twelve-metre shaft, in places barely wide enough to squeeze through, but eventually it widened into a sloping passage that ascended a further thirty metres. Finally, he struggled through a narrow crevice that brought him out into daylight. He found himself at the bottom of a five-metre, brick-lined shaft, overgrown and forgotten, half-way up the hill behind the spring.

Immediately, his discovery caused a sensation amongst biblical scholars of the day. Was this the gutter that David's troops had used to capture the city? There could be little doubt that some ancient inhabitants had gone to considerable effort to dig down through solid rock to connect a shaft to the spring waters at the bottom of the hill. However, there was a serious snag to this theory: the walls of ancient Jerusalem were thirty-five metres further up the hillside. The shaft would have been useless to David, it seemed, as it would not have allowed his men entrance to the city.

In 1961 the British archaeologist Kathleen Kenyon was the first properly to excavate the remains of the walls on the crest of the hill and, to her surprise, discovered that they dated only from around 600 BCE and had probably been built in an attempt to defend the city against the Babylonians. Determined to discover the course of the original walls, she dug at various locations on Ophel Hill. At first she discovered the foundations of a wall some twenty metres down the escarpment that had been built around 850 BCE, probably to defend the city against the Syrians. Eventually, thirty metres further down the hill, she unearthed the foundations of a thick city wall that dated from the tenth or eleventh century BCE. She concluded that she had found the line of the eastern wall of the Jebusite city. Incredibly, it was twenty metres below the entrance to the shaft and above the Spring of Gihon. This prompted her to excavate the brick-lined shaft that led down into the gutter passage. It was contemporary, she discovered, with the Jebusite wall.

The fact that there was a means of entering the Jebusite city, just as described in the Samuel account, was fascinating enough, but what made the narrative seem all the more authentic was that the shaft opening would have been outside the city walls after the mid-ninth century. Even if the story had been invented, it must at least have been composed before this time.

Leaving aside the possibly exaggerated reign of Solomon, the Old Testament account of the Hebrews back to the time of King David, around 1000 BCE, seems to fit into a reasonable historical context. But what about the all-important period when the Israelites were said to have first settled Canaan? In the biblical narrative the interval between the Hebrews' first arrival in Palestine and the unification of Israel was the age of the judges, Israelite tribal leaders who fought for ten generations to protect their newly acquired land from incursions by surrounding kingdoms. Preceding the Books of Samuel in the Old Testament is the Book of Judges, named after a series of the judges, such as Gideon, Jephthah and Samson. 'Judges' is a misleading term to modern readers: 'chieftain' would probably be more accurate.

One, Deborah, was even a warrior prophetess who led the Israelites into battle against the Canaanites, the indigenous population of central Palestine. The book covers a period of some ten generations, in which the twelve tribes of Israel fight a precarious existence in Canaan, opposed by a series of surrounding peoples, chief of whom are the Philistines, a seafaring race who had established a powerful kingdom along the Palestinian coast. During this time the Israelite tribes were scattered over a wide area along the length of the river Jordan, although in times of crisis they occasionally joined forces. By modern reckoning, ten generations would be around two hundred years. Is there any evidence of an entrenched Israelite presence in Canaan for two centuries before 1000 BCE?

The oldest contemporary reference to the Hebrews in Canaan comes from an inscribed stone found at the funerary temple of the Egyptian pharaoh Merenptah at Thebes. Now in the Cairo Museum, it has become known as the Israel Stela because it includes the only known mention of Israel in an Egyptian text. In a list of Merenptah's campaigns are included the words: 'Plundered is Canaan with every evil' and 'Israel is laid waste'. Whether this refers to Egyptian military activity or some natural catastrophe, such as an epidemic or famine, is difficult to tell, although we can infer from their inclusion in the list that the pharaoh had sent troops to oppose the Israelites. If the pharaoh saw it necessary to send his army against the Israelites, the Hebrews must have been there in considerable numbers. Moreover, the reference to Israel means that they must have established some kind of kingdom.

The inscription dates the event to the fifth year of Merenptah's reign – around 1200 BCE. This is precisely the time that the period of judges seems to have begun. According to the biblical narrative, immediately before the age of judges the Hebrew chieftains were united behind one military leader, Joshua, which was how they came to conquer Canaan. However, before too long the tribes became divided and the period of judges began. In 1978 Robert Hoffman, Professor of Biblical Studies at the University of Toronto, suggested that Merenptah's campaign might have led directly to the break-up of the Hebrew tribes, after their unifying leader, perhaps Joshua's successor, perished in battle.

On the balance of evidence, the Book of Judges account of this period of Israelite struggle to retain a tenuous foothold in Canaan sits well with what is known of the historical period 1200–1000 BCE. Shortly before this time Canaan was wedged between the mighty empires of Egypt and the Hittites, who had expanded south from Turkey. It had been a sort of demilitarized zone in which dozens of so-called city-states had evolved. Despite their name, these were little more than fortified hillocks from where native chieftains controlled an area of surrounding countryside. Such peoples were the Jebusites, from whom David eventually seized the fortified citadel of Jerusalem. During the period of the Hittite and Egyptian empires these city-states were afforded protection from the surrounding kingdoms, but once these empires fell into decline in the thirteenth century BCE, a power vacuum resulted that the surrounding kingdoms were quick to exploit. The city-states were soon overrun. From the archaeological evidence, it was the Israelites who best exploited the situation, abandoning their nomadic existence and moving in from the Sinai wilderness.

Even after the conquest of Canaan the indigenous inhabitants, the Canaanites, were still something of a threat as can be gleaned from the story of Deborah and her battle against them. As time went on, however, it was the more powerful surrounding kingdoms that posed the greatest threat. To the Israelites' immediate south was the kingdom of Edom, which seems to have been friendly, as the Book of Judges provides no account of Edomite hostility. The other surrounding kingdoms were not so affable.

To the south-west there was Midian, against which the judge Gideon is said to have struggled. To the east was Moab, from which the judge Ehud delivers the tribe of Benjamin. Also to the east, and north of Moab, was Ammon, from which the Hebrew tribes of Manasseh, Gad and Reuben repelled invasion under the leadership of the judge Jephthah. Then there were the most formidable of all the Israelite enemies, the Philistines, against whom Samson and the tribes of Dan, Simeon and Judah fought.

Little is known about these kingdoms at this early period, except that of the Philistines. Philistia was established along the Mediterranean coast to the south of Canaan and stretched to the borders of Egypt and the Nile delta. The name Philistine comes from an Egyptian word meaning 'sea peoples' and they are first recorded in the reign of Ramesses III, around 1185 BCE. Archaeology shows them to have been of Aegean origin and that they first settled in Canaan around the same time as the Israelites. The Philistines probably began as seafaring raiders, much like the Vikings of later Europe. Soon, however, they managed to establish a foothold along the coast of what is now the Gaza Strip. We even know what they looked like. Carved reliefs from the reign of Ramesses III, at his mortuary temple of Medinet Habu in Thebes, show them wearing headdresses of feathers, rising vertically from a horizontal band, and wielding lances, long broadswords, triangular daggers and round shields. According to the Bible, David eventually overcame the Philistines, although their kingdom continued as a vassal state of Judah until its absorption into the Babylonian Empire four centuries later. The Philistines seem to have risen to prominence again after the collapse of the Babylonian Empire, as the Greek historian Herodotus refers to them around 450 BCE. Indeed, they ultimately lent their name to the area as a whole. Palestine, the Roman name for Canaan, actually meant 'land of the Philistines'. So it is fairly safe to assume that the biblical period outlined in the Book of Judges also fits into a reliable historical context. We come, therefore, to the beginnings of Hebrew presence in Canaan. When did they first arrive?

Placed before the Book of Judges in the Old Testament is the Book of Joshua, named after the leader of the Israelites at the time of the conquest of Canaan. In the Book of Joshua, Joshua leads the Israelites across the river Jordan into Canaan and besieges the city of Jericho. Following God's instructions, the Israelites march around the city walls, led by the priests who carry the Ark of the Covenant. When, at last, the priests all blow a blast from their ram's horns, the walls miraculously collapsed and the city is taken. There follows a series of battles in which, one by one, the cities of Canaan are conquered, ending with the sacking of Hazor, during which its pagan inhabitants are mercilessly slaughtered by Joshua's troops.

This final stage of the conquest of Canaan, as described in the Bible, has not only been verified but also dated. The Old Testament Book of Joshua describes Joshua's destruction of Hazor:

> And they smote all the souls that were therein with the edge of the sword, utterly destroying them; there were not any left to breath, and he burned Hazor with fire. (JOSHUA. 11:11)

In the 1950s excavations were conducted at the site of ancient Hazor, modern Tell-el-Qedah, some fourteen kilometres north of the Sea of Galilee. Here the Israeli archaeologist Dr Yigael Yadin unearthed the remains of a huge fortified palace that had been destroyed by fire sometime between 1300 and 1200 BCE. Dating was possible from broken Mycenean pottery found lying at the level of destruction. Such ceramics were popular throughout the Near East during the thirteenth century BCE, but had ceased to be imported into Palestine by the twelfth century BCE. The destruction of the city had almost certainly been the work of an enemy, rather than accidental, as statues and temple decorations had been deliberately defaced. The remains of hearths, tent bases and hut footings, with a characteristic desert-style pottery, led Yadin to conclude that tent dwellers – a previously nomadic people – had settled there afterwards. Part of the area had been rebuilt again as a fortified city in the tenth century BCE, and distinctive artefacts, such as beads, showed this to have been the work of the Israelites.

Dr Yadin was satisfied that the discoveries at Hazor matched the biblical account of Joshua's conquest in a number of ways. The conquerors had razed the city to the ground, just as the Bible says; they had attempted to destroy the cultic practices of the Canaanites, as we are told God charged the Israelites to do; and they had been a nomadic people, just as the Israelites had recently been. Dr Yadin was certain that the Israelites had occupied the area from the time of the burning, but had had neither the power nor the motivation to rebuild the city until the creation of the unified kingdom after the time of David.

So the conquest appears to have ended during the thirteenth century BCE. When, however, had it started?

According to the Bible, the conquest began with the fall of Jericho. Although the story of the miraculous fall of the city walls might have been a later exaggeration of events, there is considerable archaeological evidence that Jericho was destroyed by foreign invaders around half a century before the destruction of Hazor. In 1952 the British archaeologist Kathleen Kenyon excavated a Bronze Age fortification at Tell-es-Sultan near the Dead Sea, thought to be the site of ancient Jericho. She concluded that from 1900 BCE the city was a prosperous walled town, just as the Bible describes, until it was destroyed by fire around 1500 BCE. Until recently, archaeologists took this as evidence against the story of the destruction of the city by Joshua because of its early date – at least two and a half centuries before the Israelite conquest of Hazor. However, recent radiocarbon tests, at the Centre for Isotope Research at Groningen University in Holland, have now determined a much later date for the carnage. In July 1996, Hendrik J. Bruins and Johannes van der Plicht published their findings in *Nature* magazine, after they had dated ancient cereal grains found in the burned layer of the citadel excavation. (The samples had actually been excavated by Kathleen Kenyon in the 1950s.) Caution is called for with regard to radiocarbon dating, due to the margin of error involved. In this case, however, six separate sets of samples were available for testing, and provided dates spanning a period of 150 years. The dates ranged from 1397–1244 BCE, the average being around 1320 BCE, which is not too long before the period in which Dr Yadin's excavations indicated Hazor was conquered.

Although there is no collaborative evidence for the existence of Joshua, archaeology shows that the Israelites conquered Canaan in much the way the Bible relates sometime during the late fourteenth or early thirteenth century BCE.

Before we can examine the all-important period in which the Old Testament tells us the Hebrew religion came into existence – during the forty years the Israelites are said to have wandered in the Sinai wilderness to the south of Canaan – we need to examine how they came supposedly to be in the wilderness in the first place. This early period of Israelite history, which is outlined in the first two books of the Bible, Genesis and Exodus, seems to the modern reader to be as mythological as the stories of the Garden of Eden and Noah's flood. We are told that the entire nation of Israel descended from just one family who settled in Egypt at some unspecified period and that, following centuries of slavery under the pharaohs, God helped the Israelites escape by cursing the Egyptians with preternatural plagues and enabled them to leave the country by miraculously parting the waters of the Red Sea. From the historical perspective such fantastic claims need considerable supportive evidence if they are to be believed, and the official records of Egypt make no reference to any of these events. In fact, for years historians and Egyptologists doubted that the Israelites had ever been in Egypt at all.

Summary

• A number of foreign inscriptions survive that not only confirm the existence of certain Hebrew figures and their military campaigns as referenced in the Old Testament but have made it possible to date many of the events in the biblical narrative. The most important is an inscribed stone from the kingdom of Moab, which can be positively dated to around 850 BCE. Now in the Louvre in Paris, the Moabite Stone has proved of immense importance to biblical historians. It enabled an approximate dating for events in the Old Testament, and confirmed that Israel was worshipping the one God, referred to in the Bible as Yahweh, as least as early as the mid-ninth century BCE.

• From the biblical narrative we can determine that around 930 BCE the Hebrews split into two kingdoms: Israel and Judah. Israel, with its capital at Samaria, was by far the larger of the two kingdoms as it consisted of ten of the twelve Hebrew tribes. It was only because of their well-defended, strategic position in Jerusalem that the tribe of Judah survived as the independent kingdom of Judah. Archaeology has confirmed the existence of these two kingdoms and that the kingdom of Israel was ultimately wiped out by the Assyrians in the late seventh century BCE. It was, therefore, in Judah that the Hebrew religion survived. Indeed, it is from the name Judah that the term Judaism is derived and its adherents, the Jews, were the people of Judah.

- In recent years various earlier biblical episodes once thought fanciful have been afforded historical credence. King David's capture of Jerusalem is one such example. According to the Old Testament account, David discovered a secret method of entry into the walled city, through a water-shaft or underground gutter that led from inside the city down to a spring outside the walls. It was by a sneak attack through this tunnel that the city is said to have been taken. In 1876 a tunnel was discovered that exactly matched the biblical descriptions. In 1961 the British archaeologist Kathleen Kenyon excavated the ancient walls of Jerusalem to discover that the tunnel indeed led inside the city as the Old Testament relates.

- The Old Testament account of the even earlier Israelite conquest of Canaan has also been supported by archaeology. According to the Book of Joshua the conquest ended with the sacking of Hazor. In the 1950s excavations were conducted at the site of ancient Hazor, modern Tell-el-Qedah, some fourteen kilometres north of the Sea of Galilee. Here the Israeli archaeologist Dr Yigael Yadin unearthed the remains of a huge fortified palace that had been destroyed by fire sometime between 1300 and 1200 BCE. Dr Yadin was satisfied that the discoveries at Hazor matched the biblical account of Joshua's conquest in a number of ways.

- A precise dating of the original arrival of the Israelites in Canaan was not possible until the late 1990s. According to the Bible, the conquest of Canaan began with the fall of Jericho. In 1952 the British archaeologist Kathleen Kenyon excavated a Bronze Age fortification at Tell-es-Sultan near the Dead Sea, thought to be the site of ancient Jericho, discovering that it had been a prosperous walled town until it was destroyed by fire and abandoned. In 1996 radiocarbon tests carried out at the Centre for Isotope Research at Groningen University in Holland determined that the carnage occurred around 1320 BCE.

4 SLAVERY IN EGYPT

The Old Testament story of how the Israelites came to be in Egypt is contained in the Book of Genesis and the story of Joseph – the boy with the 'coat of many colours'. During his time, we are told, the Hebrews consist merely of one family who had descended from Joseph's great-grandfather Abraham. Abraham is said to have lived in the land of Haran, in what is now Turkey, many generations before the time of Joshua and the battle of Jericho. The Book of Genesis relates how, because he is a good and righteous man, God decides that Abraham and his descendants are to be his chosen people. Abraham is instructed to move to the land of Canaan. Here, he is succeeded by his son Isaac, who in turn has two sons, Jacob and Esau. As eldest son, Esau, is Isaac's rightful heir but Jacob swindles him out of his inheritance. One day Esau returns from a hunting trip on the brink of starvation to discover Jacob boiling a pot of stew. He asks to be fed but Jacob refuses unless he sells him his birthright. Ravenous with hunger, Esau agrees.

When Isaac is old Esau conspires to kill his brother and Jacob is forced to flee. While in hiding Jacob has a dream in which he sees a ladder to heaven. In the dream God tells Jacob that it is now only his, and no longer his brother's, descendants who are the chosen ones. It seems that God has lost faith in Esau for taking his birthright so lightly. Later God renames Jacob, calling him Israel – meaning 'God strives' – so his offspring become 'the children of Israel': the Israelites, God's chosen nation. When

Jacob awakes from the dream he decides that the place he slept is the gateway to heaven and calls it *Beth-el* – 'house of God' – and there erects a pillar of stone. Ultimately he is reunited with his brother Esau, whose descendants continue to live in the land of Edom (southern Jordan) around Mount Seir, while Jacob makes his home to the north, in Shalem in the land of Canaan.

Joseph is a younger son of Jacob, whose older brothers grow jealous of him because he becomes their father's favourite. Eventually they come to detest him when he develops prophetic powers and tells them of a dream in which he sees them paying him homage. One day the brothers seize Joseph, strip him of his 'coat of many colours', with which Jacob has honoured him, and sell him as a slave to a caravan of traders heading for Egypt.

In Egypt, Joseph is sold to an official named Potiphar, who soon promotes him to the position of chief steward of his household. Eventually, when Potiphar's wife tries to seduce Joseph and he refuses her, she falsely accuses him of trying to seduce her and he is thrown into prison. There, he develops a reputation as an interpreter of dreams, and when the pharaoh himself is disturbed by a series of strange dreams, Joseph is summoned to interpret them. Joseph tells the pharaoh that his dreams predict a period of seven years of abundance in Egypt, followed by seven years of famine. He advises the pharaoh to appoint someone to oversee the gathering of stockpiles of food to tide the country over the lean years that are to follow. The grateful pharaoh accepts Joseph's interpretation and appoints him as his grand vizier, or chief minister, to supervise the seven-year plan.

Eventually, when the famine occurs as predicted, it also afflicts Canaan and Jacob sends his sons into Egypt to buy corn. When they appear before the chief minister to beg for help, they do not recognize him as their grown brother Joseph. He, however, recognizes them and makes them humble themselves before him, just as his dream had once foretold. Ultimately, he reveals his true identity, forgives his brothers and sends for his father. The entire family settles in Egypt and are raised to high estate. Over the following centuries the descendants of Jacob – the children of Israel – remain in Egypt, their numbers growing until they are thousands.

The narrative tells us that the Israelites in Egypt are comprised of twelve tribes, each descended from, and named after, a son of Jacob: Reuben, Levi, Issachar, Joseph, Dan, Gad, Simeon, Judah, Zebulun, Benjamin, Nephtali and Asher. They live in an area known as Goshen, north-east of the Nile delta, around the Egyptian city of Avaris.

According to Genesis, therefore, the nation of Israel originated with Jacob and his twelve sons. The pharaoh at the time the family settled in Egypt is unnamed, but we are told that they moved there 470 years before the conquest of Jericho. From the radiocarbon dating at Groningen University (see page 63) we know that the fall of Jericho occurred around 1320 BCE. Accordingly, the story of the Israelites' arrival in Egypt is apparently set sometime around 1790 BCE. Historically this would have been during the so-called fourteenth dynasty, a succession of kings who ruled Egypt from around 1800 to 1700 BCE.

Because various radical theories have attempted to redate Egyptian history in recent years, it is important to explain how the standard Egyptian chronology, which we will be employing here, was first reconstructed. It is the chronology on which nearly all mainstream Egyptologists, historians and archaeologists, concur.

Since the early days of Egyptology in the nineteenth century, five ancient Egyptian inscriptions have been discovered to reveal the names and order of succession of many of Egypt's pharaohs. The Palermo Stone, a black diorite slab, recorded a series of early kings; a Royal List from the city of Karnak included the names of those who preceded the eighteenth-dynasty pharaoh Tuthmosis III; a Royal List from the city of Abydos, made by the nineteenth-dynasty pharaoh Seti I, named the seventy-six kings who preceded him, as did two duplicates made by his son Ramesses II. Unfortunately, as an historical chronology these lists were originally useless on their own, as they fail to provide the length of each reign. Luckily, however, one ancient text was discovered that does: a list of some three hundred kings on a long sheet of papyrus dating from the late nineteenth dynasty. Now in the Turin Museum, the so-called Royal Canon not only gives the order of succession but provides the exact period of each reign, right down to the months and days. The problem, however, was that at the time it was rediscovered there was no way to determine how the list related to the modern calendar. In which year did it start and in which did it end? Consequently, the dating of Egyptian history originally proved a nightmare, and scholars disagreed with one another sometimes by centuries. Historians needed points of reference, other datable events with which to link the pharaohs' reigns. It fell to astronomy eventually to resolve the matter. Some of the pharaohs' reigns could be precisely dated due to ancient astronomical observations and a lucky mistake in the Egyptian calendar.

The ancient Egyptians knew that the year consisted of 365 days, but they made no adjustment for the additional quarter day, as we do now by adding a day every fourth year. Civic activities, administrative meetings, tax collections, censuses, and so forth, were arranged according to a 365-day calendar, but religious activities were tied to celestial events, such as the midsummer sunrise, or the spring equinox, which occur at the same time each 365-and-a-quarter-day solar year. Accordingly, the Egyptian civil and solar calendars gradually moved out of synchronization by a day every four years until, after 730 years, midsummer's day fell in the middle of winter. Because they had no idea that the year was determined by the length of time it took the earth to orbit the sun, this discrepancy perplexed the ancient Egyptians, who every few centuries would find the seasons apparently reversed. On one papyrus dating from the thirteenth century BCE, a mystified scribe has recorded: 'Winter has come in summer, the months are reversed, the hours in confusion.' It would take a further 730 years for the solar calendar to catch up with the civil calendar, so only every 1460 years would the two calendars properly align.

As the brightest star in the sky, Sirius was considered of great magical importance, and each year on the day of its heliacal rising – its annual reappearance in early July – an important religious festival took place. Accordingly, when this festival coincided with the first day of the civil calendar, every 1460 years, it was considered a particularly special time: the beginning of a new aeon called the Sothic Cycle (after Sothis, the ancient name for Sirius). Such an occasion is known to have been celebrated by the Roman occupiers of Egypt in the second century CE: a coin was issued to commemorate the event during the reign of the emperor Antoninus Pius in 139 CE. As this occurred only every 1460 years, by counting backwards we can work out that the same thing had also happened in 1321 BCE and 2781 BCE.

Against these important dates, specific years in the reigns of kings from the Royal Canon of Turin could be determined. One of the kings included in the list was Senusret III, and a contemporary inscription records that in the seventh year of his reign the heliacal rising of Sirius occurred on the 226th day of the civil calendar. As it took four years for the calendars to move out of alignment by one day, then for the calendars to be out of alignment by 226 days meant that 904 years (226x4) must have transpired since the beginning of the last Sothic Cycle in 2781 BCE. Accordingly, the seventh year of Senusret III's reign must have been in 1877 BCE. Another such sighting is recorded in the ninth year of the reign of the pharaoh Amonhotep I. It happened on the 309th day of the civil calendar, meaning that 1236 years had transpired since the beginning of the Sothic Cycle in 2781 BCE, making the ninth year of Amonhtep's reign 1545 BCE. With these and other such recorded sightings it was possible to date the reigns of a number of kings recorded in the Royal Canon. As this list gave both the successive order of the kings, together with the length of their reigns, by counting backwards and forwards from the known dates, it was possible to work out when each king's reign had begun and ended. For example, if the seventh year of Senusret III's reign was 1877 BCE, his reign must have begun in 1884 BCE; the recorded nineteen-year reign of his predecessor, Senusret II, must therefore have begun in 1903 BCE; the recorded thirty-four-year reign of this king's predecessor, Amenemhet III, must have begun in 1937 BCE, and so on. From this a chronological framework of Egyptian history emerged which has on numerous occasions been corroborated by the radiocarbon dating of ancient Egyptian finds. Accordingly, the Standard Egyptian Chronology was assembled.

Returning to the Old Testament account that would seem to place Jacob and his family in Egypt in the fourteenth dynasty during the eighteenth century BCE: is there any historical evidence that they were really there at this time? Although there are no contemporary references to Jacob and his family, or to a chief minister named Joseph, this is not necessarily indicative. Knowledge of this dynasty is somewhat scanty at best, as few of its monuments survive. The kings themselves are only known from odd fragmentary inscriptions, and some of them remain nameless. Nonetheless, it seems most unlikely that the hundreds of thousands of Hebrew slaves, which the Bible records at the time of the Exodus, were all descended from one man who lived only four centuries before. If it has any historical basis, the story of Jacob and his family was probably a simplified account of the migration of the Hebrew people into Egypt during the eighteenth century BCE.

From later archaeological finds, it is known that the Israelites belonged to a group of Asiatic people collectively called Semites who occupied much of the eastern Mediterranean around the time that the Joseph story is set. Like the story of Jacob's family travelling to Egypt to buy corn, Semite trading journeys into Egypt occured by this time. A wall painting in the tomb of the Egyptian nobleman Khnumhotep, near Cairo, dating from around 1850 BCE, shows a group of thirty-seven Semites entering Egypt at a border post to be met by frontier officials. Described as traders, they are depicted wearing colourful striped garments, which some biblical commentators have associated with Joseph's 'coat of many colours', as described in Genesis 37:3. It is unlikely, though, that these first Semite traders have any link with the Joseph story. There is no evidence of them ever having settled in Egypt. However, around a century and a half later the Semites began to settle in Egypt in large numbers.

In the Genesis narrative, Jacob and his family came from Shalem, close to Shechem in the centre of what is now the West Bank. During the eighteenth century BCE, the Semites who controlled this area were a formidable people who came originally from the kingdom of Mari in Syria. The site of the Mari capital city lies on the west bank of the Euphrates, just inside Syria on a hill called Tell Hariri, about twenty kilometres north of what is now the Iraq border. In 1933 a team of French archaeologists, led by Professor André Parrot, began excavating the site. Here they discovered a splendid royal palace dating from around 2000 BCE, which had more than three hundred rooms, richly furbished with statues and ornate frescoes. Since 1933, the Mari excavations have unearthed thousands of inscribed clay tablets that provide valuable information about the history of the Mari kingdom and its vassal states.

The Mari kingdom was invaded by the Babylonians around 1800 BCE, and its capital was taken and destroyed. With the overthrow of their kingdom, the Mari migrated south into Canaan and within a few years had formed themselves into an effective alliance of tribes. By the end of the next century they were even powerful enough to threaten Egypt. The Egyptians at the time refer to the Mari as the *Hikau khasut*, 'rulers of the desert uplands', a term the Greeks later rendered as Hyksos, 'desert princes', the name by which historians still refer to them today. If they represented an historical people, therefore, Jacob and his family would evidently have been a Hyksos tribe.

The first references to the Hyksos in Egyptian records appear shortly after the collapse of the Mari kingdom. Unlike the previous Semitic traders, these people seem to have been settling in Egypt. A text dating from around 1745 BCE, for instance, in the reign of the pharaoh Sobekhotep III, contains a list of the Hyksos servants in the king's household. Before long, however, it was the Hyksos who became the masters. Over the next half-century increasing numbers of Hyksos moved into the Nile delta as the Egyptian kingdom fell into decline. Within fifty years they outnumbered the local population to the extent that they seized control of northern Egypt. For the next century and a half Egypt was divided. In the north, the Hyksos kingdom was centred on the city of Avaris, and in the south, the pharaohs still controlled their shrunken kingdom with its new capital at Thebes. It is around the Hyksos capital of Avaris, in the land of Goshen, that the Bible tells us that Jacob and his family settled.

According to the Exodus account, Jacob's descendants flourish so well in Egypt that within a few generations they number thousands. According to Exodus 1:7: 'The children of Israel were fruitful and increased abundantly, and multiplied, and waxed exceedingly mighty; and the land was filled with them.' In fact, there are so many of them that the pharaoh complains: 'Behold,

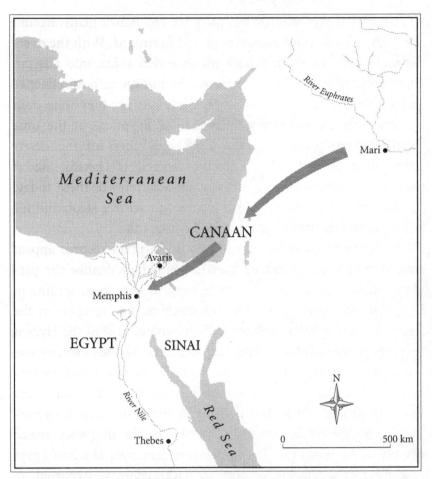

Migration of the Hyksos in the eighteenth century BC

the people of the children of Israel are more and mightier than we.' There was only one period in Egypt's history when the Semites were so mighty and numerous within its borders – during the time the Hyksos controlled the north, between 1700 and 1550 BCE.

According to the Greek historian Manetho, writing in the fourth century BCE, the Hyksos not only conquered northern Egypt, they emulated the Egyptians and set themselves up as pharaohs. These Hyksos pharaohs, whom Egyptologists refer to as the fifteenth and sixteenth dynasties, built a massive new palace at Avaris that has recently been unearthed. Excavations by the Austrian archaeologist Dr Manfred Bietak, of Vienna University, reveal that the Hyksos lived as opulently as the Egyptians they replaced.

During this period the Israelites could well have achieved the high status within Egyptian society that the Bible maintains. Northern Egypt was a Semite kingdom and, like the Israelites, its rulers were Hyksos. One of the Hyksos pharaohs was actually called Yakob, the Hebrew rendering of Jacob, a common name amongst the Israelites. As he seems to have been one of the last Hyksos kings, it might be that by the time the Egyptians retook the north the Israelites were themselves the ruling élite.

In Thebes the Egyptian monarchy ultimately devised plans to reconquer the north. The first Egyptian king to lead the offensive was Seqenenre II, around 1570 BCE. The incursion failed and Seqenenre was killed. His mummified body, found in 1881, shows that he had five sword wounds to the neck and head, indicating that he had been literally hacked to death. His son and successor, Kamose, launched a full-scale attack on the Hyksos king Apophis, and drove him back to the walls of Avaris. The account of his campaign was discovered in 1954, on a limestone stela from the temple of Amon-Re at Thebes. According to the account, Kamose's younger brother and successor, Ahmose, kept up the pressure: he laid siege to Avaris, which fell sometime around 1550 BCE, and pursued the defeated Hyksos into Canaan. Under Ahmose, and the new eighteenth-dynasty kings, Egypt was once again reunified under Egyptian rule. This might have been the period referred to in the first chapter of the Book of Exodus that continues the story of the Israelites in Egypt:

> Now there arose a new king over Egypt which knew not Joseph. And he said unto his people, Behold, the people of the children of Israel are more and mightier than we. Come on, let us deal wisely with them; lest they multiply, and it come to pass that, when there falleth out any war, they join also unto our enemies, and fight against us, and so get them up out of the land.
> (EXODUS 1:8–10)

Historically, the Hyksos were eventually enslaved by the triumphant Egyptians. Under a series of eighteenth-dynasty pharaohs, Egyptian armies repeatedly swept through Canaan, laying the country waste. Tuthmosis III, often referred to as the Napoleon of ancient Egypt, was the most formidable campaigner: he finally crushed the Hyksos in Canaan at the decisive battle of Megiddo somewhere around 1500 BCE. During his reign, thousands of the Hyksos were returned to Egypt in chains. This may be the time referred to in Exodus 1:11, when the Israelites are enslaved:

> Therefore they [the Egyptians] did set over them [the Israelites] taskmasters to afflict them with their burdens.

Tomb illustrations of the eighteenth dynasty include scenes showing Hyksos slaves making bricks, while taskmasters stand over them, rods in hand. According to Exodus, this is precisely the fate of the Israelites: 'So they were made to work in gangs, with officers set over them, to break their spirit with heavy labour' (EXODUS 1:11). 'And they made their lives bitter with hard bondage, in mortar, and in brick' (EXODUS 1:14).

Until recently, however, there appeared to be no direct historical or archaeological evidence that any of the Hyksos slaves were actually the Israelites, as no surviving records specifically refer to any of them by that name. However, the ancestors of the Israelites who conquered Canaan in the thirteenth century BCE might not have been called Israelites at this time. According to Dr Mordechai Snyder, of the Hebrew University, the name Israel might not have come into usage until after Joshua's conquest of Canaan:

Israel [meaning 'God strives'] implies a nation intent on maintaining its geographical integrity. As such, the term would have no meaning before the entry into the Promised Land [of Canaan].

Dr Snyder suggests that Genesis 35:10, where God renames Jacob Israel, was only interpolated into the narrative after Joshua's time to provide a genealogical link between the nation and its ancestral founder. This would be typical of the common ancestor myth that occurs in many cultures: the mythical Romulus, for example, who was said to have co-founded Rome. It might account for why the Bible uses two names for its chosen people: Israelites and Hebrews.

In the original Hebrew Bible the word Hebrew is rendered as *Habiru*, meaning 'people from across the river'. This, Dr Snyder proposes, is the name by which the Israelites were first known. It is in this form that the world's oldest reference to the Hebrews appears in an inscription from the original Hyksos kingdom of Mari. In 1978 Snyder examined an inscribed clay tablet in the Louvre that had been found during the Mari excavations. In the text, dating from around 1820 BCE, he discovered a line in which King Zimri-Lim of Mari records a people described as 'the Habiru' residing in his kingdom. On examining Egyptian texts, Snyder discovered that a people with a similar name – Hapiru – appear in Egyptian records of Hyksos slaves:

Circa 1500 BCE: The oldest reference to the Hapiru is on a scene from the tomb of Tuthmosis III's great herald Antef, which lists them among the prisoners of war captured during the pharaoh's campaigns.

Circa 1475 BCE: A scene on the tomb of the noble Puyemre at Thebes, dating from the reign of Tuthmosis III, shows four men working a wine press and accompanying hieroglyphics read 'straining out wine by the Hapiru'. It is accompanied by another inscription telling us of the location: 'wine of the vineyard of War-Hor'. This was in the land of Goshen where the Bible has the Israelites enslaved.

Circa 1430 BCE: A list of foreign captives found on an inscribed stone discovered at Memphis, dating from the reign of Amonhotep II, includes 3600 Hapiru.

Circa 1270 BCE: The Leyde Papyrus, concerning the reign of Ramesses II, mentions the Hapiru being used as hard labour to make repairs to a temple at Memphis.

Circa 1270 BCE: In the reign of Ramesses II the Hapiru are recorded being used to make bricks at Miour in the province of Fayum.

Circa 1180 BCE: During the reign of Ramesses III one inscription lists the Hapiru working the land at Heliopolis in northern Egypt, while another lists them working as quarrymen in the same district.

Although Snyder's theory was criticized by other biblical scholars, who contended that the term Hapiru referred to a particular category of workmen, prisoners-of-war or class of slave, this, he countered, was unlikely. Similar workers are shown on reliefs throughout the eighteenth and nineteenth dynasties without being referred to by any name other than captives, foreigners or slaves. The only distinctions usually made are by words such as *fa-kat*, 'workers', or *yus*, 'builders'. Chiefly through the textual studies of the award-winning historian Dr Maurice Bucaille, of the University of Paris, in the 1980s, who further examined the Hapiru references, many biblical scholars and Egyptologists alike now accept that the Hapiru were the Hebrews and that these inscriptions attest to the presence of Hebrew slaves in Egypt for two centuries before the Israelite conquest of Canaan.

We move on, then, to the crucial period of Moses, when the biblical narrative appears to swing back into an ambience of mythology. According to the Book of Exodus, the pharaoh of Egypt, concerned about the growing number of Hebrew slaves, gives orders that their newborn sons should all be killed. Although many are murdered, the baby Moses escapes when his mother places him in a basket and hides him in the bulrushes at the riverside. The daughter of the pharaoh then discovers the child and decides to raise him as her own son. Years later, although he has been brought up as an Egyptian prince at the royal court, Moses still has compassion for his countrymen, and when he sees an Egyptian beating an Israelite slave he kills the man. When the deed is discovered, the pharaoh orders Moses to be executed. However, he escapes and settles in the land of Midian, east of the Red Sea, where he marries and raises a family.

One day, while tending his father-in-law's flock on Mount Sinai, Moses sees a bush that burns without being consumed. God then speaks to Moses from within this bush and charges him to return and confront the new pharaoh of Egypt. Moses does as God commands and, accompanied by his brother Aaron, appears before the pharaoh with God's command: he must free the Israelites and let them return to Canaan – the Promised Land. When the pharaoh refuses and actually makes life harder for the Hebrews, God punishes the Egyptians with a series of plagues: bloodied water, frogs, lice, flies, cattle deaths, boils, fiery hail storms, locusts and days of darkness. Ultimately, the Israelites escape Egypt when God strikes down all the first-born Egyptians and miraculously parts the waters of the Red Sea to allow them to escape the country. (This is the Exodus of the Israelites from Egypt after which the Book of Exodus is named.) The Israelites are then condemned to remain in the Sinai wilderness for forty years until, after Moses' death, Joshua leads them in the conquest of Canaan.

Could there be any truth in this apparently far-fetched account? In order to examine this question, we need to establish when these events are supposed to have occurred. It is clear from the narrative that this is many generations after the Israelites were first enslaved. According to Exodus 1:12, the following separates the original enslavement of the Israelites from the birth of Moses:

> But the more that they [the Egyptians] afflicted them [the children of Israel] the more they multiplied and grew . . .

If the enslavement of the Israelites occurred following the overthrow of the Hyksos and the campaigns of Tuthmosis III around 1500 BCE (see page 77), then the Exodus from Egypt has to have taken place some generations after Tuthmosis' reign. The Bible does not name the pharaoh at the time of the Exodus, nor does it name any other Egyptian official, so we have no direct chronological reference to determine the period in which the Exodus story is set. However, if the Hebrews were only enslaved in Egypt after 1500 then there are only two periods during which the account fits into an historical context. According to Exodus 1:11, the Israelites were employed in a massive construction project: 'And they did build for Pharaoh treasure cities, Pithom and Ramesses.' This was the biblical name for the city of Pi-Ramesses, which was basically two cities in one: an administrative centre and a palace and suburban district, built over the ruins of the old Hyksos capital of Avaris. The city was rebuilt only twice during the post-Hyksos era and before the Israelite conquest of

Canaan. The second of these rebuildings was during the reign of Ramesses II.

Ramesses II came to the throne at the age of twenty-five in 1280 BCE and soon earned his title, Ramesses the Great. He reigned for a remarkable sixty-seven years, making him one of the oldest men recorded in Egyptian history. During his reign he did everything on a gigantic scale: he added to the great temples of Karnak and Luxor and built one of his own at nearby Abydos. In Nubia, at Abu Simbel, he built the Great Temple. Well deserving its name, it is a remarkable piece of engineering, even by today's standards: a huge artificial cavern cut into a mountain, some sixty metres deep and forty metres high. Inside the vast excavated dome is a series of temples and outside, the imposing entrance is flanked by four eighteen-metre-high statues of the king, hewn from solid rock. His grandest scheme, however, was the reconstruction of Avaris. Although they do not mention the Habiru by name, inscriptions from the city have shown that a vast slave labour force was used.

The first and original rebuilding of the city was about a century earlier, during the reign of Amonhotep III, *circa* 1385–1360 BCE. At this time Egypt was at the height of her power. Amonhotep III's great-grandfather, Tuthmosis III, had laid the foundations of the new empire and the land of Egypt was filled with abundance. Amonhotep used this new-found wealth to erect great buildings and monuments throughout Egypt. In Thebes, he built his enormous Malkata palace, as splendid as any before it, and he embellished the already massive temple of Amun-Re at Thebes. The largest project of all, however, was the rebuilding of Avaris, which had been levelled after the defeat of the Hyksos. Recent excavations of the city led by Dr Manfred Bietak, of Vienna University, have unearthed numerous inscriptions attesting to foreign slave labour being employed.

Traditionally, biblical scholars have tended to place the Exodus during the Ramesses period, the reason being that the Bible refers to the city as Pithom and Ramesses – Pi-Ramesses being the new name for the city during Ramesses' reign. They also draw attention to another biblical reference concerning the flight of the Israelites during the Exodus. 'And the children of Israel journeyed from Ramesses to Succoth' (EXODUS 12:37). Pi-Ramesses literally means 'city of Ramesses' and was renamed after Ramesses II. As the city would not have been known as Ramesses or Pi-Ramesses during Amonhotep's reign, a century earlier, then, it is argued, the Exodus must have been set during the time of the second rebuilding of the city.

However, as we saw in chapter 2, the Old Testament does not appear to have been compiled in its present form until many centuries later and anachronisms are often employed in the narrative in the form in which they existed by the seventh century BCE. In the case of the city of Ramesses, the Bible certainly uses its name anachronistically on one occasion. In Genesis 47:11, Ramesses is the name given for the city where the Israelites are allowed to settle on their arrival in Egypt: 'And Joseph placed his father and his brethren, and gave them a possession in the land of Egypt, in the best of the land, in the land of Ramesses.' This was many years before the time of Ramesses II, seemingly during the Hyksos era – the Bible itself tells us that this was over four centuries before the Exodus (EXODUS 12:40). The city was certainly not named after Ramesses at this time. We know for certain, therefore, that the city was referred to at least once in the Old Testament by the name it only acquired at a later date. The same could equally be true during the Exodus account.

The other principal argument placing the Exodus during the time of the second rebuilding of Avaris concerns the references to the Hapiru. If they are the Hebrews, it is reasoned, then they are still in Egypt after the time of the first rebuilding. Indeed, they are actually recorded during the time of Ramesses II.

However, the Hapiru are still in Egypt well after Ramesses' reign. The last record of them is around 1180 BCE, a century later. This is well after archaeology has shown that Jericho and Hazor had been conquered, and the Israel Stela records that the Israelites had established some kind of kingdom in Canaan. If the Exodus was an historical event, and the Hapiru are the Hebrews, then the ones recorded in 1180 were either recaptured or descendants of slaves who did not manage to escape. The same, therefore, could equally be true of the Hapiru recorded after Amonhotep's reign.

So we are back to square one. During which of these periods is the Exodus set?

One particular Hapiru reference supports the argument that the Exodus occurred during the first rebuilding of Avaris. In this instance, the Hapiru are recorded not as slaves in Egypt but as a free people who reside in the city of Beisham in central Canaan. On the Hypostyle Hall at Karnak a relief celebrates the battles of the pharaoh Seti I. In one scene the king is shown riding in his chariot as foreign soldiers fall before him. Beneath it is the inscription: 'Fallen are the Hapiru at Beisham.' If the Hebrews were in Canaan, and in large enough numbers for the pharaoh to lead his army to oppose them, this would suggest that the Exodus had already occurred and the Israelite occupation of the area was already under way by Seti's reign. As Seti was Ramesses II's predecessor, and reigned from 1305–1292 BCE, then, if the Hapiru are the Hebrews, the Exodus must have happened before the second rebuilding.

The radiocarbon dating of the fall of Jericho would also tend to place the Exodus during the time of Amonhotep III (see page 63). The six dates obtained range between 1397 and 1244 BCE, giving a central date of 1320 BCE. Jericho, then, had already fallen to the Israelites four decades before Ramesses II's reign even began. Moreover, if the Exodus occurred forty years before the conquest of Jericho as the Bible maintains, then its most probable date, based on these radiocarbon tests, would be about 1360 BCE. This was around the end of Amonhotep III's reign when Avaris was rebuilt for the first time.

On the balance of evidence it seems more likely that the Exodus story is set at the time of the first rebuilding of Avaris rather than the second, at some time during the reign of Amonhotep III. Based upon the archaeological evidence, therefore, this would appear to be the chronology of events concerning the period of the early Hebrews.

Approximate Chronology BCE

2000 The birth of the Mari kingdom at Tell Hariri in Syria.

1820 Mari king Zimri-Lim records the Habiru as one of his peoples.

1800 The Mari kingdom is invaded by the Babylonians. The Hyksos migrate south into Canaan.

1750 The Hyksos establish a powerful presence in Canaan.

1745–1700 Increasing numbers of Hyksos continue to settle the Nile delta as Egypt's power declines. Hebrews first settle in Egypt.

1700 The whole of northern Egypt falls to the Hyksos.

1700–1550 The Hyksos kings govern northern Egypt, establishing their capital at Avaris. Southern Egypt remains in the hands of the Egyptian kings with their capital at Thebes.

1550 The Egyptian king Ahmose reconquers northern Egypt.

Some Hyksos are enslaved while others retreat into Canaan.

1500–1450 Reign of Tuthmosis III.

1500 Tuthmosis III conquers the Hyksos in Canaan and returns with many new slaves. The oldest reference to the Hapiru slaves in Egypt. Israelites enslaved.

1385–60 Reign of Amonhotep III. Rebuilding of Avaris. Possible period of the Exodus.

1320 Israelite conquest of Jericho.

1300–1287 Reign of Seti I.

1290 Egyptians fight the Hapiru at Beisham in Canaan.

1287–20 Reign of Ramesses II. Rebuilding of Avaris as Pi-Ramesses.

1200 Israel Stela mentions the Israelites having some kind of kingdom in Canaan.

It seems, then, that the pharaoh whom Moses is portrayed as confronting was Amonhotep III and that the Exodus story is set around the end of his reign. However, if the Hebrews managed to escape Egypt in vast numbers, as the Exodus account maintains, why is no reference to the event found in contemporary Egyptian records? The answer may be that the event was on a much smaller scale than the Bible implies. Perhaps, however, many would argue, it never happened at all.

Although there might well have been Hebrew slaves in Egypt, and they might have been there in considerable numbers, they might simply have left Egypt gradually and in smaller groups during a turbulent period in Egyptian history that followed

Amonhotep's reign. For two decades after the death (or, in some theories, abdication) of Amonhotep, Egypt experienced a period of religious upheaval in which the empire shrank and the country was almost bankrupted (see chapter 5). Although records from the period are somewhat sketchy and there is no direct reference to the wholesale desertion or freeing of slaves, it seems reasonable to assume that during this economic recession many Egyptian nobles found it impractical to keep large numbers of slaves. First, they would no longer have been able to afford to feed and control them, and second, there would have been no large-scale projects to keep them employed. Merely setting the slaves free would impose a considerable burden on the beleaguered economy, so it is quite possible that they were expelled from Egypt. Was this how vast numbers of Israelites came to be in the Sinai wilderness? It would certainly make poor reading for the proud Jews of later years to read that their nation was founded because the Egyptians had thrown their ancestors out. Was the fabulous story of God's divine intervention to free his chosen people from bondage simply a piece of religious propaganda?

Although there is no contemporary Egyptian record of a mass exodus of slaves from Egypt, a reference does survive of a large-scale slave revolt during Amonhotep III's reign in the work of a later Greek historian. It is found in Manetho's *Aegyptiaca*, a history of Egypt compiled in the fourth century BCE from extant Egyptian records preserved at the temple of Heliopolis near modern Cairo. Interestingly, the revolt is said to have taken place in Avaris, where the Israelites seem to have been enslaved. According to Manetho, Amonhotep was advised by one of his officials to purge the country of 'undesirables' and set them to work in the stone quarries of Avaris. For many years they were forced to work as slaves until they were joined by a priest from the temple of the god Ra in Heliopolis. Evidently, the priest had abandoned the gods of Egypt and had been condemned to bondage. He had, Manetho tells us, once been a soldier and during his captivity he trained the 'undesirables' to fight. When he ultimately led them in rebellion, thousands managed to escape and return to their homeland. The 'undesirables' are not named, neither is their homeland, while the priest is simply referred to as called Osarseph, which means 'leader'. In the first century CE, the Jewish historian Josephus read the account and concluded that the undesirables were the Israelites and that Osarseph was Moses. However, there is presently no way of knowing one way or the other. Nevertheless, as Manetho had nothing to gain from inventing the story, and he appears to have consulted surviving Egyptian records, it does seem that a large number of foreign slaves escaped Egypt at the time and from the location the Bible portrays the Exodus as having occurred.

Nevertheless, although it is possible that Hebrew slaves did affect a mass revolt and escape Egypt to settle eventually in Canaan, the actual events of the Exodus outlined in the Old Testament concerning the so-called plagues scarcely seem credible. However, as we saw in Chapter One, they can all be explained by a terrifying but natural event – the volcanic eruption of Thera. The question is did this eruption occur during the likely period in which the Exodus story appears to be set, during the reign of Amonhotep III?

Over the years the Thera eruption was variously dated between 1600 and 1300 BCE. Compelling scientific evidence for a more precise dating, however, appeared in the 1970s with ice-core samples from Greenland. Every winter a fresh layer of ice-forms on the Greenland ice cap, creating clearly defined strata, one for each year. Every layer contains trapped air, holding a sample of the earth's atmosphere as it was when the ice formed. In the 1970s Danish geophysicists began taking core samples many metres down into the ice, so as to recover a year-by-year record

The enigmatic pharaoh Akhenaten. (*Egyptian Museum, Cairo.*)

Limestone relief from Amarna showing Akhenaten worshipping the Aten disc. (*Ny Carlsberg Glyptotek, Copenhagen.*)

A wide angle picture of the Attuf Ridge. (*Jane Taylor.*)

The outer siq.
Was this the biblical
Kadesh? (*Jane Taylor.*)

Colossal statue of
Amonhotep III with his wife
Queen Tiye. Was he the
pharaoh of the Exodus?
(*Egyptian Museum, Cairo.*)

The pool of Gibeon at El-Jib where the army of David triumphed.
(*David Deissmann.*)

The spring of Gihon in the Kidron Valley where David discovered a secret
tunnel that led inside the Jebusite stronghold of Jerusalem. (*David Deissmann.*)

The walls of the ancient city of Dan dating from the tenth century BC.
(*Sally Harper.*)

The excavated altar at Dan where I Kings says that Jeroboam
erected the golden statue of a calf. (*Hebrew University.*)

OPPOSITE: The tomb of Aaron on Jebel Haroun. (*Jane Taylor.*)

One of the bronze bulls discovered during the excavations of Samaria. Was there a relationship between such images and the golden calf fashioned by Aaron at mount Sinai? (*Hebrew University.*)

The excavated altar at the ancient Israelite capital of Samaria, thought to be the altar of Baal destroyed by Jehu around 840 BCE. (*University of Toronto.*)

Michelangelo's statue of the horned Moses made for the tomb of Pope Julius II. Exodus 34:35 suggests that Moses wore a horned headdress during his ascent of Mount Sinai. (*Saint Peter's, Vincoli.*)

Sandstone head discovered at Karnak in 1920, thought to depict the young Prince Tuthmose wearing the royal serpent of co-regency. Is this the face of the historical Moses? (*Museum of Fine Arts, Boston.*)

The High Place on Attuf Ridge. (*Jane Taylor.*)

The Israel Stela, dating from the reign of Merenptah around 1200 BCE. Amongst a list of the pharaoh's campaigns its inscription contains the oldest known reference to the land of Israel.

The Maobite Stone, circa 850 BCE, discovered in Dhiban in 1868. When translated its inscription was crucial in establishing Old Testament chronology. (*The Louvre, Paris.*)

The King Zimri-Lim inscribed clay tablet from the Mari excavations. Dating to around 1830 BCE, it contains the oldest reference to the Hebrews yet discovered. (*The Louvre, Paris.*)

Fragmentary relief from Memphis showing Prince Tuthmose officiating as high priest at the temple of Ptah. (*Egyptian Museum, Cairo.*)

of the earth's atmospheric conditions going back some 100,000 years. The team, led by Drs C. U. Clausen, H. B. Hammer and W. Dansgard, soon observed that from years when there had been major volcanic eruptions, such as the one that destroyed Roman Pompeii in 79 CE, the samples evidenced high levels of acidity. In an article in *Nature* magazine in November 1980, the team reported that there had been a massive eruption somewhere in the world around 1390 BCE, with a margin of error of some fifty years either way. The only eruption large enough to have resulted in the atmospheric conditions recorded by the Danes, and known by geologists to have occurred within two hundred years either side of this date, was the Thera eruption. This means that Thera could well have erupted at the time the Exodus story appears to be set, during the reign of Amonhotep III: 1385–360 BCE.

Archaeological collaboration of this dating had actually been discovered, on the island of Crete, as long ago as the 1930s. However, it had remained stored away in the vaults of the National Archaeological Museum of Athens for almost seventy years.

In the early fourteenth century BCE Crete was the heart of the Minoan civilization: they were a race of master ship-builders who had dominated the Aegean for centuries. Through trade, rather than conquest, Crete had become one of the wealthiest powers in the entire Mediterranean. It is only 112 kilometres south of Thera, so would have suffered the effects of the eruption on a far greater scale than Egypt. The first evidence that a massive catastrophe had occurred on Crete in ancient times came to light in 1901, when the Boston archaeologist Harriet Boyd excavated the Minoan town of Gournia at the eastern end of the island. Ms Boyd was shocked by what she found: everywhere there was evidence that the last Minoans who had lived in the town had suddenly dropped everything and fled. Personal belongings and workmen's tools were found abandoned and cooking hearths still had their utensils in place as if in preparation for a meal. The cause of the panic was clear: a layer of charcoal revealed that the town had been razed by fire.

Gournia was not the only Minoan community to suffer this fate. In 1906, another American archaeologist, Richard Seager, excavated the Minoan port on the island of Mochlos, a couple of kilometres off the north coast of Crete. He discovered that this community had also come to a sudden and violent end in the late Minoan period. As at Gournia, tools and other personal effects had been abandoned when fire swept the town. Here, however, the occupants seemed to have been overwhelmed more quickly, as the charred remains of townsfolk were found amongst the ruins.

Over the following decades many more Minoan sites were discovered on Crete that revealed an almost identical picture of sudden calamity. For some time it was thought that the Minoan civilization had been overwhelmed by invaders: possibly the Greek Mycenaeans who had later established their own power-base on Crete. However, in the 1920s, when the Greek archaeologist Stephanos Xanthoudidis uncovered the remains of the once magnificent villa of Nirou Khani on the north coast of the island, the invasion theory was discounted. Like the other sites, it had been destroyed by fire. However, at the time disaster struck it was crammed with valuable objects, such as jewellery and expensive ceramics, some of which had escaped the fire and lay exactly were they had been left. Surely, if marauders had sacked the villa they would not have left such valuable items behind. Most indicative of all were the bronze battle-axes that remained in the armoury, stacked neatly against the wall. The guards had clearly not attempted to repel a human foe.

In the 1960s another Greek archaeologist, Professor Nicholas Platon, discovered the remains of Crete's easternmost Minoan palace at Kato Zakro. Once more it had been destroyed by fire, and again precious objects had been left behind – elephant tusks, bronze ingots and exquisitely made vases, together with tools and cooking utensils – all hurriedly abandoned. Professor Platon noticed something even stranger:

> Huge stones, some dressed, some not, had been hurled to a distance or had fallen and shattered, blocking passages and filling open spaces. Whole sections of the upper storey had been thrown down . . .

This was a clear indication of seismic upheaval. However, the disaster seemed to have been more than simply an earthquake. Professor Platon also noticed that many storage jars had been compressed and squeezed as if by the enormous pressure of an explosion, as were the walls, having fallen from their foundations in one piece, as if toppled by some massive external force. Moreover, the ruins were full of volcanic pumice. There could be little doubt that Kato Zakro had suffered the effects of a volcanic eruption.

The Thera firestorm may have devastated life on Crete, but the fallout was not the greatest danger. Based on the Krakatau event (see Chapter I), it has been estimated that a *tsunami*, a tidal wave, a staggering ninety metres high would have thrashed the coast of Crete after the eruption of Thera. The towering wall of water would have lashed the densely populated north coast, sweeping through the great ports, pulverizing towns and villages – no doubt claiming countless lives. In the 1930s the Greek archaeologist Spyridon Marinatos found evidence of just such an occurrence. Excavating the site of Amnisos, once the harbour town for the capital at Knossos, he uncovered a villa whose walls bulged outward in a curious way. Large upright stones seemed to have been prised out of position as if by some huge external force, suggesting that they had been hit by the backwash of an enormous tidal wave. It seemed that the harbour town had been drowned by a towering wall of water, evidently the result of the Thera eruption. An Egyptian artefact found here by Marinatos showed that the Thera eruption could not have taken place until at least the reign of Amonhotep III.

From the seventeenth century BCE there was close commercial contact between the Minoans and Egypt. Minoan pottery, with its distinctive geometric patterns and naturalistic wildlife, turned up frequently in Egypt over the next three centuries, and by the eighteenth dynasty the two countries had forged strong diplomatic ties. In the tomb of Queen Hatshepsut's chief minister Senenmut, dating from around 1480 BCE, we see scenes of foreign envoys, each in their national costume. Some are called *Keftiu* and from the goods they bear it is clear that they are Minoans. During the next fifty years or so the Minoans are depicted regularly on tomb reliefs, where they appear as emissaries to the Egyptian court, and by the early fourteenth century BCE relations between the two empires had reached an all-time high. By this time the Minoans had adopted Egyptian building techniques for their new temples on Crete, while the Egyptian place of Malkata at Thebes was lavishly decorated with Minoan frescoes. One example of an exchange of goods between the two nations was found by Marinatos in the ruins of Amnisos beneath the fallen walls of the villa – the broken fragments of an Egyptian alabaster jar. Since the 1930s it has been housed in the National Archaeological Museum of Athens. However, it was not until 1999 that Greek archaeologist Kristos Vlachos examined the artefact and realized its implications. If Amnisos was destroyed in the Thera event, then for the artefact to have been found beneath its fallen walls means that the eruption could not have taken place until after the jar was made. And its date of manufacture was inscribed upon it. It was decorated with a hieroglyphic inscription that made reference to the thirty-third year of the reign of Amonhotep's father, Tuthmosis IV. As Vlachos points out:

> From KV 43 [Tuthmosis IV's tomb in the Valley of the Kings] we know that this was the last year of the king's reign. The find implies that the Santorini [Thera] eruption occurred no earlier than the reign of his successor Amonhotep III.

So the Thera eruption seems to have occurred after 1385 BCE, which fits with the dating of the Danish geophysicists. But if the Thera eruption was responsible for the story of the plagues of the Exodus and the Exodus took place during the reign of Amonhotep III, why is there no historical record of such a catastrophe in Egypt? Most Egyptian writings that survive are inscriptions on stone monuments and tombs. These were almost exclusively of a religious nature or were written to commemorate the accomplishments of the pharaohs: battles won, captives taken, possessions acquired. Nearly all the records we have examined here are of that type. The day-to-day records that might have included historical reference to the Thera eruption would have been on perishable papyrus and few of these have survived. There is, however, indirect contemporary evidence that an unprecedented major catastrophe did occur during Amonhotep's reign.

In the last year of his reign Amonhotep III erected literally hundreds of statues to honour the goddess Sekhmet. At Asher, half a kilometre to the south of the Temple of Amun, Amonhotep was in the process of rebuilding a temple to the chief goddess Mut, when he suddenly reconsecrated it to Sekhmet. Furthermore, he decreed that Sekhmet should replace Mut as the principal goddess. So many statues did he erect of Sekhmet, here and elsewhere, that nearly every Egyptological collection in the world can boast at least one example. The British Museum has the largest number: over thirty specimens in various states of preservation. Hundreds still remain *in situ* in Egypt, the majority being at the temple of Luxor. It has been estimated that there were originally around 700 here alone. In fact, as the Egyptologist Cyril Aldred pointed out in 1988, no other deity of ancient Egypt is represented by so many large-scale statues – and nearly all erected by order of Amonhotep III. These statues of Sekhmet are a clear indication that, despite the apparent stability and wealth of the country, something was wrong. Sekhmet was the goddess of devastation.

Why these monumental statues of the goddess exist in such unrivalled numbers has never been satisfactorily explained. The fact that Amonhotep erected more statues to her – by far – than he did to the chief god Amun-Re, suggests that something had occurred to make him question the power of the principal deity. Sekhmet was represented as a lioness or a woman with a lion's head. In Egyptian mythology she was the daughter of the sun god Ra and she had once almost annihilated mankind. She had obscured the sun and rained down fire from heaven, and humanity was only saved through Ra's personal intervention. Sekhmet's mythical vengeance is markedly similar to the calamity that would have been caused by the Thera eruption. Believing her responsible for the catastrophe, Amonhotep might well have erected the statues in an attempt to appease her.

These statues were erected in the last year of Amonhotep's reign. If they were a response to the Thera eruption, then it would date the event to somewhere around 1360 BCE when his reign ended. Interestingly, this is exactly forty years before the central radiocarbon date for the fall of Jericho. From the Bible we can gather that the plagues of the Exodus occurred forty years before the Israelites began their conquest of Canaan.

The Thera eruption might well have made possible the Exodus itself by enabling the Israelites to escape. Amongst the panic and terror, they might have overpowered their captors and fled into the desert. Yet the plagues were not the only extraordinary episodes to have aided the Israelites' flight that Thera might have caused. There was also the parting of the Red Sea.

According to the Book of Exodus, the Israelites begin their trek out of Egypt once the plagues have finally persuaded the pharaoh to free them. However, before long, the pharaoh has a change of heart and orders his army to pursue them. With their backs to the Red Sea, all seems lost until God again intercedes and causes the waters to part. The Israelites are thus able to walk across the seabed, but when the Egyptian army tries to follow the waters return and the pursuers are drowned.

The event is covered in the original Hebrew Bible just as it is in the modern translation. The miraculous escape, however, might not have happened at the Red Sea but in the Nile delta. It is now generally recognized that the name Red Sea is a mistranslation in the Greek version of the Bible that has been preserved into modern times. First pointed out to western Biblical scholars by the American Egyptologists N. Gunn and A. H. Gardiner in 1918, the original Hebrew Bible describes the place where the Israelites crossed out of Egypt as *Yam Suph* – 'Reed Sea' or 'Sea of Reeds'. The Sea of Reeds was the name used by the ancient Egyptians for Lake Manzala on the Mediterranean coast of the Nile delta, at the extreme north-east of Egypt. Its original name was appropriate at the time as it was a shallow lake covered in reeds. Its modern name, Lake Manzala, is somewhat misleading, as it is actually open to the sea. However, this was not always the case: in ancient times, when sea levels were lower, it was divided from the Mediterranean by a narrow ridge of dry land some fifty kilometres long, broken here and there by a few hundred-metre stretches of water at high tide. At low tide, however, this ridge formed a causeway that could be crossed on foot. If this is the location the Exodus author had in mind, then the route taken by the Israelites makes geographical sense. The best place from Avaris to escape Egypt in the direction of the Sinai wilderness, avoiding the patrolled eastern frontier, would have been to head north then cross the Manzala causeway at low tide. The muddy ground would make it difficult for armed soldiers and heavy chariots to pursue.

The first Egyptologist publicly to consider a connection between the Thera eruption and the Exodus events was Dr Hans Goedicke, the chairman of the Department of Near Eastern Studies at Johns Hopkins University, Baltimore. He concluded that a tidal wave created by the eruption might have been responsible for the miracle at the Sea of Reeds.

When the volcano on the island of Krakatau erupted in 1883, it created a massive *tsunami* some thirty metres high that thrashed the coasts of nearby Sumatra and Java resulting in a terrible loss of life. Within an hour of the Thera eruption a *tsunami* would have hit the Egyptian coast. Although 800 kilometres from Thera, it was well within the danger zone. A very much smaller seismic event, an earthquake in Japan in the 1940s, created a devastating ten-metre *tsunami* on the other side of the Pacific in California. During the Krakatau eruption, a series of *tsunami* occurred over a period of two days. The same would certainly have been true for Thera. In fact, a succession of *tsunami* might have hit the Egyptian coast for much longer, swilling up and down the Mediterranean like water in a bath.

Preceding the arrival of a *tsunami*, the sea withdraws, sometimes for hours. After the Krakatau eruption, a huge coral reef on the coast of Java, usually two metres under sea level, even at low tide, was completely exposed for more than an hour before the wave hit. (It is basically the same phenomenon that causes the sea to withdraw before the breaking of a normal wave, only over a longer duration.) Such a phenomenon might have worked to the Israelites' advantage. From Avaris, the Israelites could easily have reached the Manzala causeway within a couple of days of the initial eruption. If a section of the causeway, usually under

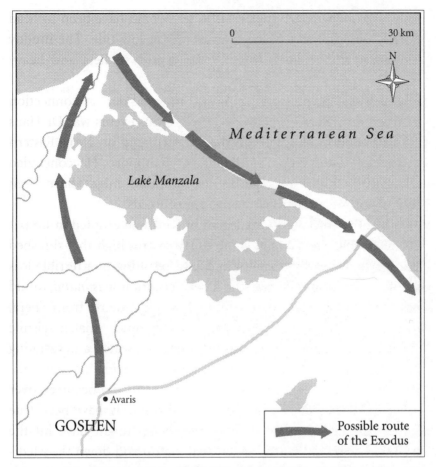

Possible route of the Exodus from Goshen

water, had been exposed by the pre-*tsunami* conditions, then the Israelites could have crossed in much the way the Bible relates:

> And the Lord caused the sea to go back by a strong east wind all that night and made the sea into dry land, and the waters were divided. (EXODUS 14:21)

This is an excellent description of what would have happened at the Manzala causeway, with the waters of the Mediterranean having divided from the waters of the Lake Manzala. The pressure drop over the lowering coastal waters of the Mediterranean might even have caused a strong wind to blow from the east. The Israelites could have made it safely across and, if the timing was fortuitous, the pursuing soldiers might have been attempting to follow when the *tsunami* hit, washing them all away.

> And the waters returned and covered the chariots, and the horsemen and all the host of Pharaoh that came into the sea after them; there remained not so much as one of them.
> (EXODUS 14:29)

From the scientific perspective, therefore, the Exodus could indeed have happened pretty much as the Bible describes.

So it seems that the Biblical history of the Hebrews does appear to fit within a reasonable framework of historical events – at least where it can be tested against external evidence – and that the all-important period of the Exodus and the forty years in the wilderness happened between around 1360 and 1320 BC. The archaic episodes, such as the Garden of Eden and Noah's flood, might be mythological. Some events, such as the reign of Solomon, might have been exaggerated, while others, such as the arrival of Jacob's family in Egypt, might have been over-simplified. Nevertheless, there seems no serious reason to doubt that the general history of the Hebrews was something along the lines the Old Testament relates. The religious elements – how the Hebrew religion came into being – we shall examine shortly. First we must investigate the figure at the very heart of the mystery: Moses himself. It was he, the Old Testament tells us, who first revealed God's laws to the Israelites during the forty years they spent in the wilderness. It was from Moses that the Israelites not only acquired their religion but first learned about the one God.

Summary

- According to the Book of Genesis the Israelites first arrive in Egypt from Canaan when the Patriarch Joseph is made chief minister by the pharaoh and he settles his family in the kingdom. Historically, the Israelites belonged to a large group of Asiatic people collectively called Semites, and Semite trading journeys into Egypt, as described in the Joseph story, occurred as early as the nineteenth century BCE. The Book of Exodus tells us that the period the Israelites spent in Egypt before the Exodus was 430 years, and that following the Exodus they spent forty years in the wilderness before conquering Jericho. As the radiocarbon dating of the fall of Jericho provides a central date of 1320 BCE, the Joseph story appears to be set some time in the eighteenth century BCE.

- The Semite peoples who occupied much of Canaan at this time were called the Hyksos. Around 1750 BCE they began to settle in northern Egypt and, because Egypt was suffering a period of decline, within fifty years they had set up their own rival kingdom in the area with their capital at Avaris. It is certainly feasible that the Hyksos rulers of northern Egypt appointed as their chief ministers those of Canaanite extraction as they were from Canaan themselves.

- It is possible that the biblical enslavement of the Israelites reflects the historical period when the Egyptian pharaohs of the south – the seventeenth-dynasty Theban kings – eventually overcame the Hyksos rulers of the north. That many of the Hyksos were enslaved around 1500 BCE is known from tomb inscriptions of the period. There is even evidence of a people who might have been the Israelites being prominent amongst the Hyksos slaves. They are specifically referred to as *Hapiru* – a name that some scholars believe to have been the origin of the word Hebrew.

• The Exodus can be dated to around 1360 BCE, at the end of the reign of the pharaoh Amonhotep III. This is not only because of the dating of the fall of Jericho to around forty years later but also because of the eruption of the Aegean volcano of Thera, whose effects match the description of the biblical plagues. The Thera eruption can be dated from both ice-core samples taken from Greenland, which show high levels of volcanic dust in the earth's atmosphere of this time, and the dating of the resultant devastation on the nearby island of Crete.

• The 'parting of the Red Sea' may also be accounted for by the eruption of Thera. The name 'Red Sea', used in Exodus for the place were the waters miraculously part to allow the Israelites to escape Egypt, comes from a mistranslation of the Hebrew words *Yam Suph*, which actually mean 'Sea of Reeds'. The 'Sea of Reeds' seems to have been the ancient name for a broad inlet on the delta coast now called Lake Manzala. In biblical times it was divided from the Mediterranean by a narrow ridge of dry land some fifty kilometres long, broken here and there by a few hundred-metre stretches of water at high tide. If the Israelites tried to cross here, a tidal wave created by the Thera eruption might have worked to their advantage. Preceding the arrival of such tidal waves, the sea withdraws, sometimes for hours. If a section of the causeway, usually under water, had been exposed by such conditions, then the phenomenon might indeed have saved the Israelites if the Egyptians were in close pursuit.

5 MOSES: MAN OR MYTH

Although the Old Testament portrays God as speaking directly to a few of Moses' forebears, such as Abraham and Jacob, there is no worship or acceptance of Yahweh by the Hebrews as a whole. It is Moses who first discovers God and reveals him to the Israelites. This would certainly appear to fit with the archaeological evidence that has discovered no indication of the one God religion in Canaan prior to the fall of Jericho around 1320 BCE. On the contrary, the Israelites' ancestors who dwelt there at the time of the Hyksos appear to have been pagan.

Genesis tells us that Jacob and his family lived in the area around Schechem in central Canaan and the Book of Joshua describes how the Hebrews eventually returned here after they left Egypt. Joshua is said to have made it his capital where he built a High Place – an important open-air temple – that continued for centuries as a major centre of worship. The site of biblical Schechem was excavated in the late 1980s and early 1990s by the Israeli archaeologist Dr Isaac Yonah. The dig, in the Samarian mountains just to the north of Nablus, revealed one of the best-preserved early Hebrew religious sites yet discovered. It was found to have consisted of three distinct levels of occupation: a Hyksos period from around 1800 BCE to 1500 BCE; a Canaanite period until around 1300; and an Israelite period until the Assyrian conquest in the late eighth century BCE.

As anticipated, the Israelite level produced no evidence of pagan worship, with the exception of a small bronze bull. Burials around the site had been simple and lack the grave goods typical of pagan burials. The Canaanite level was also as expected: a pagan period with numerous effigies, small statues of various deities and more elaborate interments accompanied by various cultic offerings. The Hyksos level, however, was both surprising and revealing. It was hoped that the site might produce evidence of early Hebrew monotheism, reflecting the biblical period of Jacob and his family. However, although markedly different in character from the later Canaanite finds, numerous clay and stone effigies were found. Whoever was living around Schechem during the biblical period of Jacob, they had many gods, chief of which were what Dr Yonah termed the cardinal deities. These four gods seem to have represented the celestial guardians of the north, south, east and west. Three were depicted in animal form – an ox, a lion and eagle – and one was represented in human form.

We only have the Genesis account to tell us that the Hebrews really were in Schechem before the sojourn in Egypt, but the discovery of these effigies very much confirms that the contemporary inhabitants were indeed the direct Israelite ancestors. These four cardinal deities are reflected in the Old Testament. In the Book of Ezekiel, the prophet has a vision of four winged messengers of God:

> As for the likeness of their faces, they four had the face of a man, and the face of a lion, on the right side: and they four had the face of an ox on the left side; they four also had the face of an eagle. (EZEKIEL 1:10)

These 'living creatures', as Ezekiel first describes them, are said to be the guardians of God's heavenly throne. (Their symbolism was even to influence later Christians who used the ox, lion, eagle and man to represent the four gospel writers, Matthew, Mark, Luke and John.) It is surely indicative that these same four beings should be represented together. Why, though, should the Ezekiel author employ such symbolism? The answer can be found later in his narrative. During a further vision described in chapter nine of the Book of Ezekiel, the prophet identifies the beings as 'cherubim'. The word cherubim is the plural of cherub, which roughly translates as 'celestial being'. To the ancient Israelites, cherubs were not the cute winged babies they became in later Christian art, but fully grown warriors of God. After he expelled Adam and Eve from the Garden of Eden, for example, God places 'Cherubims [sic] with a flaming sword' to guard the Tree of Life. More specifically, they were the guardians of God's throne. In Ezekiel's vision they are depicted as bearing it aloft. The cherubim were such an important motif in the Hebrew faith that they were regularly represented in religious art. According to I Kings 6:23–30, Solomon erected two giant statues of cherubim either side of the entrance to the inner sanctum of the Jerusalem Temple, and Exodus 25: 18–22 describes two golden cherubim figures that adorned the lid of the Ark of the Covenant.

The Old Testament Book of Daniel actually names two of them as Gabriel and Michael. Gabriel means 'man of God', referring to him as the cherub with the face of a man. Michael, on the other hand, was the cherub with the face of an eagle. The New Testament authors later adopted these two beings. The Gospel of Luke has Gabriel appear to the Virgin Mary to announce the birth of Christ, while the author of Revelation has Michael fighting the devil in the form of a dragon. Here they are called by the more familiar term – angels. In fact, the four cherubim were the chief angels, or archangels, the other two being identified in Jewish writings of the second century BCE as Raphael and Uriel: the lion and the ox.

The finds at Schechem suggest that these four archangels were originally the chief Hebrew gods. In all probability, they were absorbed into the new religion in the same way that early saints of the Christian Church were derived from the earlier European gods. Many pagan practices were absorbed into early Christianity. Pagan festivals became Christian holy days, for instance, such as the festival of Eostre, which celebrated the annual resurrection of the summer goddess, becoming Easter when the resurrection of Jesus was celebrated. Some of the chief pagan gods were retained in a similar fashion. For example, the Celts of Britain worshipped a fertility goddess called Briganta. In the British Church she became St Brigit, the patron saint of childbirth. Something similar seems to have occurred with the four cardinal gods of the ancient Hebrews, who became the cherubim.

The discovery of effigies of these four cardinal deities in Schechem, dating from the sixteenth century BCE, is a strong indication that the contemporary inhabitants were not only pagan but Hebrews. It seems that when they were taken into captivity in Egypt, around 1500 BCE, the Israelites were venerating many gods, but by the time they returned to Canaan, around two hundred years later, they had a new, single deity – Yahweh, the one God. If the Bible is right then the Israelites in Egypt had no knowledge of the one God before Moses revealed him to them. According to Exodus 3:13 even Moses has no idea who this God is when he first confronts him at the burning bush – like the Hebrews still in captivity, he is completely ignorant of the God of Israel:

> And Moses said unto God, Behold, when I come unto the children of Israel, and shall say unto them, The God of your fathers hath sent me unto you; and they shall say to me, What is his name? what shall I say unto them?

The story of Moses and his teachings is covered in four books of the Old Testament. The Book of Exodus relates the story of Moses' background as well as the Exodus itself. It ends with the first few months spent in the Sinai wilderness. The narrative relates how Moses has been told by God to lead the Israelites back to their ancestral land of Canaan. Having been divinely promised to the Israelites, Canaan is often referred to as the Promised Land. However, it is to be another forty years before God allows the Israelites to enter it. According to the Book of Exodus, having led the Israelites out of Egypt, Moses leads them to Mount Sinai where he communes alone with God, receiving the Covenant – God's holy laws – and the Ten Commandments, written on two stone tablets. Here God also instructs Moses to make the Ark of the Covenant, a golden container to house the sacred tablets. When he returns from the summit of the mountain, Moses discovers that many of the Israelites have reverted to idolatry and have fashioned a golden calf. Accordingly God punishes them by condemning them to wander in the wilderness for forty years, so that an entire generation will expire before they enter the Promised Land.

The Mosaic Law, the detailed religious doctrine God is said to have revealed to the Israelites through Moses, is primarily contained in the next three books of the Old Testament: Leviticus, meaning 'the priestly book'; Numbers, named after a census it includes that numbers the Israelites; and Deuteronomy, meaning 'the second law'. Together with Genesis and Exodus, these first five books of the Old Testament were and still are the holiest scriptures for the Jews. Collectively called the Torah – the Book of the Law – their Christian name is the Pentateuch, from the Greek meaning 'five volumed'. Traditionally, both Jews and Christians alike attribute all five of these books to the authorship of Moses, although, as we have seen, it seems most unlikely that they were contemporary accounts.

So who exactly was Moses? Was he really an historical figure – a remarkable leader and religious visionary? Or was he simply a legend – the personification of a religious system that actually developed over many years?

According to chapter two of the Book of Exodus Moses was born into a family of Hebrew slaves, although his parents remain unnamed. A later passage, Exodus 6:16–20, suggests that Moses' parents were called Amram and Jochebed. However, the same passage tells us that Amram was the grandson of Joseph's brother Levi, which would seem to be well over two centuries too early to have any connection with an historical Moses. After he is saved from the pharaoh's purge in the little boat of bulrushes (see Chapter IV), he is actually raised by the pharaoh's daughter:

> And the child grew, and she [Moses' sister] brought him unto Pharaoh's daughter, and he became her son. (EXODUS 2:10)

According to Exodus 2:14, Moses even becomes an Egyptian prince. Surely, such a high-profile individual should be found somewhere in Egyptian records? However, there is no record of a Moses during the reign of Amonhotep III, or indeed any Egyptian pharaoh. The name Moses, however, may be misleading. It might not have been his true name.

The modern translations of the Old Testament took the name Moses from the Greek Bible, where it is rendered as Mosis. This, in turn, was taken from the Hebrew Bible, where it appears in its original form as Mose. Exodus 2:10 tells us that the pharaoh's daughter decided to name him this 'because I drew him out of the water'. It is generally assumed that the Exodus author is referring to the similarity between Mose and the Hebrew word *masa*, which means 'to draw forth'. In 1906 the German historian Eduard Meyer contended that this passage was inserted by a later Old Testament copyist to provide a Hebrew origin for what was really an Egyptian name. The episode, he argued, made no sense in the context of the narrative as it now survived. If the princess wished to keep Moses' nationality a secret from the court – which she must have done, since the pharaoh ordered the killing of the

Hebrew babies – then she would not have given her adopted son a Hebrew name. As Meyer's contemporary, the famous Egyptologist Flinders Petrie, pointed out, *mose* is an Egyptian word meaning 'son'. It is a common suffix in many Egyptian names. It is found, for example, in Ahmose, the first king of the eighteenth dynasty, whose name means 'son of the moon'.

In 1995 Israeli historian David Ullian speculated that Mose might have been a title rather than a personal name, just as the term Christ – 'the anointed one' – later became the epithet for Jesus. He suggested that it might have been the shortening of 'Son of God'. In later times the kings and prophets of Judah were often described as the 'sons of God'. It is possible, then, if such a figure did lead the Israelites to freedom, that he appears in Egyptian record under another name. Is there anyone, therefore, of any name, at the court of Amonhotep III who fits Moses' profile?

To start with, it is doubtful that we are looking for an adopted Israelite. The entire story of Moses' Hebrew origins seems to have been an interpolation for two crucial reasons. First, the bulrushes story appears to have been taken from Babylonian legend. In Exodus 2:3 we are told how Moses' mother hides him:

> And when she could no longer hide him, she took for him an ark of bulrushes, and daubed it with slime and with pitch, and put the child therein; and she laid it in the flags of the river brink.

Babylonian mythology includes the markedly similar legend of a certain King Sargon of Akkad. He, too, is floated on a river in a basket of bulrushes when his mother tries to hide him. Like Moses he is found and adopted by someone else:

> My changeling mother conceived me, in secret she bore me. She set me in a basket of rushes, with bitumen she sealed my lid. She cast me in the river which rose not over me.

Second, and more importantly, the story of Moses' adoption fails to withstand historical scrutiny. The Exodus account holds that the pharaoh's daughter adopted Moses and he was raised as a prince. In ancient Egypt the bloodline of the royal family was strictly controlled and manipulated. The pharaohs were considered gods and their daughters could only conceive children with someone of the king's choice: very often himself. Adoption was out of the question. At the time, it is inconceivable that a pharaoh's daughter would be allowed to adopt a son.

It is clear why a story of Moses' origins might have needed to be concocted. Later Israelite nationalists would have found it hard to accept that their great law-giver was a foreigner. If Moses was a prince at the Egyptian court then he is far more likely to have been a native Egyptian. Remarkably, there is one Egyptian prince from Amonhotep's reign who has much in common with Moses – Prince Tuthmose. Tuthmose was the king's eldest son and heir to the throne. As a young man he acted as governor of Memphis, before being appointed commander of the king's chariot forces and seeing active service against the Ethiopians. After a successful campaign he turned to the religious life and was installed as high priest at the temple of Ra in Heliopolis. In the twenty-third year of Amonhotep's reign he suddenly, and for no given reason, resigned his position as high priest and mysteriously disappeared. Two years later, when Amonhotep's reign ended, it was his younger brother Akhenaten who ascended the throne.

Prince Tuthmose fits the Moses profile in a number of ways. He commanded the army during an Ethiopian campaign. So also, it seems, did Moses. Although the Bible tells us next to nothing about Moses' time as an Egyptian prince, the first-century Jewish historian Josephus provides an entire chapter on the subject. In what seems to have been the accepted version of events around two thousand years ago, we are told that the pharaoh appointed

Moses commander of an army he sent to fight the Ethiopians. It was his success in the campaign that led to his exile. Jealous of Moses' popularity amongst the soldiers, the pharaoh eventually orders his arrest but, forewarned, Moses escapes the country. The Josephus account seems to have greater historical validity than the biblical narrative regarding the reason for Moses' exile. In the Book of Exodus we are told simply that Moses is forced to flee Egypt after he saves the life of an Israelite by killing a vicious slave driver. In reality, an Egyptian prince could order a common slave driver executed on the spot if he so desired. This was probably another episode that was added to make Moses an Israelite.

If Moses was the priest who appears in Manetho's *Aegyptiaca*, then Tuthmose further fits the profile (see Chapter IV). Manetho tells us that the priest was a servitor at the temple of Ra in Heliopolis before he abandoned the Egyptian gods. This was precisely the position held by Prince Tuthmose before he disappeared.

Like Moses, Tuthmose might also have been driven into exile, the reason being that his tomb was never used. The explorer Giovanni Belzoni discovered Tuthmose's tomb at the far end of the Valley of the Kings in the early nineteenth century and it immediately posed an enigma. Royal tombs were prepared while the owner was still alive; only the final funerary decorations were added after death. This tomb, however, was finished but the usual illustrations depicting the owner's funeral and mummification were absent. This meant that the tomb was empty not because it had been robbed but because it had never been used. Why not?

It is possible that Tuthmose had commissioned another tomb, although this seems most unlikely. Tombs were an expensive and time-consuming business. It took years to cut out the hundreds of square metres of solid rock to create the burial and treasury

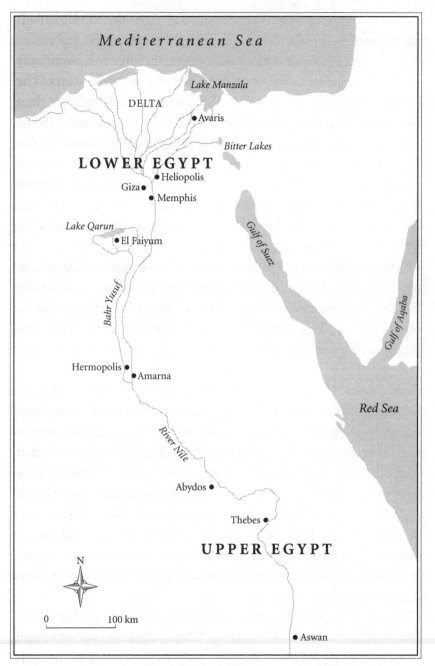

Mediterranean Sea

Lake Manzala

DELTA

● Avaris

Bitter Lakes

LOWER EGYPT

● Heliopolis

Giza ●

● Memphis

Lake Qarun

● El Faiyum

Bahr Yusuf

Gulf of Suez

Gulf of Aqaba

Hermopolis ●

● Amarna

Red Sea

River Nile

Abydos ●

Thebes ●

UPPER EGYPT

N

0   100 km

● Aswan

Ancient Egypt

chambers deep underground. Masons' graffiti discovered in Tuthmose's tomb showed that it was completed in the twenty-second
year of Amonhotep's reign: only a year before the prince van-
ished. There was simply not enough time to build a new one.
Coupled with his sudden and unexplained disappearance from
the temple of Ra and the lack of any memorials or obituaries, the
empty tomb suggests that Tuthmose had been disgraced in some
way and had either been executed or driven into exile.

The only major difference between Tuthmose and Moses is
their ages. According to the Exodus account, it is many years
after Moses' exile that he returns to lead the Israelites to freedom,
by which time he is eighty. Based on our current calculations, the
Exodus occurred shortly before the end of Amonhotep's reign
when Tuthmosis would have been no older than around thirty-
five. Nevertheless, we have to treat biblical ages with caution. We
often read of people living to more than a century when forty or
fifty was considered a good lifespan.

If the Exodus took place during the reign of Amonhotep III,
then Prince Tuthmose is the best candidate by far for the
historical Moses. If our assumptions are correct, his background
uniquely matches Moses' in a number of ways: commander of
the army in Ethiopia; priest at the temple of Ra; and he is
disgraced or exiled. Even his name is intriguing: Tuthmose means
'son of [the god] Thoth'. If Tuthmose had abandoned the old
gods and decided to drop the god-element *Tuth* – Thoth – from
his name, then he would actually have been called Mose, the
original rendering of the name Moses.

There is, however, a problem with placing Moses in the reign
of Amonhotep III. Over recent decades archaeology has unearthed
evidence to suggest that the Hebrew religion was already established in Egypt by this time. If the Bible is right then the Israelites
in Egypt had no knowledge of the one God before Moses returned
to them. If the Hebrew religion was already established in Egypt

by Amonhotep III's time, then it would constitute a case for placing Moses during an earlier period.

Evidence that the God of Israel was already being worshipped by the Hebrew slaves by Amonhotep's reign is found indirectly in Egyptian sources. It seems that the Israelites' monotheistic religion had influenced an Egyptian sect. Known as Atenism, this sect worshipped a single universal deity and denied the existence of all other gods. Its practices were so similar to the Hebrew religion that many biblical commentators and Egyptologists alike have seen a connection, some suggesting that it was directly inspired by the religion of the Israelite slaves, in a similar manner to how early Christianity later inspired the religion of Imperial Rome.

Atenism had been growing steadily in Egypt for around a century before Amonhotep came to the throne. The sect's single god was called the Aten, and the first reference to it as a divinity appears during the reign of Tuthmosis III, around 1450. An inscription from the tomb of the army commander Djehuty at Deir el-Bahari at Thebes talks of the 'living Aten, lord of the two lands'. As the two lands were Egypt itself – Upper and Lower Egypt – then we can infer that the noble family who commissioned the inscription considered the Aten to be the supreme god of Egypt. By the end of the century such references are far more numerous, such as a commemorative scarab from the reign of Tuthmosis IV, around 1400 BCE. Here an inscription describes the peoples under the dominion of the pharaoh as 'his subjects by the will of the Aten'. It is doubtful that the king himself shared this view, but by Amonhotep III's reign the Aten was certainly accepted by the king as a legitimate deity. He actually named his state barge *Radiance of the Aten*. By the time Amonhotep's son Akhenaten came to the throne, around 1360 BCE, Atenism had grown so influential that the new pharaoh even adopted it as the state religion of Egypt.

Before we can decide if the existence of Atenism in Egypt prior to Amonhotep's reign constitutes a case for Moses living before this time, we need to ascertain if it really did spring from the religion of the Israelites.

The correlation between the two religions does seem too close to be coincidental. Apart from the fact that they both believe in a single universal god and deny the existence of all others – a concept unknown anywhere else in the world – they share a number of unique themes. First, both venerate a nameless god that is only referred to by titles. The name Jehovah, familiar to Christians today, is actually a Greek rendering of the Hebrew *Yhvh* or *Yahweh*, which actually means 'the Lord'. The God of Israel has no name. Neither does the god of the Atenists. No matter how reverently, in Egypt gods were usually addressed directly. Indeed, the name of the god was thought to invoke its presence. However, the god of the Atenists was a unique exception. The common name used by Egyptologists for the Atenist god is 'the Aten'. However, this was not actually the god's name, but the name for the glyph that represented it. A direct transliteration of the word Aten is 'giver of life'. Aten was not the name of the Atenists' deity it was merely a description. Its other titles and forms of address are identical to those used for the Hebrew God. This is known from a chance discovery made at Thebes.

In the first years of his reign, Akhenaten erected a new temple to the Aten at Karnak in Thebes. However, shortly after his reign, when Egypt abandoned Atenism and reverted to the pantheon of traditional gods, the temple was torn down. By chance many of the sculpted blocks that decorated the temple were preserved inside two giant gate towers that were erected in front of the nearby temple of Amon-Re. In the 1930s, when these towers were dismantled for structural repairs, over forty thousand of these sculpted blocks were found inside, which had been used as filling over three thousand years ago. Now called the Karnak Talatat, many are inscribed with Atenist prayers that bear a striking resemblance to Hebrew texts.

In the biblical account, when Moses first asks God to reveal his name at the burning bush he is told, 'I am who I am' (EXODUS 3:14). He was simply God – the only God. The Hebrew word for 'god' was *El*. This had various forms such as *Elyon*, 'god most high', and *Elohim*, 'your god', or *El Shaddai*, 'god Almighty'. The word *Yahweh*, 'the Lord', is used often as in *Yahweh-tsidkenu*, the 'Lord of hosts'. (The Hebrew word *tsidkenu*, which modern translations render as 'hosts', actually refers to armies, such as the hosts of Judah, the hosts of Israel or hosts of angels.) However, because the Hebrews even considered *Yahweh* too personal, the word *Adonai* – 'my Lord' – was substituted in prayer.

In the Karnak Talatat inscriptions we find the Aten addressed in almost identical fashion. One reference is highly reminiscent of the 'I am who I am' in the burning bush episode: 'Thou art what thou art, radiant and high over every land.' Others refer to the Aten, just as the Bible repeatedly refers to God, as God almighty and God most high. For example: 'O great Aten, god almighty, who furnishest man's sustenance' and 'O great Aten, god most high, who drivest away the dark.' The Aten is even referred to as lord of armies, just as the God of Israel is called the Lord of Hosts: 'Thou who art Lord of all the armies of the world.' Most frequently, however, the Aten is addressed in a similar fashion to the way God is addressed as *Adonai*, using the word *Neb*, the Egyptian word for lord.

It is not only the forms of address that are so alike but the very way the two religions perceive their deities. A lengthy prayer to the Aten survives in a number of reliefs in the city of Amarna in middle Egypt. Known as 'The Hymn to the Aten', it was seen by the American Egyptologist James Henry Breasted, as early as 1909, to bear a striking similarity to Psalm 104 in the Old

Testament. Both prayers describe in identical terms how God and the Aten are respectively seen as creators, nurturers and prime movers of all phenomena on earth. God and the Aten are also regarded as heavenly kings. Like the name of a pharaoh, the Aten's hieroglyphic titles are always enclosed in a royal cartouche (an oval design). The God of Israel, too, is spoken of as a king. For example, in Isaiah 44:6: 'Thus saith the Lord the King of Israel', or Psalm 47, which tells us that, 'God is the King of all the earth.'

Another unique correlation between the God of Israel and the Aten is that neither deity was permitted to be represented in effigy. Although, as we shall examine shortly, the early Israelites did make icons to represent aspects of God's power, Israelite religion proscribed the making of effigies of God himself. Traditionally, in Egypt, an effigy or statue of a god was an essential part of cultic practice. The Egyptians believed that the deity actually inhabited the image and the making of them was rigidly described in ancient texts. Exclusively in Egypt, Atenism diverged from this practice. The Atenists proscribed the making of any idols and effigies of the Aten. According to one of the Karnak Talatat: 'No form in all the earth can reflect thy glory.'

Both religions managed to get round the problems that such a doctrine created by employing a symbol to represent the deity's presence. When they eventually settled in Canaan, the Israelites used the menorah, a holy seven-branched candelabrum, to represent God's light and presence in the temple. The practice still survives in modern synagogues and Jewish homes. The Atenists also used a symbol of light to represent the Aten. It was a glyph: a disc with arms extending downward to end in hands holding the ankh, the symbol for life. It actually depicted the sun with its rays bringing life-giving light to the earth. Early Egyptologists interpreted this to be evidence of sun worship. However, as more archaeological finds were made during the twentieth century, it became clear that the glyph represented sunlight and not the sun itself. (The sun was actually portrayed as a winged disc.) Atenism forbade the representation of its god in any other form. It is now clear that sunshine – which brings warmth, light and life – was the way the sect conveyed the idea of an omnipresent, all-providing god.

The only exception the Atenists made to the making of images is exactly the same exception the early Israelites seem to have made: the image of a sacred bull. Even after Akhenaten abandoned all the traditional deities and everything associated with them, he made specific instructions for the Mnevis bull, an animal sacred to Ra, to be brought to his new capital at Amarna and buried in a special tomb in the nearby hills. The Mnevis Bull, or Nemur, was a living animal worshipped at the temple of Heliopolis, which, when dead, was buried with great pomp and ceremony and replaced by a new one located in the wild according to prescribed portents. A number of hand-size effigies of such a bull, in both stone and bronze, have been discovered at the ruins of Amarna.

The early Israelites, too, continued to venerate a sacred bull, much to the annoyance of Moses. A sacred bull is echoed in the biblical story of the golden calf. According to chapter thirty-two of Exodus, when Moses is absent communing with God on Mount Sinai, his people, fearing some ill has befallen him, ask his deputy Aaron to make sacred images to protect them. Agreeing, Aaron collects golden jewellery from the people and makes a 'molten calf'. In fact, contrary to the popular Hollywood image, it is not one calf they make but many, as the others are said to follow Aaron's lead. Aaron declares that these calves are 'thy gods, O Israel, which brought thee up out of the land of Egypt' (EXODUS 32:4). Furthermore, they do not seem to be life-size representations either. We are not told how big they are, but the inference is that, like the Egyptian bull effigies, they are small enough to be held in the hands. When the people gave Aaron their golden earrings to make the idol, 'he received them at their hand and fashioned it with a graving tool' (EXODUS 32:4).

That the early Israelites venerated such idols is supported by archaeological evidence. A number of hand-size carved bulls have been found at early sites throughout Palestine. Perhaps the most interesting was a bronze bull, some twenty centimetres long, found at the site of Schechem and now in the possession of the Israeli archaeologist Dr Amihay Mazor, of the Hebrew University, Jerusalem. This was the biblical Schechem, one of the holiest sites in ancient Israel where Joshua raised an altar to God. The artefact dates from the twelfth century BCE, a time after the period of Moses and consequently a time when the Hebrew faith was apparently fully established.

If the Old Testament story of the Israelite conquest of Canaan is true, then the site of Schechem was an extremely important centre of worship. According to the Book of Joshua, after Canaan was conquered Joshua erected an altar to give thanks to God:

> So Joshua made a covenant with the people that day, and set them a statute and an ordinance in Shechem. And Joshua wrote these words in the book of the law of God, and took a great stone, and set it up there under an oak, that was by the sanctuary of the Lord. And Joshua said unto all the people, Behold this stone shall be a witness unto us; for it hath heard all the words of the Lord which he spake unto us: it shall be therefore a witness unto you, lest ye deny your God. (JOSHUA 24:25–27)

The bronze bull, coming from this highly revered site, is clear evidence of the continued veneration of the bull, certainly by some Hebrews, well after they had returned to Canaan. Of all the hundreds of religious practices that there were in the world, that both the Atenist and Hebrew religions should seemingly have retained the same pagan one is surely more than coincidence.

Perhaps the most compelling evidence that Atenism and the religion of the Israelites were related came with an astonishing archaeological discovery made in 1989. In that year the French archaeologist Alain Zivie discovered a rock-cut tomb in the Bubasteion cliff at Sakkara, near Cairo. The man interred in the tomb was both a priest of the Atenist and an Israelite priest.

The tomb was still sealed, but it had been plundered in antiquity and patched up by necropolis attendants at the time. Inside was the decomposed mummy of one Aper-el. A number of items remained, including the coffin, wine jars, a number of *ushabti* figures, statuettes, jewellery, and a complete set of Canopic jars for the mummy's removed organs. Most important of all, however, were the inscriptions that still remained intact, identifying the occupant and his place in Egyptian history.

Aper-el was practically unknown before the discovery, which made the find all the more exciting. It turned out that he was one of the most important figures in Akhenaten's government. He was a grand vizier, the chief minister of northern Egypt. The remarkable thing was that Aper-el was not a native Egyptian but a Semite, which in itself would have been unusual enough. More specifically, however, he seems to have been an Israelite. His name, Aper-el, Alain Zivie realized with surprise, appeared to have been a title. Translated, it means literally 'servitor of [the god] El'. As we have seen, *El* was the Hebrew word for God. His name clearly implied that Aper-el was a chief practitioner of the Israelite religion during Akhenaten's reign. The most astonishing discovery, however, was the tomb illustrations revealing that Aper-el was also the high priest of the Atenist temple in the city of Memphis. Here we have not only evidence of a shared link between the Hebrew religion and Atenism, but an example of someone who seems to have been a priest of both religions and saw no contradiction in that.

That two different cultures in the same place and the same

time should both have practised such a similar religion is surely beyond coincidence. All the more so because the Hebrews and the Atenists are the only peoples on earth for over another millennium known to conceive of monotheism. There would seem little reason to doubt, therefore, that Atenism sprang from the religion of the Israelites as some scholars suspect.

If Atenism and the Hebrew religion are related then it appears that, although the Egyptians may have oppressed the Israelite peoples, they had no problem with their religion, certainly not by Akhenaten's time. Why Akhenaten opted to establish Atenism as the state religion of Egypt, though, is something of an enigma. It is possible that if the Israelites had interpreted the cataclysm brought about by the Thera eruption as an act of their God then, perhaps, from Akhenaten's perspective, this was the god to follow.

So we are left with a problem concerning Moses. Although Atenism did not become the state religion of Egypt until Akhenaten's time, it had been a steadily growing sect in the country for around a hundred years. It might only have been a minority cult before Akhenaten's reign, but it existed nevertheless. If it was inspired by the Hebrew religion then it would seem that if Moses existed then he lived before Atenism came into being in the early fifteenth century BCE. Yet, as we have seen, there is much evidence to place the Exodus in the mid-fourteenth century BCE, during Amonhotep's reign. If the Old Testament account of Moses first revealing God to the Israelites in any way reflects historical events, then there must have been two Moses': one who led them to freedom at the time of the Thera eruption about 1360 BCE, and another, earlier Moses, who first revealed God to the Israelites at some point before Atenism made its appearance around a hundred years earlier.

If we look again at the Exodus story, it does seem that two distinct historical periods were involved. There are, in fact, two separate pharaohs in the Exodus story. The one who enslaves the Israelites, the pharaoh of the oppression, and the one who is in power at the time of the Exodus, the pharaoh of the Exodus. From Exodus 1:19 we can see that it is the first of these pharaohs who is on the throne when Moses first leaves Egypt. When he eventually returns to lead the Israelites to freedom a new pharaoh is in power. According to Exodus 2:23:

> And it came to pass in the process of time, that the king of Egypt died: and the children of Israel sighed by reason of the bondage, and they cried, and their cry came up unto God by reason of the bondage.

In the popular Hollywood version of events, the second pharaoh is the other's son and successor. However, it is clear that a considerable period of time has elapsed between Moses' exile and the Exodus itself. According to Exodus 1:12, the following separates the two events: 'But the more they afflicted them, the more they multiplied and grew.' This has to be some generations. Two Moses figures, separated by a century or so, would seem to fit with the biblical narrative. It is possible, then, that the character represented first communing with God at the burning bush and the character who ultimately leads the Israelites out of Egypt are two separate figures that the passage of time confused as one. If the name Moses was a title, as David Ullian believes, then such confusion might have arisen due to the misinterpretation of Mose as a personal name.

The Exodus narrative does retain one passage that appears to betray that, in its original rendering, the story concerned two different men. Moses' father-in-law seems to have been two separate people. A few verses before he encounters God in the burning bush, Moses saves seven sisters from a group of marauding shepherds. In gratitude, their father Reuel offers him one of his daughters in marriage:

Now when Pharaoh heard this thing, he sought to slay Moses. But Moses fled from the face of Pharaoh, and dwelt in the land of Midian: and he sat down by a well. Now the priest of Midian had seven daughters: and they came and drew water and filled the troughs to water their father's flock. And the shepherds came and drove them away: but Moses stood up and helped them, and watered their flock. And when they came to Reuel their father, he said, How is it that ye are come so soon this day? And they said, An Egyptian delivered us out of the hand of the shepherds, and also drew water enough for us, and watered the flock. And he said unto his daughters, And where is he? why is it that ye have left the man? call him, that he may eat bread. And Moses was content to dwell with the man: and he gave Moses Zipporah his daughter. (EXODUS 2:15–21)

Moses then marries Reuel's daughter and settles down to raise a family. Later when Moses leads the Israelites out of Egypt, his father-in-law receives the news:

When Jethro, the priest of Midian, Moses' father in law, heard of all that God had done for Moses, and for Israel his people, and that the Lord had brought Israel out of Egypt. (EXODUS 18:1)

Although he is again described as 'the priest of Midian', this time Moses' father-in-law is called Jethro, as he is elsewhere during the account of the flight from Egypt. There seems to have been some confusion here. At no point are we told that Moses had more than one wife, so it would seem that the Moses who first encounters God in the burning bush has a different father-in-law from the Moses who led the Exodus.

An original Moses – a visionary who first inspired the Israelite religion well before the Exodus – would certainly fit into a feasible historical context during the early fifteenth century BCE. As we have seen, based on the available archaeology and historical evidence, this was when Tuthmosis III first hauled the Israelites back from Canaan. With the defeat and humiliation of the

Hyksos and the recent enslavement of the Israelites, the climate was ripe for new religious thought. Especially one that set the Israelites apart as a chosen people, uniquely selected for salvation and deliverance.

The circumstances are, in fact, uncannily similar to the inception of Christianity, at the time when the Jews in Judah were first brought under direct Roman rule. The teachings of Jesus quickly gained a hard-core following amongst the Jews, whose traditional religion seemed to have failed them. Moses' new faith may also have inspired Atenism amongst Egyptians under the same circumstances as Jesus's teachings inspired Christianity amongst the first-century Romans. Because of its concept of a universal God, Christianity quickly appealed to many liberal Romans, uneasy with the new imperial establishment and the tyranny and excesses of the emperors. (Rome had been a republic before Augustus.) The Christianity that eventually became Roman Christianity, however, was somewhat different from that perceived by Christ's original followers. This we know from chapter two of St Paul's letters to the Galatians in the New Testament, where he complains that the Christians in Jerusalem believed that Jesus's teachings were intended only for the Jews. In a similar manner, the Hebrew religion might have inspired the Atenist variation amongst disgruntled Egyptians, now under the iron rule of Tuthmosis III, the so-called Napoleon of ancient Egypt.

If the Moses in the Old Testament was originally two separate men, is there any evidence of the first during the reign of Tuthmosis III? There is certainly someone who may be the woman depicted as the princess who adopted Moses. Although she is anonymous in the Bible, Josephus names her. He calls her Thermuthis. No royal princess called Thermuthis is recorded during Amonhotep III's reign, or indeed in the reign of any pharaoh. However, there is a princess at the court of Tuthmosis III whose name is remarkably similar.

In July 1916 a group of British explorers discovered a tomb, half-way up a cliff-face some distance west of Deir-el-Bahari at Thebes. It proved to be the tomb of a princess who died during the reign of Tuthmosis III. Her name was Termut, 'Daughter of [the goddess] Mut'. This name could well have been rendered as Thermuthis in the Greek translation of Josephus' original text, which still survives. The Greeks often wrote the T pronunciation in Egyptian names as a letter *theta* – TH – and appended the *is* sound to the end of names. Tuthmose, for example, is transliterated as Tuthmosis. Termut could well have been the original rendering of Thermuthis.

Termut, however, was her adopted Egyptian name: inscriptions on the walls of the tomb identify this woman as a Syrian princess. It was the common practice at the time for foreign kings' daughters to be exchanged as royal hostages with the Egyptians to seal an alliance against their common enemy, the Hittites. There were, in fact, no fewer than nine such princesses from various kingdoms and city states at the court of Tuthmosis III. Some ended up in the king's harem but other, more important princesses had their own estates and were granted the honorary title *Tet-sa-pro* – 'daughter of pharaoh', which meant that they were under the king's personal protection. As the daughter of one of Tuthmosis' chief allies in his struggle against the Hittites, Termut was afforded such privileges.

The only real restraint on such women was celibacy. If the alliance fell apart, the girl would either be executed or, more likely, end up with the others in the king's harem. Accordingly she was expected to remain a virgin and not to marry. Although she could not have children of her own, she might act as nanny or tutor in foreign matters to royal princes and princesses. Termut must have been good at this job for she is described in the tomb as tutor in Semitic languages to the queen, Merytre, and her son Amonhotep (later to become Amonhotep II). She was also tutor to three other courtly officials. Two were the sons of military officers recorded elsewhere during the reign of Tuthmosis III, and one was a mysterious figure who appears to have come from nowhere. His name was Kamose, and in the thirty-fourth year of Tuthmosis reign (around 1470 BCE) he became chief steward or foreign minister to the king.

Kamose appears a number of times in monuments of the period, but nowhere are his parents named. This was unusual and can only mean that they were not of the nobility. Kamose, it seems, was a self-made man. Or, to be more accurate, Termut made him the man he was. In her tomb Kamose is mentioned because, as the author of the inscription boasts, Termut tutored him from an early age. Termut arrived in Egypt in the tenth year of Tuthmosis' reign, which would be around 1494 BCE. The inscription says that she tutored Kamose from the fourteenth year. The first time Kamose appears in Egyptian records he is a minor priest at the temple of Heliopolis in the twenty-ninth year of Tuthmosis' reign. As priests were appointed around the age of fifteen, this would mean that he was only a very young child when Termut took him under her wing. In all probability his parents had been killed and she became his guardian. As his parents do not seem to have been of noble birth, then it is possible that he was the son of one of the princess's countrymen. Was Kamose the first Moses?

Kamose must have been an exceptional young man as five years after becoming a priest in Heliopolis he was appointed by the king as his chief steward. The position was similar to a foreign minister so would have made him one of the most important civil servants in the kingdom. Kamose's main responsibility would have been to deal with diplomatic envoys and foreigners living in Egypt. He was also chiefly responsible for the deployment of any captive workforce. Slaves in Egypt were usually overseen by their own countrymen: slaves who had been freed to act as taskmasters because they understood the customs and, more importantly, the language of the slaves. Kamose's job would have been to liaise with these people. There is no doubt, therefore, that if the Israelites were slaves in Egypt at this time Kamose would have been in close contact with them. Perhaps he might even have come to sympathize with their plight. To be outspoken on such matters would almost certainly have led to his dismissal from office and perhaps also to exile.

Kamose was still alive and was chief steward when Termut died, which is why his education is included amongst her achievements in the tomb inscriptions. However, he no longer appears after year forty of Tuthmosis' reign when he is replaced by the grand vizier Rekhmire, when the office of chief steward was joined to this minister's existing office of chief minister. What happened to Kamose is a mystery, but there is some evidence that he was disgraced or dismissed. Rekhmire's tomb still survives in the Valley of the Kings, and here Kamose's name is found amongst those who were subordinate to the grand vizier. The tomb was prepared, no doubt, some time before the minister's death. When it was finally used, however, the name of Kamose was scratched out. The name is now discernible only through modern ultraviolet analysis of the inscription. This selective vandalism would not appear to have been the work of tomb robbers as the rest of the inscription is fully intact. For the name to have been erased strongly suggests that Kamose was disgraced.

No tomb of Kamose has been found in Egypt, although, if he was not of noble birth, this may not necessarily be indicative. Then again, neither was Menkheperresoneb, who rose to be high priest of Amon-Ra at Thebes, and he had a splendid tomb in the Valley of the Kings. As chief steward, Kamose would presumably have been rich enough to have afforded a similar burial. Like Prince Tuthmosis, almost a century later, therefore, there is a case to be made for Kamose having been forced into exile.

So was Kamose the original Moses – the man who found God in the burning bush? He fits the profile in a number of ways:

- His parentage is unknown and seems to have been lower class, even foreign.

- He was raised by a 'daughter of pharaoh' with the same name as Moses' adopted mother.

- He held high office at the pharaoh's court.

- He was in close contact with foreign slaves, which might have included the Israelites.

- He left office mysteriously and seems to have been disgraced.

- His eventual whereabouts are unknown.

Finally we have his name. Once more, the name might have been rendered as Mose. His name Kamose means 'son of the spirit'. 'Ka' was the Egyptian name for the soul, but it also referred to a divine spark of life, such as the Great Spirit in Native American religion. In this respect, the name is not so different from what David Ullian believes was the origin of the name Moses, 'Son of God'. The fact that both candidates for the composite Moses have this 'son' element in their names may account for why they became confused as one character when the Old Testament was committed to writing many years later. The Israelites would have dropped the Egyptian Ka element from his name as they may have dropped the Tut from Prince Tuthmose's name. It betrayed both pagan and Egyptian origins. Two men called Mose: one discovered God and inspired the Israelites with a new religion, the other freed the Israelites and revealed God's laws. It is understandable that later they became confused as one man – a man who was required to live to well over a hundred years of age.

If Kamose and Prince Tuthmose were the first and second Moses, then they had a common religious background. Both men were, for a while, priests of the temple of Ra in Heliopolis. Although the cult of the sun god Ra bears little resemblance to the Hebrew religion, it does show that both men were trained in religious matters. In Kamose's case, disillusionment at the treatment of the foreign slaves might have made him question the traditional gods of Egypt. If he was forced to leave the country, it is quite likely that such a man would have found another religion: one that he might have returned to bring to the Israelites.

The burning question, however, is not so much who Moses was but where this religion came from. In order to answer it we need to examine the actual nature of ancient Israelite religion. Remarkably, considering that the Hebrews are thought of as a people united under one God, for much of their history they were split into two rival factions, each having different cultic practices and, more importantly, completely different concepts of God.

Summary

• If the Bible is right, then the Israelites in Egypt had no knowledge of the one God before Moses returned to them. Although God is portrayed as speaking directly to a few of Moses' forebears, such as Abraham and Jacob, there is no reference to the worship or acceptance of God by the Israelites as a whole. Even Moses has no idea who this God is when he first confronts him at the burning bush. Like the Hebrews still in captivity, he is completely ignorant of the God of Israel.

• Moses appears in the original Hebrew Bible under the name Mose. The word *mose* is in fact an Egyptian word meaning 'son'. In 1995 Israeli historian David Ullian speculated that Mose might have been a title rather than a personal name, just as the term Christ – 'the anointed one' – later became the epithet for Jesus. He suggested that it might have been the shortening of 'Son of God'. In later times the kings and prophets of Judah were often described as the 'sons of God'. It is possible, then, if such a figure did lead the Israelites to freedom, that he appears in Egyptian record under another name.

- The historical Moses seems to have been two separate men: one who lived in the mid-fifteenth century BCE and another around a century later. The first Moses discovered God in the burning bush and the second led the Israelites out of Egypt. Two distinct historical periods were involved in the Exodus story. There are two separate pharaohs: one who enslaves the Israelites and another who is in power at the time of the Exodus. According to Exodus 1:12, the following separates the two events, 'But the more they afflicted them, the more they multiplied and grew.' This has to be some generations. Two Moses figures, separated by a century or so, would seem to fit with the biblical narrative.

- The first-century historian Josephus tells us that Moses' adopted mother, the daughter of the Pharaoh, is called Thermuthis, the Greek rendering of the Egyptian name Termut. There is only one Egyptian princess recorded with this name: a woman who lived during the reign of Tuthmosis III. Around 1494 BCE she adopted the young boy called Kamose. Later Kamose became an Egyptian priest and then the foreign minister to Tuthmosis III around 1470 BCE. This man seems to have been the Moses who discovered God in the burning bush. He matches the profile in a number of ways. His parentage is unknown and seems to have been lower class, even foreign. He was raised by a 'daughter of pharaoh' with the same name as Moses' adopted mother. He held high office at the pharaoh's court. He was in close contact with foreign slaves, which included the Israelites. He was dismissed from office and disappeared from the records around 1460 BCE.

- In the fourth decade of the following century, the pharaoh Amonhotep III was on the Egyptian throne and his son Prince Tuthmose was his heir. However, Tuthmose mysteriously disappeared around 1363 BCE. He might have been a second Moses, the man who led the Israelites out of Egypt. He matches the Moses profile in a number of ways: commander of the army in Ethiopia, as Josephus tells us Moses was, and priest at the temple of Ra, as the Greek historian Manetho suggests Moses was. Furthermore, he was disgraced or exiled, as his brother Akhenaten was named heir and his tomb remained unused.

6 A PEOPLE DIVIDED

According to the Old Testament, after the reign of Solomon it was not only the Hebrews' kingdom that was split in two but their religion. For much of three centuries, from the time the monarchy divided until the period of the Assyrian invasion, the two Hebrew kingdoms of Judah and Israel were apparently worshipping different gods. According to the Books of Kings and Chronicles Judah stayed faithful to Yahweh, the one Hebrew God, whereas Israel, from the moment it separated from Judah, began worshipping another god.

The first Book of Kings describes how Jeroboam was the first king to build a temple to this other god. His immediate act on becoming the first king of lesser Israel, around 930 BCE, was to order the making of two effigies of calves, one of which he erected in the city of Dan (the capital of Israel before Omri made it Samaria), and the other at a new temple he had constructed as his country's principal religious centre.

> Whereupon the king took council, and made two calves of gold, and said to them ... behold thy gods, O Israel, which brought thee up out of the land of Egypt. And he set one in Beth-el, and the other he put in Dan. And he made an house of high places, and made priests of the lowest of the people, which were not of the sons of Levi ... So he did in Beth-el, sacrificing unto the calves that he had made: and he placed in Beth-el the priests of the high places which he had made. So he offered upon the altar which he had made in Beth-el ... (1 KINGS 12:28–33)

We are not told where the shrine of Beth-el actually is but the reference to a 'house of high places' suggests that it was a large open-air temple common to the period. Archaeologists have discovered a number of holy sites described in the Bible as High Places, such as the one at Schechem in central Israel (see Chapter 5): large and sophisticated, open-air temples, consisting of a paved area sometimes surrounded by pillars. The site of biblical Dan, however, where the second calf is said to have been erected, has been identified with Tell el-Qadi, a large mound of some fifty acres at Mount Hermon in northern Israel. In the 1970s excavations at the site were conducted by a team of archaeologists led by Professor Avraham Biran, director of the Nelson Glueck School of Biblical Archaeology in Jerusalem. At the entrance to the site, they uncovered the remains of a massive gatehouse, consisting of two towers, either side of what appears to have been a main concourse, flanked by the foundations of various dwellings. The concourse terminates at what appears to have been an open-air forum: a paved square with a raised stone platform surrounded by four decorated columns, set before a long stone bench. Various ceramic finds at the site led Professor Biram to date the town's construction to the early tenth century BCE, which means that it would indeed have been occupied at the time that Jeroboam seems to have been king.

Over a period of ten years the dig uncovered spectacular evidence of ancient cultic activity. Higher up the hillside, directly above the site, there is a spring, said to be the source of the river Jordan. Here the team uncovered an imposing structure that Professor Biram believes could have been the High Place where the calf was erected. It consists of a paved area before a raised platform carved from solid rock. The platform supports an altar, some thirty-five centimetres high and forty centimetres square, cut from a single block of limestone. Remarkably, its surface was still scorched from the burning of incense in ancient times.

Although no statue of a calf was found, the excavations have demonstrated that the site was in use during Jeroboam's reign just as the Old Testament purports.

The reference in the above passage to the sons of Levi refers to the priests of Solomon's temple in Jerusalem, as the tribe of Levi had become the priestly caste amongst the Hebrews. Jeroboam, we are told, rejected their authority and established another priesthood. As such, he had severed all ties with the religious practices of Judah. Moreover, the calves would, on the face of it, appear to represent a completely different god from the God of Israel, as Yahweh was proscribed under Hebrew doctrine from being represented by idols or images of any kind.

This new god is apparently identified later in the first Book of Kings when we are told how King Ahab of Israel, some fifty years after Jeroboam, continued to sanction the cult:

> And Ahab the son of Omri did evil in the sight of the Lord above all that were before him. And it came to pass, as if it had been a light thing for him to walk in the sins of Jeroboam the son of Nebat . . . and went and served Baal and worshipped him.
> (I KINGS 16:30–31)

It seems, then, that the god is a deity called Baal. Ahab's son and successor Ahazaih also continued to venerate this apparently pagan god:

> Ahaziah the son of Ahab began to reign over Israel in Samaria . . . And he did evil in the sight of the Lord, and walked in the way of his father, and in the way of his mother, and in the way of Jeroboam the son of Nebat, who made Israel to sin: For he served Baal, and worshipped him . . . (I KINGS 22:51–53)

After Ahaziah's death his brother Jehoram succeeded him as king, and he, too, continued to sanction Jeroboam's sacrilegious cult:

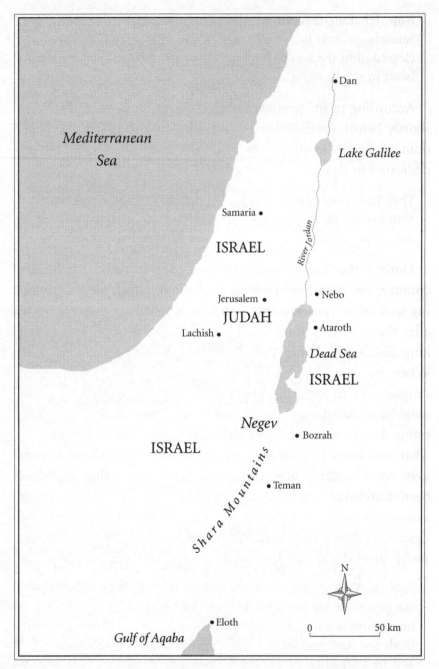

Israel and Judah at the time of Jeroboam

> Now Jehoram the son of Ahab began to reign over Israel in Samaria ... And he wrought evil in the sight of the Lord ... he cleaved unto the sins of Jeroboam the son of Nebat, which made Israel to sin; he departed not therefrom. (II KINGS 3:1–3)

According to the prophet Jeremiah, who preached in the years shortly before the Babylonian conquest, by the end of the kingdom of Israel's existence the High Places of Israel had all been dedicated to Baal.

> They have built also the high places of Baal, to burn their sons with fire for burnt offerings unto Baal, which I commanded not, nor spake it, neither came it to my mind. (JEREMIAH 19:5)

During the kingdom of Judah's time as an independent country, on the other hand, its citizens are portrayed as remaining faithful to Yahweh. The second Book of Kings describes how, after the Assyrians annihilated the kingdom of Israel, the Judean king Josiah seized the opportunity to eradicate the cult of Baal. When he came to the throne, around 640 BCE, the Assyrian Empire was in rapid decline due to the growing power of its neighbour Babylonia, and its forces had withdrawn from Palestine. Josiah was therefore free to expand Judah's influence into what had been Israel's territory. Although Israel had ceased to exist some eighty years earlier, and most of its inhabitants had been butchered, enslaved or dispersed, there were apparently isolated pockets of Hebrews living in the mountains and the deserts. It seems that Baal worship was still continuing here, as Josiah immediately made plans to exterminate the sect.

> And the king [Josiah] commanded Hilkiah the high priest, and the priests of the second order, and the keepers of the door, to bring forth out of the temple of the Lord all the vessels that were made for Baal, and for the grove, and for all the hosts of heaven: and he burned them without Jerusalem in the fields of Kidron, and carried the ashes of them unto Beth-el. (II KINGS 23:4)

It was against Beth-el, the chief shrine to Baal, that Josiah focused the brunt of his religious purge. It seems that Hebrews from the kingdom of Israel had taken refuge around the Beth-el sanctuary and that some of the Jews from Judah had joined them. Josiah accordingly attacked and sacked Beth-el. He drove out its priesthood, destroyed the site and slaughtered its devotees, who dwelt in a nearby settlement. Even the dead were not left in peace. So ferocious was Josiah's carnage that bones were removed from graves around Beth-el and pulverized to dust.

> Moreover the altar that was at Beth-el, and the high place which Jeroboam the son of Nebat, who made Israel to sin, had made both that altar and the high place he brake down, and burned the high place, and stamped it small to powder, and burned the grove. And as Josiah turned himself, he spied the sepulchres that were there in the mount and sent, and took the bones out of the sepulchres, and burned them upon the altar, and polluted it, according to the word of the Lord which the man of God proclaimed, who proclaimed these words ... And he slew all the priests of the high places that were there upon the altars, and burned men's bones upon them, and returned to Jerusalem. (II KINGS 23: 15–20)

Who was this god Baal, to whom such a large faction of the Hebrew people had evidently devoted themselves for so long? Traditionally, biblical scholars have interpreted Baal as having been a Phoenician deity, introduced into Israel by Ahab's Phoenician wife Jezebel around 870 BCE. The reasoning is based on the first direct reference to Baal worship in association with the kingdom of Israel, in I Kings 16:31:

> And it came to pass, as if it had been a light thing for him to walk in the sins of Jeroboam the son of Nebat, that he took to wife Jezebel ... and went and served Baal and worshipped him.'

However, although she is portrayed as a chief adherent of the deity, nowhere in its account of Jezebel does the Old Testament narrative actually say that it was she who introduced Baal to Israel. Indeed, the god seems to have been worshipped by Jeroboam half a century before Jezebel's time. Although Baal is not specifically named in association with the passage describing Jeroboam erecting the calf effigies and building the temple at Beth-el, every time either book of Kings describes a king of Israel worshipping Baal it talks of him following 'in the sins of Jeroboam'. Indeed, archaeology has unearthed no evidence that the Phoenicians ever had a god called Baal. Historically, the Phoenicians worshipped a pantheon of gods, but nowhere do any of their inscriptions or texts, of which many survive, record one by this or a similar name.

In fact, *baal* is actually a Hebrew word, meaning 'lord'. It is used on many occasions throughout the Bible where it has nothing to do with the God worshipped by the kingdom of Israel. It is affixed to personal names to denote status, such as Baal-Hanan, an Edomite king (1 CHRONICLES 1:49) and Baal-Is, a king of the Ammonites (JEREMIAH 40:14). Sometimes it is used as a title applied to leading figures of the Hebrew tribes, such as Baal, a Reubenite elder just before the Assyrian conquest (1 CHRONICLES 5:5), and Baal, a chief of the tribe of Benjamin during Joshua's time (1 CHRONICLES 8:30). It is also used as a prefix to place names, presumably after a city's founder, such as Baal-Hamon, a city near Samaria where Solomon had a vineyard (SONG OF SONGS 8:11), and Baal-Meon, a city the Reubenites seized from Moab (1 CHRONICLES 5:8). The latter is also described as Beth-Baal-Meon – the 'house of Lord Meon' (JOSHUA 13:17).

Baal, 'Lord', is simply a title for the deity, therefore, not its name, just as Yahweh, 'The Lord', was a title for the Hebrew God. So who exactly was this god being worshipped in the kingdom of Israel? One thing that is apparent is that the deity was associated with a bull or calf. Not only did Jeroboam erect the calf effigies but, according to I Kings 18:26, the priests of Baal prepared a bullock in the name of the god:

> And they took the bullock which was given them, and they dressed it, and called upon the name of Baal . . . and they leaped upon the altar that was made.

Bull horns are described as adorning the high altar at Beth-el in the Old Testament Book of Amos. Amos was a prophet from Judah who preached against the priests of Beth-el during the reign of Jeroboam II, around 750 BCE. According to Amos 3:14: 'I will also visit the altars of Beth-el: and the horns of the altar shall be cut off and fall to the ground.'

Archaeology has confirmed that the god to whom the Old Testament authors refer as Baal was indeed associated with the bull. According to the second Book of Kings, during the reign of Israel's king Jehoram, around 840 BCE, one of his generals, Jehu, is persuaded by the prophet Elisha to destroy a temple to Baal:

> Jehu said to the guard and to the captains, Go in and slay them, let none come forth. And they smote them with the edge of the sword; and the guard and the captains cast them out, and went to the city of the house of Baal. And they brought forth the images out of the house of Baal, and burned them. And they break down the image of Baal, and brake down the house of Baal . . .
> (II KINGS 10:25–27)

This temple is not the one at Beth-el or the one at Dan, but a temple built later by King Ahab, around 870 BCE. According to I Kings 16:32, Ahab decided to build a new temple to Baal right in the heart of his capital: 'And he reared up an altar for Baal in the house of Baal, which he had built in Samaria.'

Excavations carried out at the site of this ancient capital of Israel in the late 1980s, by a team from the University of Toronto, uncovered the remains of a temple that was built about the time of Ahab's reign. Interestingly, a charred level in the foundations revealed that it was destroyed by fire within a few years of its construction. Both the dating and burning of the building suggest that this was the temple destroyed by Jehu around 840 BCE. Although no large-scale statues were found, a number of bronze bull and calf effigies were unearthed. If this was Ahab's temple of Baal – and at present there is no stronger contender – then Baal was indeed being venerated with images of the bull.

The veneration of a bull or calf as a sacred animal goes back much further into the Hebrews' past than the period of Jeroboam. At the time of the Exodus, over four centuries earlier, Moses' brother and deputy Aaron made the golden calves at Mount Sinai:

> And all the people brake off the golden earrings which were in their ears, and brought them unto Aaron. And he received them at their hand, and fashioned it with a graving tool, after he had made it a golden calf: and they said, These are thy gods, O Israel, which brought thee up out of the land of Egypt.
> (EXODUS 32:3–4)

Interestingly, these last words are paraphrased in the passage in I Kings 12:28, when Jeroboam makes his calves for Beth-el and Dan: 'Behold thy gods, O Israel, which brought thee up out of the land of Egypt.' As *The Oxford Dictionary of Jewish Quotations* points out, in the Hebrew original the plural 'gods' refers to the effigies themselves and not the deity they represented. What can be inferred by cross-referencing these two verses is that the god being venerated by Jeroboam is the same god venerated by Aaron many years earlier. It seems, therefore, that Baal was being worshipped four centuries before Jeroboam's time. This biblical link between the calves of Aaron and Jeroboam betrays evidence that Baal might not have been a foreign god at all, but the Hebrew God himself.

The Exodus narrative portrays Aaron as one of God's chosen messengers. He is not only second to Moses but God speaks to him directly and Aaron speaks for God:

> And the Lord said unto Aaron, Go into the wilderness to meet Moses. And he went, and met him in the mountain of God . . . And Moses told Aaron all the words of the Lord who had sent him, and all the signs which he had commanded him. And Moses and Aaron went and gathered together all the elders of the children of Israel: And Aaron spake all the words which the Lord had spoken unto Moses, and did the signs in the sight of the people. (EXODUS 4:27–30)

Moreover, Aaron himself believes that it was the one God of Israel who led the Hebrews out of Egypt:

> These are that Aaron and Moses, to whom the Lord said, Bring out the children of Israel from the land of Egypt . . .
> (EXODUS 6:26)

As Aaron, by the Old Testament authors' own admission, clearly believed that Yahweh was the only god, and that it was his power that delivered the Israelites from bondage in Egypt, then the calves had to have represented this same Hebrew God. It seems that what the Old Testament authors referred to as the cult of Baal was actually an intrinsic and important sect within the Hebrew religion. After all, Aaron was Moses' deputy and Jeroboam was chosen by the prophet Ahijah to succeed Solomon. In fact, as ten of the Hebrew tribes – all except the tribe of Judah and the Levite priests – followed Jeroboam, we must assume that it was the majority sect during his time.

Archaeological confirmation that Israel was still venerating Yahweh at the time the Old Testament portrays it as being totally devoted to the worship of Baal comes with the Moabite Stone. According to its inscription, King Mesha of Moab raided the temple at Nebo and 'took from there the altar stones of Yahweh' (see Chapter III). Mount Nebo, modern Jebel Neba, some thirty kilometres south-west of Amman, was one of the most important religious sites in the kingdom of Israel as it marked the spot from which the Book of Deuteronomy (32:49) says that Moses bade farewell to the Israelites just before he died. From the inscription we can gather that the king against whom Mesha was conducting his campaign was Omri's grandson Jehoram, around 853 BCE. This is confirmed by II Kings 3:1–4. The same biblical passage also tells us that Jehoram 'cleaved unto the sins of Jeroboam, the son of Nebat, which made Israel to sin'. The Moabite Stone inscription therefore concerns a time when Baal was supposed to be Israel's god, yet it tells us that Mesha sacked one of Israel's most important temples that was still dedicated to Yahweh. The Old Testament specifically makes reference to Mesha's raiders taking away idols of Baal from the temple at Nebo:

> Bel [a variation of the word Baal used on three occasions in the Bible] boweth down, Nebo stoopeth, their idols were upon the beasts, and upon the cattle. (ISAIAH 46:1)

As Mesha's inscription identifies these same 'idols' as stones from the altar of Yahweh, then Yahweh and Baal were evidently one and the same.

Yet if the kingdom of Israel was actually worshipping the God of Israel why do the Old Testament authors portray it as a sin, and why use the name Baal? When we examine the Old Testament further, we can infer that it was not so much the god they were worshipping that was the point of contention but the way in which they were worshipping him – namely, by making idols. According to the second of the Ten Commandments:

> Thou shalt not make unto thee any graven image, or any likeness of any thing that is in heaven above . . . Thou shalt not bow down thyself to them, nor serve them . . . (EXODUS 20:4–5)

It is important to remember that those who eventually compiled the Old Testament around the time of the Babylonian Exile (see Chapter II) were scribes from the kingdom of Judah. By the time the scriptures were committed to writing in their present form, the kingdom of Israel had ceased to exist. It might only have been by this much later period of Hebrew history that the calf and bull effigies came to be seen as contravening this divine precept. It seems that in earlier times such effigies were not considered a 'likeness of any thing that is in heaven' at all. During the time of the Exodus, Moses himself made what the Judeans would later regard as a graven image.

One image to which the Judeans took particular exception was a bronze serpent. Around 725 BCE, when Israel was invaded by the Assyrians, many of its citizens fled to the safety of Judah. The Judean king, Hezekiah, was willing to accept these refugees on condition that they swore allegiance to the Jerusalem Temple. As their priests entered Jerusalem, Hezekiah seized and broke one of their most treasured relics: a staff with a bronze serpent coiled around it, which had been made by Moses himself while the Hebrews had wandered in the wilderness. The people, we are told, had come to revere the staff and Hezekiah saw it as a form of idolatry forbidden by God's law:

And he [Hezekiah] did what was right in the sight of the Lord . . .
and brake in pieces the brazen serpent that Moses had made.
(II KINGS 18:3–4)

By Hezekiah's time the Judeans might have come to regard such an object as a graven image, but Moses, the great law-giver himself, had not. The making of the serpent staff during the time in the wilderness is described in the Book of Exodus:

And the Lord spake unto Moses, Make thee a fiery serpent, and set it upon a pole . . . And Moses made a serpent of brass, and put it upon a pole . . . (EXODUS 21:8–9)

It seems that by the late eighth century BCE the Judeans had taken the Second Commandment much further than Moses had originally perceived it. The serpent staff was not the only such icon that Moses had endorsed. He even venerated the bull and had horns attached to an altar, just like the later priests of Baal:

> And thou shalt take the blood of the bullock, and put it upon the horns of the altar . . . (EXODUS 29:12)

One controversial Old Testament passage has even been interpreted to associate Moses himself with horns. Exodus 34:35 concerns Moses' return to the Israelites with the Ten Commandments at the foot of Mount Sinai. According to the original Hebrew Bible his head was *qaran*. In Mishnaic Hebrew, which developed after the Assyrian period (see Chapter II), the word was no longer in usage. There were, however, two similar words: *qalen*, 'shining' and *qalan*, 'horns'. When the first English translation of the Bible was made in the early sixteenth century the word was translated as the former: 'Moses' head was shining.' The King James Bible of the early seventeenth century took the translation one stage further and accordingly substituted the word face for head: 'And they saw that the face of Moses when he came was shining.' However, an earlier translation of the Old Testament, made by the Italian scholar Jerome around 400 CE, translated the passage as: 'And they saw that the head of Moses when he came out had horns . . .' This was the version of the Bible familiar to Michelangelo when he created his famous horned statue of Moses for the tomb of Pope Julius II in 1515. Now in the church of St Peter in Vincoli in Rome, it stands alone but was originally intended as the centrepiece in a spectacular design for the pope's tomb. The bearded figure of Moses sits contemplating the Ten Commandment tablets that he holds in his hands. It is his head, however, that immediately draws our attention. On his head are two small horns, making the great law-giver look more like the ancient depictions of the Greek god Pan.

This particular passage from the Book of Exodus seems to have created problems even for the Hebrew scholars who compiled the oldest surviving copies of the Old Testament as they are divided equally on which word they employ. We only know that the word *qaran* was originally used as this is the way it appears in the oldest surviving copy of the Old Testament in Hebrew: a second-century copy in the National Library of Israel in Jerusalem (see Chapter VII). As the Hebrew linguist Dr Benedek observed, it is quite possible that the verse did refer to some manner of head-dress as the word *qaran* appears on one other occasion, in Psalm 69:31, where the word clearly refers to horns: 'This also shall please the Lord better than an ox or bullock that hath *qaran* and hoofs.'

Hezekiah's hostility towards the serpent motif certainly represents a later amendment to religious thought. From the Exodus account we can gather that the Hebrews in Moses' time must have interpreted it very differently. The staff Moses uses during the Exodus is also equated with the serpent, where it is clearly seen as a symbol of God's authority:

> And the Lord said unto him [Moses], What is that in thine hand? And he said, A rod. And he said, Cast it on the ground. And he cast it on the ground, and it became a serpent. (EXODUS 4:3)

God then tells Moses to take the same staff with him when he confronts the pharaoh:

> Get thee unto Pharaoh in the morning; lo, he goeth out unto the water; and thou shalt stand by the river brink against he come; and the rod which was turned to a serpent shalt thou take in thy hand. (EXODUS 7:15)

Here there is a clear indication of the allegorical significance of the serpent. In Egypt, the serpent was a symbol of kingly authority. From Egyptian art we can gather that all the pharaoh's chief ministers were given a staff with a handle carved into the shape of a royal cobra. Moses' staff is presumably a symbol of God's authority over the pharaoh. There was, however, more to the serpent staff than an image of kingly power: Exodus 4:20 even describes it as 'the rod of God':

> And Moses took his wife and his sons, and set them upon an ass, and he returned to the land of Egypt: and Moses took the rod of God in his hand.

It is the conduit through which God's power flows. It is depicted as being used by Moses, amongst other things, to turn the Nile to blood, part the sea and bring forth a miraculous stream.

> Thus saith the Lord, In this thou shalt know that I am the Lord: behold, I will smite with the rod that is in mine hand upon the waters which are in the river, and they shall be turned to blood. (EXODUS 7:17)

> But lift thou up thy rod, and stretch out thine hand over the sea, and divide it: and the children of Israel shall go on dry ground through the midst of the sea. (EXODUS 14:16)

> And the Lord said unto Moses, Go on before the people, and take with thee of the elders of Israel; and thy rod, wherewith thou smotest the river, take in thine hand, and go. Behold, I will stand before thee there upon the rock in Horeb; and thou shalt smite the rock, and there shall come water out of it, that the people may drink. (EXODUS 17:5–6)

What this clearly shows is that at the time of the Exodus the serpent staff would not have been considered idolatrous as it was by Hezekiah's time. In fact, the perspective had changed so much by the time of the Babylonian Exile that the Judeans had come to regard the serpent as a symbol of evil. It is a serpent that persuades Adam and Eve to sin in the Garden of Eden account.

We have seen how the Garden of Eden story was evidently a late addition to the biblical narrative, being taken from the Babylonian myth of the Garden of Dilmun. The serpent, though, does not appear in the Babylonian version. It would seem, then, that the serpent was yet another interpolation to equate with corruption the brand of the Hebrew religion practised in the kingdom of Israel. If the serpent was equated with evil at the time of the Exodus, it would not have been employed in the account as a symbol of God's authority.

In fact, over three centuries after Moses' time, the Second Commandment was still not being observed in the way in which the Judeans eventually interpreted it. Idolatry was being practised at the very highest level. Solomon had two massive statues of cherubim erected at either side of the temple portico:

> And in the most holy house he made two cherubim of image work, and overlaid them with gold. And the wings of the cherubims were twenty cubits long... (II CHRONICLES 3:10)

Here, Solomon has made two huge statues of angels with ten-metre wingspans. If this is not making a 'likeness of any thing that is in heaven above', then what is? Regardless of the truths or exaggerations concerning the biblical accounts of Solomon's reign, the fact remains that during a time centuries before Hezekiah, Josiah or the Babylonian Exile, the united kingdom of Israel is portrayed as practising what was later regarded as idolatry without the slightest implication of any infringement of God's holy laws.

It seems, therefore, that the reason why the authors of extant Old Testament texts leave us with the impression of the kingdom of Israel as a nation of heathens is that by the time it was compiled two different interpretations of Hebrew religion had developed. The situation was probably not dissimilar to the Catholic and Protestant churches of the European Reformation, each worshipping the same God, but considering the other's to be the church of the Antichrist. In the case of the ancient Hebrews, however, only the Judean version of events survives. If the kingdom of Israel had survived to compile the Old Testament we might well have read of Judah being a land of heretics.

Why, though, does the Old Testament use the name Baal for God as he is perceived in the kingdom of Israel? It seems that this was actually an ancient title for God. There is a direct reference in the Old Testament book of Hosea to the God of Israel once being referred to as Baal. Hosea, a prophet who preached in the kingdom of Israel at the time it was being conquered by the Assyrians, reminds his reader that the name should no longer be used:

> And it shall be at that day, saith the Lord, that thou shalt call me Ishi; and shalt call me no more Baali. (HOSEA 2:16)

Ishi is a shortened version of the term 'the God of Israel', and the *i* syllable suffixed to Baal is the personal pronoun, making the word mean 'the Lord'. The verse is referring to a time after the Exodus when God had apparently told the Israelites that henceforth he should be known only as 'the God of Israel' rather than 'the Lord'. Nevertheless, it seems that the word Yahweh eventually replaced this form of address. Although Yahweh and Baali both mean 'the Lord', the term Baal or Baali had become associated with the Philistine god Zebub. It seems, at some point, that Israelite converts to this foreign deity had come to refer to him as Lord Zebub or Baal-Zebub (II KINGS 1:1–16), from where the later New Testament term, Beelzebub, the name of the devil, came. To completely dissociate their God from this pagan deity, the Baal form of address was proscribed. The Judeans might therefore have employed the earlier form of address, Baal, in reference to God as he was perceived in Israel, not so much to imply a pagan religion but a more primitive one. To them the citizens of Israel were not so much pagans as unenlightened, in the same way that the early Christians considered the Jews un-enlightened for not accepting Jesus as the Messiah.

However, although it might have been the more primitive form of the religion, from what we have so far examined, it seems to have been the more original. Before the time the monarchy divided, the Second Commandment can only have been taken to refer to specific images. The serpent, the bull and the calf were certainly not amongst them, if the practices of Moses, Aaron and Solomon are anything to go by. As all of these figures evidently accepted the Ten Commandments, it would seem more likely that these particular icons were considered to represent some aspect of God's power rather than having been images of God himself. They may have served a similar symbolic purpose for devotional practices as later Christians employed a lamb motif to represent the power of Christ and a fish to represent his Church. After all, as the Book of Genesis stated that 'God made man in his own image', if God had been represented as a statue then it would have been fashioned in wholly human form.

Nevertheless, if Solomon's cherubim are any indication, back at the time the country divided idolatry was not the divisive issue. So what really did cause the Hebrews to split into two rival factions? The initial impression is that it was purely political. Solomon's successor, Rehoboam, the grandson of David, was of the tribe of Judah. This notion of a wholly Judean dynasty – the house of David – was not accepted by Israel as a whole. The moment Rehoboam is proclaimed king, many of the Hebrews object:

> So when all Israel saw that the king harkened not unto them, the people answered the king, saying, What portion have we in David?
> (I KINGS 12:16)

So there was certainly disagreement concerning the royal lineage. Should only the descendants of David be kings of Israel, as

Solomon's priests maintained, or should, as the prophet Ahijah proclaimed, Jeroboam and his house of Joseph become the monarchy of Israel? However, if this had been the chief point of contention, we should not expect every Hebrew tribe but two to have endorsed Jeroboam as king. This was simply replacing one authoritarian dynasty with another. Jeroboam might have been able to rely on the support of his own tribe of Joseph, but why should virtually every other tribe have followed him? If the kingdom broke up due to the dynastic issue alone, surely we should expect either a more even division of support or, more likely, a fragmentation of the Hebrews into the earlier tribal states. The first proclamation Jeroboam makes on becoming king is presumably the most telling and seems to provide us with the fundamental reason for the schism:

> If this people go up to do sacrifice in the house of the Lord ...
> then shall the heart of this people turn against unto their lord ...
> (I KINGS 12:27)

This house of the Lord that Jeroboam is condemning is the Jerusalem Temple, recently built by Solomon. It was to remain the most sacred site in Judah until the time it was destroyed by the Babylonians around 597 BCE. When the Jews returned from exile it was rebuilt and restored and was later vastly extended by Herod the Great around the birth of Christ. Even today, the Wailing Wall, all that remains of Herod's temple complex, is still considered Judaism's most sacred site. However, from the above verse we can see that this was certainly not what Jeroboam and his followers believed. In fact, the Jerusalem Temple is being condemned as sacrilegious. It appears to have been the status of the Jerusalem Temple that was the essential issue that first divided the Hebrews.

In the second Book of Chronicles, Solomon explains why the temple has been built:

> I have built a house of habitation for thee [God], and a place for
> thy dwelling for ever. (II CHRONICLES 6:1)

According to Solomon, then, the Jerusalem Temple is to be for
ever more the one and only house of the Lord. Unlike later
Christian or Judaic notions of any church or synagogue being the
house of the Lord, to the ancient Israelites there was only one
such place. There were other temples and shrines where God
could be worshipped, but there could be only one 'house of
habitation'. On dozens of occasions when the Jerusalem Temple
is referenced in the Old Testament it is called the 'house of God'.
In the reign of Ahaz: 'And Ahaz gathered together the vessels of
the house of God' (II CHRONICLES 28:24). In the reign of
Hezekiah: 'And in every work that he began in the service of the
house of God' (II CHRONICLES 31:21). In the reign of Josiah:
'They delivered the money that was brought into the house of
God' (II CHRONICLES 34:9). Throughout its long history, the
kingdom of Judah regarded the Jerusalem Temple as, quite
literally, the house of God.

The reason for Jeroboam's grievance with the Jerusalem Temple is revealed by his response to its construction – by building
the new chief shrine for his kingdom at Beth-el. In Hebrew, *Beth-
el* translates directly as 'house of God'. This name was not used
allegorically. Before Solomon built the temple, the Hebrews had
considered Beth-el to be the 'house of habitation', where God
was thought to reside.

According to the Book of Genesis, Beth-el was where God
selected Jacob to be the father of all his chosen people. It was the
place where the nation of Israel was founded. According to the
account, while he is hiding from his brother, Jacob has a dream
in which God first speaks to him:

> And he lighted upon a certain place, and tarried there all night,
> because the sun was set; and he took of the stones of that place,

and put them for his pillows, and lay down in that place to sleep. And he dreamed, and behold a ladder set up on the earth, and the top of it reached to heaven: and behold the angels of God ascending and descending on it. And, behold, the Lord stood above it, and said, I am the Lord God of Abraham thy father, and the God of Isaac: the land whereon thou liest, to thee will I give it, and to thy seed. (GENESIS 28:11–13)

Jacob then decides that the place he had slept was the house of God – the very gateway to heaven:

And Jacob awaked out of his sleep, and he said, Surely the Lord is in this place; and I knew it not. And he was afraid, and said, How dreadful is this place! this is none other but the house of God, and this is the gate of heaven. And Jacob rose up early in the morning, and took the stone that he had put for his pillows, and set it up for a pillar, and poured oil upon the top of it. And he called the name of that place Beth-el.
(GENESIS 28: 16–19)

From these verses we learn that Beth-el is a special and unique location, set apart for Jacob's descendants, the Israelites, to commune with God. In Genesis 31:13 God specifically identifies himself with this particular site and no other: 'I am the God of Beth-el.' Regardless of whether or not Jacob was an historical figure, or whether or not he really spoke with God, the fact remains that this is what the Bible tells us the early Hebrews believed – the house of God was Beth-el.

After the Exodus Beth-el became the Israelites' most sacred shrine. Although Jeroboam might have built a new temple at the site, the Old Testament refers repeatedly to religious practices taking place at Beth-el well before his time. From this we can infer that there was already a temple or High Place at the site. In fact, from Genesis we can gather that the original altar at the shrine was attributed to Jacob himself:

> And let us arise, and go up to Beth-el; and I [Jacob] will make there an altar unto God. (GENESIS 35:3)

Jeroboam, it seems, had merely elaborated the High Place that already existed at Beth-el. We can gather that it was being used as the principal site of worship and was regarded as the holy habitation of God just prior to David's reign. After Samuel has anointed Saul, the prophet tells the king:

> Then shalt thou go on forward from thence, and thou shalt come to the plain of Tabor, and there shall meet thee three men going up to God to Beth-el. (I SAMUEL 10:3)

When Solomon built the Jerusalem Temple, however, he expected all his subjects to accept it as the new 'house of God':

> And they went about in Judah, and gathered the Levites out of all the cities of Judah, and the chief of the fathers of Israel, and they came to Jerusalem. And all the congregation made a covenant with the king in the house of God. (II CHRONICLES 23:2–3)

In this passage in the Hebrew original, the term 'house of God' is actually rendered as *Beth-el*. Solomon had not just created another temple or shrine, but another Beth-el. Moreover, it was thereafter to be the only Beth-el: 'a place for thy dwelling for ever' (II CHRONICLES 6:1). By doing this, the king was challenging one of the Israelites' most fundamental beliefs. He had decreed, in no uncertain terms, that God had moved house. Much of Israel would surely have seen this as sheer blasphemy. It would be like a Muslim decreeing that Mecca was no longer Islam's holy city.

Solomon's own reasons for doing this were apparently more political than religious. According to the first Book of Chronicles it was God's will that Solomon build the temple to establish Jerusalem, and so the house of David, as the heart of the Hebrew nation:

He shall build an house for my name; and he shall be my son, and I will be his father; and I will establish the throne of his kingdom over Israel for ever. (I CHRONICLES 22:10)

However, Solomon seems to have underestimated the extent of the hostility this would arouse. It was the matter of Beth-el versus the Jerusalem Temple more than anything else, it would seem, that split apart his kingdom.

Before the Jerusalem Temple was built, however, Beth-el had evidently remained unchallenged for generations as the Hebrews' most holy shrine. Moreover, it would appear to have been so from the Israelites' earliest days. If it can be found, therefore, Beth-el may provide a unique insight into the Hebrew religion in its original form. Here we may even discover archaeological evidence of how this faith was born. Unfortunately, locating Beth-el is easier said than done. In modern times historians have proposed various sites, and biblical atlases suggest almost as many locations as there are editions, the reason being that whenever the Old Testament narrative provides reference to Beth-el's geographical setting it seems to be in a different place.

According to Genesis 35:16:

And they journeyed from Bethel; and there was but a little way to come to Ephrath.

This verse tells us that Beth-el is close to Ephrath, an early name for Bethlehem, some twelve kilometres south of Jerusalem. According to Judges 21:19, however, Beth-el is to the north of Jerusalem:

Then they said, Behold, there is a feast of the Lord in Shiloh yearly in a place which is on the north side of Bethel.

Here we are told that Beth-el is in the district of Shiloh. Once again, this location is no mystery. It has been identified by archaeology as the region of Khirbet Seilun – some twenty-seven kilometres to the north of Jerusalem.

Another verse in the book of Judges places Beth-el even further to the north, above the Sea of Galilee. According to Judges 4:5:

> And she dwelt under the palm tree of Deborah between Ramah and Bethel.

This suggests that Beth-el is somewhere close to Ramah, but Ramah, the birthplace of the prophet Samuel, is located over two hundred kilometres to the north of Jerusalem.

Joshua 18:12–13, however, suggests it is right next to Jerusalem:

> And the goings out thereof were at the wilderness of Beth-aven. And the border went over from thence towards Luz, to the side of Luz, which is Bethel, southward.

According to this, Beth-el is south of Beth-aven. I Samuel 13:5 describes Beth-aven as being west of Michmash, a mountain pass some twelve kilometres north-east of Jerusalem, where Saul fought the Philistines in I Samuel 13:23. By this reckoning Beth-el must be close to Jerusalem, somewhere to the immediate north-east.

Yet another verse in the Book of Joshua, however, places Beth-el in the kingdom of Moab, at the southern end of the Dead Sea:

> And goeth out from Bethel to Luz, and passeth along unto the borders of Archi to Ataroth. (JOSHUA 16:2)

According to this, the journey from Beth-el to Luz takes the traveller first through Archi and then through Ataroth. Archi was the modern river Arnon, which flows northwards into the eastern shore of the Dead Sea and Ataroth was a Moabite city, mentioned in the Mesha inscription, due east of the central Dead Sea. By this reckoning Beth-el has to be somewhere in southern Moab, at least sixty kilometres south-east of Jerusalem. This last passage, by making reference to the city of Luz, makes matters even more confusing. The site of Luz is now unknown, but according to this it must be somewhere to the northern end of the Dead Sea. It is here that Genesis 35:6 places Beth-el: 'So Jacob came to Luz, which is in the land of Canaan, that is, Bethel.'

So Beth-el is beside Jerusalem, it is twenty-seven kilometres north of Jerusalem, it is twelve kilometres south of Jerusalem, it is two hundred kilometres north of Jerusalem, it is thirty kilometres due west of Jerusalem and it is sixty kilometres south-east of Jerusalem. Although there might perhaps have been more than one place that eventually came to be called Beth-el, all these references make it quite clear that the Beth-el in question is the shrine founded by Jacob. Many biblical sites are relatively easy to locate as they still bear their ancient names in Greek and Roman times, from which maps and other relevant documentation survive. Even those that have been forgotten are not given so many wildly dispersed points of reference. Although it is possible that the true location might have been forgotten by the time the Old Testament was committed to writing, this seems unlikely. Josiah had known of its location only three decades before the Babylonian Exile. It seems more probable that the Judean scribes deliberately chose to confuse the issue.

We can tell from various references in the Old Testament that as the two kingdoms' religious perspectives grew further apart, the shrine at Beth-el came to be as loathed by the kingdom of Judah as the Jerusalem Temple was loathed by the kingdom of Israel. During the reign of Jeroboam II, around 750 BCE, Judah's chief prophet Amos vehemently condemns Beth-el:

> For thus saith the Lord unto the house of Israel, Seek ye me, and ye shall live. But seek not Bethel ... and Bethel shall come to

nought. Seek the Lord, and ye shall live; lest he break out like fire in the house of Joseph, and devour it, and there be none to quench it in Bethel. (AMOS 5: 4–6)

So does the prophet Hosea, at the time the Assyrians are conquering Israel around twenty years later. He goes so far as to attribute the Assyrian invasion to God's punishment for the kingdom continuing to venerate Beth-el:

So shall Bethel do unto you because of your great wickedness.'
(HOSEA 10:15)

After Israel has been eradicated by the Assyrians, the prophet Jeremiah links the national shame of Beth-el with the pagan temples of the Moabite god Chemosh:

And Moab shall be ashamed of Chemosh, as the house of Israel was ashamed of Bethel. (JEREMIAH 48:13)

Then, finally, around 630 BCE, Josiah destroys the site. Judging by the ferocity of Josiah's carnage, as described in II Kings 23:15–20, by the time the kingdom of Israel ceased to exist Bethel was detested by the Judeans. It is quite possible, then, that the authors of the extant Old Testament attempted to obscure Beth-el's true location to hide it from future generations.

Nevertheless, there still survives evidence in the Old Testament to link Beth-el with another important religious site: Mount Sinai, also called Mount Horeb or the Mountain of God. In the Books of Exodus, Leviticus, Numbers and Deuteronomy, the Mountain of God, like Beth-el, is portrayed as the most sacred site to the Hebrew God. Although Beth-el is depicted as the chief Israelite shrine in Genesis and thereafter in the Books of Joshua, Judges, Samuel, Kings and Chronicles, in these four books that fall between Genesis and Joshua, it goes unmentioned. Instead it is the Mountain of God where God resides. It is even described, as is Beth-el, as the 'holy habitation'. Deuteronomy 26:15 describes the Mountain of God in this way as does Exodus 15:13. It is on the Mountain of God that Moses first encounters God in the burning bush; it is here that Moses first leads the people of Israel after their flight from Egypt; and it is here that God makes his Covenant with the Israelites, gives them the Ten Commandments and proclaims the religious laws. Even though the Israelites are said to wander in the Sinai wilderness for the next forty years, they frequently return to the Mountain of God for divine revelation and guidance. Like Beth-el, it is thought to be where God resides. Deuteronomy 4:10, for instance, talks about the children of Israel when they 'stood before the Lord God in Horeb'. Exodus 24:16 goes further and actually says that, 'the Lord abode upon Mount Sinai.' In the original Hebrew Bible, God is repeatedly referred to as *El Elyon* – 'the most high God'. As the linguist Dr David Benedek, of the Hebrew University in Jerusalem, pointed out in 1982, this does not mean most high as most important but most high as one who dwells on high.

The first-century Jewish historian Josephus confirms that God was actually believed to reside on the mountain. Referring to Moses' encounter with the burning bush, he writes:

> Now this is the highest of all the mountains thereabouts, and the best for pasturage, the herbage being there good; and it had not been before fed upon, because of the opinion men had that God dwelt there. (ANTIQUITIES II: 12:1)

If God was thought to reside at Beth-el at the same time as he was thought to dwell on the Mountain of God, then Beth-el must be on the Mountain of God. The first Book of Samuel even describes Beth-el as being a mountain:

> Saul chose him three thousand men of Israel; whereof two thousand were with Saul in Michmash and in Mount Bethel. (I SAMUEL 13:2)

What the Old Testament authors refer to as Beth-el, therefore, might well have been a High Place – an ancient Hebrew temple – on the Mountain of God. The sacred mountain was certainly portrayed as the place where Moses first discovered God and the Israelites first learned his holy laws. It was the very place where their religion is said to have come into existence. Find the Mountain of God and we may discover the very origins of the Hebrew faith.

Summary

• According to the first Book of Kings, when Solomon died, around 930 BCE, the Hebrews split into two kingdoms: Israel and Judah. It was only because of their well-defended, strategic position in Jerusalem that the tribe of Judah survived as the independent kingdom of Judah. Israel was the primary kingdom of the Israelites – it was still called Israel, even though it had lost its capital. However, this kingdom was ultimately to be wiped from the map by the Assyrians around 720 BCE, leaving Judah as the last independent vestige of the Hebrew nation. It was here that the Hebrew religion survived. Indeed, it is from the name Judah that the term Judaism derived, as did the name of its adherents, the Jews. As it was here and at this time that the Hebrew Bible was committed to writing, the Old Testament is very much the Judean version of events.

• According to the Old Testament, the kingdom of Israel reverted to the worship of a pagan deity called Baal that continued throughout much of its existence. Traditionally, biblical scholars have interpreted Baal as having been a Phoenician deity, introduced into Israel around 870 BCE. However, archaeology has unearthed no evidence that the Phoenicians ever had a god called Baal. In fact, *baal* is actually a Hebrew word, meaning 'lord'. It is used on many occasions throughout the Bible where it has nothing to do with the God worshipped by the kingdom of Israel. Baal – 'Lord' – is simply a title for the deity, therefore, not its name, just as Yahweh – 'the Lord' – was a title for the Hebrew God.

• Archaeological confirmation that Israel was still venerating Yahweh at the time the Old Testament portrays it as being devoted to the worship of Baal comes with the Moabite Stone. Dating from around 853 BCE, its inscription says that King Mesha of Moab raided the temple at Nebo and 'took from there the altar stones of Yahweh'. Mount Nebo, modern Jebel Neba, some thirty kilometres south-west of Amman, was one of the most important religious sites in the kingdom of Israel. The Moabite Stone inscription concerns a time when Baal was supposed to have been Israel's god, yet it tells us that Mesha sacked one of Israel's most important temples that was still dedicated to Yahweh.

• According to the Bible, Baal's sacred animal was the bull. The veneration of a bull or calf by the Hebrews goes back much further into the Hebrews' past than the period of the divided monarchy. At the time of the Exodus, over four centuries earlier, Moses' brother and deputy Aaron made the golden calves at Mount Sinai. This means that Baal might not have been a foreign god at all, but an early portrayal of the Hebrew God. The Exodus narrative portrays Aaron as one of God's chosen messengers. He is not only second to Moses, but God speaks to him directly and Aaron speaks for God.

• The major point of contention between the kingdoms of Judah and Israel appears to have been the perceived status of the Jerusalem Temple. The earliest Hebrews considered God to have a special place on earth: Beth-el – literally, 'the house of God'. There still survives evidence in the Old Testament to link Beth-el with another important religious site – Mount Sinai, also called Mount Horeb or the Mountain of God. Like Beth-el, it is portrayed as the most sacred site to the Hebrew God and said to be where God resides. If God was thought to reside at Beth-el at the same time as he was thought to dwell on the Mountain of God, then Beth-el must be on the Mountain of God. During the time of Solomon, however, a new 'house of God' was built – the Jerusalem Temple. As this new centre of worship was intended to be the new Beth-el, it inevitably generated much hostility and religious discord between Israel and Judah.

7 THE LORD'S HOST

As with Beth-el, the Bible is far from clear about the location of the Mountain of God. One thing we can presume, because of the name Mount Sinai, is that it is somewhere in the Sinai wilderness. From the locations referred to in the Old Testament, we can gather that the area known as the Sinai wilderness covered a large territory, including the desert lands of Paran, Midian and Edom – the modern-day Sinai peninsula in eastern Egypt, parts of southern Israel and Jordan, and even a part of Saudi Arabia. It was not a desert, like the Sahara, with great stretches of sand, but a stony, dusty, rough country with sparse vegetation, interspersed with occasional oases of fertile ground. It measures some 400 kilometres from north to south and 350 kilometres from east to west. This is around 140,000 square kilometres. The Mountain of God could have been anywhere in this considerable expanse.

In the sixth century CE the Christian Byzantine emperor Justinian I decided that it was a particular mountain at the southern end of the Sinai Peninsula in Egypt. According to Julius Apollinaris, a seventh-century bishop of Constantinople, the emperor learned of the location in a vision. He renamed the site Mount Sinai and founded the monastery of St Catherine there, which soon became a major centre of pilgrimage. Even today, the monastery is still occupied by monks who claim it to be the oldest continuously inhabited building in the world. What the mountain had previously been called is now unknown and most western maps still refer to it as Mount Sinai, while Arab maps call it Jebel Musa – the 'Mountain of Moses'. However, modern scholars have failed to discover any biblical or historical evidence to support the emperor's belief.

Sceptical of the site, a number of modern archaeologists have proposed other locations, one of the most recent being Professor Emmanuel Anati of the University of Lecce in Italy. His theory that it was Mount Karkom near El Kuntilla in Israel, about forty kilometres north of Elat, was based on his discovery of the remains of circular dwellings at the foot of the mountain together with an altar surrounded by twelve standing stones. According to Exodus 24:4, below the Mountain of God, Moses erects an altar and twelve pillars to represent each of the twelve Hebrew tribes. Despite the initial excitement, however, a recent excavation has dated the remains to around 2000 BCE, five centuries before even the earliest dating of the Exodus.

Another recent theory identifies the Mountain of God as Jebel al-Lawz in Saudi Arabia. In 1986 two American explorers, Ron Wyatt and David Fasold, travelled to the mountain, hopingto find the Egyptian jewellery the Bible says the Israelites had with them during the Exodus. However, the pair were almost immediately arrested for illegal excavation, threatened with imprisonment by the Saudi authorities and deported. Their identification of Jebel al-Lawz with the Mountain of God was based on the hypothesis that it was to be found in what had once been the land of Midian. According to the Book of Exodus, this is where Moses flees after his exile from Egypt. As Jebel al-Lawz is the highest mountain in what some believe to have been a part of Midian, it seemed logical to Wyatt and Fasold that this would be the place where Moses would have chosen to commune with God.

More recently, another pair of American explorers decided to follow in Wyatt and Fasold's footsteps. Wall Street millionaire Larry Williams and an ex-police officer Bob Cornuke illegally

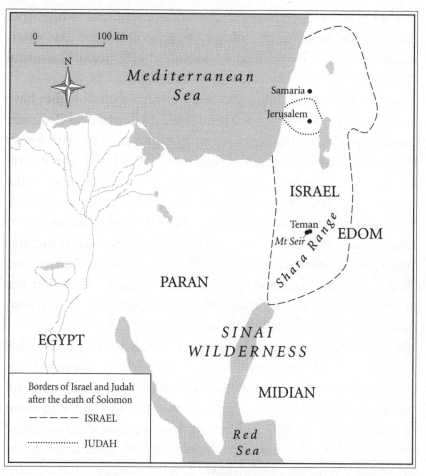

Canaan and the Sinai Wilderness

crossed into Saudi territory to search the mountain for evidence that it really was the site where Moses received the Ten Commandments. Breaking into the now fenced-off area, Williams and Cornuke searched for correspondences with the biblical record. Near the foot of the mountain, they spotted a stack of boulders bearing rock drawings of bulls. This, Williams and Cornuke decided, might be the altar where the Israelites were said to have worshipped the golden calf. Higher up the slope, Williams and Cornuke found a large stone structure, next to which were the remnants of what appeared to have been twelve stone towers, each about five and a half metres in diameter. They identified the stone structure as the altar constructed by Moses and the towers as the twelve pillars he erected nearby.

Although, unlike their predecessors, Williams and Cornuke evaded the Saudi authorities, their findings failed to convince their critics and various archaeologists questioned their theory. Allen Kerkeslager of the University of Pennsylvania, for instance, pointed out that the stack of stones they had identified with the golden calf altar, because of the bull pictographs, was actually a common construction in the area, intended in ancient times to communicate messages concerning hunting and other pastoral activities. What Williams and Cornuke identified as stone towers, Kerkeslager suggested were burial tumuli – ancient stone mounds common throughout north-west Arabia.

Lacking a proven alternative, many pilgrims and tourists alike still accept the site proposed by the emperor Justinian as the Mountain of God. However, if we examine the Old Testament narrative carefully we find evidence that the holy mountain was apparently in an altogether different part of the Sinai wilderness from that proposed by any of these conjectures.

According to the Old Testament, shortly after they escape Egypt, Moses leads the Israelites to the Mountain of God so that they might receive God's laws. When he ascends the mountain Moses receives the Covenant: religious instruction concerning priest-hood, the modes of worship and a detailed code of moral conduct. Finally he receives the Ten Commandments on two stone tablets and is given instructions on the making of the Ark of the Covenant to contain them. The events on the holy mountain fill twelve chapters of the Book of Exodus and, throughout, the mountain is merely referred to as Mount Sinai. The Book of Numbers, how-ever, uses a different name that may hold a vital clue to the mountain's whereabouts. The reason that this has been overlooked for centuries, it seems, is due to yet another mistranslation by the ancient Greeks.

On various occasions the Book of Numbers in the Christian Bible mentions a site it calls Mount Hor. In Hebrew, however, the word *hor* simply means 'mount'. If we look at Numbers 20:22, for example, we can see that a misunderstanding seems to have occurred: 'And the children of Israel, even the whole congregation, journeyed from Kadesh, and came unto Mount Hor.' When we fully translate the passage it actually reads: 'And the children of Israel ... came unto Mount mount.' This does not appear to make sense. What seems to have happened is that the Greek scribe who originally translated the passage in the fourth century BCE wrongly assumed that *Hor* was the mountain's name. When we consult the Hebrew Bible we find evidence of this. Dating from the second century CE, the oldest extant version of the Hebrew Bible is housed in the National Library of Israel on the campus of the Hebrew University in Jerusalem. Although earlier fragments survive, such as those found amongst the Dead Sea Scrolls, this is the oldest manuscript to contain the complete Torah. Called the *Alexandria Tanak*, it includes this Numbers verse, which reads: 'And the children of Israel ... came unto the mount.' It would appear, then, that the mountain was never called Hor at all.

The Mountain of God is often referred to as 'the mount' in

the Book of Deuteronomy. For example: 'And the Lord our God spake unto us in Horeb, saying, Ye have dwelt long enough in this mount' (DEUTERONOMY 1:6). Deuteronomy only once refers to it as Mount Sinai; on other occasions it is simply 'mount', 'the mount' or 'mount of God'. Mount Hor, therefore, seems to be one and the same as the Mountain of God. Nevertheless, as we can see from the above verse, Deuteronomy also names the location as Horeb. However, this is yet another untranslated word. In Hebrew *Horeb* means 'mount in the desert'. Each time Deuteronomy talks of the Covenant on the Mountain of God it refers to Horeb. For example, 'God made a covenant with us in Horeb' (DEUTERONOMY 5:2). We are left with no doubt that Horeb is the Mount of God as I Kings 19:8 tells us precisely this when talking of the prophet Elijah: 'And he arose, and did eat and drink, and went in the strength of that meat forty days and forty nights unto Horeb the mount of God.' It seems that, like God himself, the mountain was considered by some to be too sacred to be named.

So Sinai, Hor and Horeb would appear to be the same mountain. Although the word Horeb cannot in its own right help us locate the sacred mountain any more than the word Sinai, a reference to Mount Hor in the Book of Numbers can. It describes the death of Moses' brother Aaron: 'And the Lord spake unto Moses and Aaron in mount Hor, by the coast of the land of Edom ... and Aaron died there in the top of the mount' (NUMBERS 20:23–8). If Mount Hor is the Mountain of God then it is said to be in the land of Edom.

Edom was an ancient Semite kingdom in the north-west of the Sinai wilderness, in what are now parts of southern Jordan and Israel. This location fits with the Exodus account of Moses' first arrival at the Mountain of God in the burning bush episode. During his exile in Midian, Moses takes charge of his father-in-law's flock. Just like today's Bedouin, the peoples of Midian were nomadic shepherds. Entire family groups would lead their flocks of sheep and goats hundreds of miles in the course of a year around the Sinai wilderness, continually moving on to fresh grazing land. According to Exodus 3:1, Moses first discovers the Mountain of God on such a journey:

> Now Moses kept the flock of Jethro his father-in-law, the priest of Midian: and he led the flock to the backside of the desert, and came to the Mountain of God, even to Horeb.

As Midian was at the extreme south of the Sinai wilderness, the term 'backside of the desert' seems to imply its northern side. This is precisely where Edom was. The only problem with the previous reference to the mountain being 'by the coast of the land of Edom', is that Edom had no coast in the fifteenth century BCE, when the event seems to be set (see Chapter V). Although by Solomon's time Edom had a coastline on the Gulf of Aqaba, during this earlier period southern Edom was occupied by the Egyptians and had been since the time of Ahmose I, around 1550 BCE. Inscriptions from the time of Tuthmosis III reveal that they were still in possession of this territory over half a century later. From the archaeological evidence, it would seem that until the eleventh century BCE Edom was merely a valley kingdom surrounded by the Shara mountains in what is now southern Jordan. Once again, however, the ancient Greeks appear to have made a mistranslation. The Hebrew word for coast was *sup*. However, in the original Hebrew Bible the word used is *sud*, which actually means 'edge'. It is more likely that the word denoted the edge of the mountain range that delineated Edom's borders.

This location is, in fact, supported by the work of the first-century historian Josephus. According to this same Numbers reference, Aaron died on the sacred mountain: 'and Aaron died there in the top of the mount'. Josephus places Aaron's death on one of the mountains surrounding the ancient city of Petra:

> And when he came to a place which the Arabians esteem their
> metropolis, which was formerly called Acre, but has now the
> name Petra, at this place, which was encompassed by high
> mountains, Aaron went up one of them in the sight of the whole
> army, Moses having before told him that he was to die ... and
> died while the multitude looked upon him.
>
> (*ANTIQUITIES IV*, 4:7)

The city of Petra is at the north-east end of the Shara range. Built
by the Arabian Nabateans in the fourth century BCE, its spectacular ruins still survive, situated in the very valley that had once
been the heart of the kingdom of Edom.

Interestingly, recent archaeological excavations also suggest
that the site of Beth-el might have been in the mountains
surrounding Petra. Many of the traditional sites proposed for
Beth-el by biblical commentators have been in the district of
ancient Ephraim, north of Jerusalem. These locations were based
on Judges 21:19, which says that Beth-el is on the 'east of the
highway to Schechem'. It was reasoned that as the Schechem
highway – actually a track or simple trading route – ran from
Jerusalem to Schechem during the period of the judges, Beth-el
must presumably have been sited between the two cities. However, this particular area as a possible site of Beth-el long
concerned archaeologists and historians. Its geographical setting
seemed most unlikely. As we have seen, the kingdom of Judah
came to despise the shrine at Beth-el as much as the kingdom of
Israel despised the Jerusalem Temple. It was only after the
Assyrians eradicated Israel that, under Josiah, the kingdom of
Judah was able to destroy it. The area between Jerusalem and
Schechem was constantly being fought over by the two kingdoms.
On numerous occasions the armies of Judah occupied Ephraim.
In fact, during the reigns of Asa and Jehoshaphat (910–848 BCE),
the territory was actually a part of the kingdom of Judah:

And Jehoshaphat his son reigned in his stead, and strengthened himself against Israel. And he placed forces in all the fenced cities of Judah, and set garrisons in the land of Judah, and in the cities of Ephraim, which Asa his father had taken.
(II CHRONICLES 17:1–2)

If Beth-el was really in Ephraim, why did the Judeans not attempt to destroy it years before Josiah? Surely, it was reasoned, Beth-el had to have been somewhere else.

There was actually a second route also described as the Schechem highway. It was constructed during the reign of King Omri (885–74 BCE) to link Schechem with Israel's territories south of Judah. The first Book of Kings describes the extent of Hebrew territory at the time of Solomon. It was a swath of land stretching from north of Lake Galilee, as far south as the Gulf of Aqaba. After Solomon's death, when the kingdom split into two, Israel retained the lands to the north, east and south of Judah (see below). The new road began at the city of Eloth (modern Elat) on the Gulf of Aqaba, went north-east to the Shara mountains, then north-west to the Dead Sea, and finally north to Schechem. Although this road was not there during the period of the judges, we have seen how the Bible often refers to places that did not exist at the time the narrative is set. If this was the Schechem highway referred to in the above verse, then Beth-el could have been anywhere along its 280-kilometre length. In the late 1990s a new location for Beth-el was proposed, based on this particular route, by Dr Adnan Hussein of Amman University.

Although Genesis tells us that it was Jacob who first named Beth-el, its location is referenced in connection with his grand-father Abraham. According to Genesis 12:8, Abraham travelled 'unto a mountain on the east of Beth-el, and pitched his tent, having Beth-el on the west, and Hai on the east'. This verse suggests that Beth-el was due west of Hai. The site of ancient Hai

was unknown until it was uncovered in 1998 by Jordanian archaeologists led by Adnan Hussein. The dig, at modern Abu el Jordan
in southern Jordan, unearthed this ancient Semite settlement
dating from as early as the nineteenth century BCE. If Beth-el was
to the west of Hai, then these latest discoveries place the shrine in
the same area that we have placed the Mountain of God – in the
Shara mountains. In fact, the ruins of Petra are thirty kilometres
exactly due west of Abu el Jordan.

The Hebrew name for the Shara mountains was Seir. This is
known as the Bible repeatedly refers to the Edomites inhabiting
Seir (for example, Genesis 36:9). The Old Testament often links
God with this particular range. The prophet Isaiah, for instance,
tells us that when God speaks to him, 'He calleth to me out of
Seir' (ISAIAH 21:11). A particular mountain in the range is
specifically referred to as Mount Seir. The prophet Ezekiel, for
instance, tells his followers to 'set thy face against mount Seir'
(EZEKIEL 35:2). One particular passage leaves us with little doubt
that God was thought to reside there. In Judges 5:4–5, the judge
Deborah prays to God:

> Lord, when thou wentest out of Seir, when thou marchedst out of
> the field of Edom, the earth trembled, and the heavens dropped,
> the clouds also dropped water. The mountains melted from before
> the Lord, even that Sinai from before the Lord God of Israel.

Deuteronomy 33:2 is even more specific. When Moses is dying
he calls upon the Lord to bless the children of Israel and 'the
Lord came from Sinai and rose up from Seir unto them'. Not
only is this evidence that God was thought to reside in Seir but
that Mount Sinai is somewhere in the Seir range. It would appear
that Mount Seir and Mount Sinai are one and the same – one of
the Shara mountains in the land of Edom.

What do we know of this land of Edom in which the Mountain
of God was evidently to be found? Edom was originally an

independent kingdom centred on the Shara mountains in what is now southern Jordan. From the biblical descriptions, by the tenth century BCE it seems that its borders stretched from just to the south of the Dead Sea down to the Gulf of Aqaba. Much of this area was a barren and inhospitable land that formed the eastern part of what the Old Testament describes as the Sinai wilderness. During their forty years in the wilderness the Israelites frequently travelled through Edom and encountered the local inhabitants. According to the Book of Joshua, when the Israelites eventually moved north into Canaan, they initially established a presence from the source of the Jordan, at Dan, to the southern end of the Dead Sea: a swath of land about 230 kilometres long and 75 kilometres wide. By Solomon's reign, however, Edom was absorbed into the united kingdom of Israel, which now extended another 150 miles south, to the city of Eloth on the shores of the Red Sea at the Gulf of Aqaba. According to II Chronicles 8:17: 'Then went Solomon to Ezion-geber, and to Eloth, at the sea side in the land of Edom.'

Although we need to treat the accounts of Solomon's reign with some caution, there has been archaeological confirmation of a substantial Israelite presence in the Gulf of Aqaba during the period he seems to have reigned. According to I Kings 9:26: 'King Solomon made a navy of ships in Ezion-geber, which is beside Eloth, on the shore of the Red Sea, in the land of Edom.' The site of the ancient city is identified as a low mound called Tell-el-Kheleifeh, which now lies just outside the modern town of Elat. It was excavated in 1938 by an American team led by Dr Nelson Glueck, of the Hebrew Union College of Cincinnati, and distinctive Israelite-style pottery was found dating from as early as the tenth century BCE. A site for the port of Ezion-geber has also been proposed. In 1956, Dr Beno Rothenberg of Tel Aviv University suggested that Solomon's port was on the island of Jezirat Faraun, about ten kilometres down the coast from Elat. This picturesque island, about 350 metres long and 150 metres wide, has a natural lagoon on the side facing the mainland, making it a perfect harbour. It was over thirty years before underwater archaeology revealed that it had indeed been used as a port during the period Solomon appears to have lived. In 1993 an expedition by the Undersea Exploration Society of Israel discovered the remains of two ancient wrecks in the lagoon. Fragments of stone storage jars were found inside the wrecks that matched typical Israelite pottery found by Kathleen Kenyon's excavations in Jerusalem that dated from the tenth century BCE. Radiocarbon dating of timbers from the wrecks, which had been remarkably well-preserved in the mud of the seabed, also revealed a central date of around 950 BCE, the apparent time of King Solomon's reign.

The biblical descriptions of the size of Israel in the tenth century BCE have been supported by various archaeological discoveries made throughout Israel, from Dan in the north to the Gulf of Aqaba in the south. In the 1960s Kathleen Kenyon produced a map of the likely extent of Israelite occupation from the tenth to seventh centuries BCE that corresponded closely with the size of the kingdom as it is described in the Old Testament.

From various accounts in the Books of Kings and Chronicles we can gather that after the Israelite monarchy divided the land, of Edom remained a part of the kingdom of Israel. Although the kingdoms of Israel and Judah are often referred to as the northern and southern kingdoms, the kingdom of Israel actually appears to have stretched in a crescent to the east and south of Judah. The terms northern and southern evidently applied to the locations of their respective capitals, Samaria and Jerusalem. Indeed, Edom seems to have remained a part of Israel until the time of the Assyrian invasion. Although it remained free from Assyrian domination, its southern districts were seized by Judah around 735 BCE. According to II Chronicles 26:1–2:

Then all the peoples of Judah took Uzziah, who was sixteen years old, and made him king in the room of his father Amaziah. He built Eloth, and restored it to Judah.

As Uzziah was the king of Judah when the Assyrians first began their incursions into Israel, we can assume that Israel's preoccupation with defending its northern borders left the southern part of the kingdom undefended. Nevertheless, although Eloth may have fallen into Judean hands, not all of Edom fell to Judah. The Old Testament repeatedly makes reference to the Edomites after Uzziah's time, depicting them as an independent people still surviving in the Shara mountains. The Book of Ezekiel records them as late as the period of the Babylonian Exile, not only as an independent people with their own king but possessing considerable military muscle:

> There is Edom, her kings, and all her princes, which with their might are laid by them that were slain by the sword.
> (EZEKIEL 32:29)

The Edomites, however, were not regarded by the ancient Israelites as an entirely foreign people: according to the Old Testament they were actually Hebrews. All the same, they were not classed as Israelites. In the Book of Genesis, the Hebrew nation is said to have descended from Abraham, of which there were two separate peoples: the Israelites, who descended from Abraham's grandson Jacob, and the Edomites, who descended from Abraham's other grandson Esau.

Genesis tells us that these two brothers separated because Jacob tricked Esau out of his inheritance. According to Genesis 36:1–8, when the two brothers parted company Esau remained in Edom, where his descendants became the Edomites, while Jacob moved to the Samarian mountains in northern Israel, where his descendants became the Israelites. The story of Jacob and Esau appears to reflect the historical reality. Archaeology has shown that the ancient peoples of Edom were virtually indistinguishable from the Israelites. Samples of human skeletal remains found in the Samarian mountains of Israel and the Shara mountains of Edom, both dating to around 1700 BCE when the story of Jacob and Esau appears to be set (see Chapter IV), were sent for DNA tests to Japan in 2000. The tests were conducted at one of the world's leading laboratories in this field at Waseda University in Tokyo. (This was the same laboratory that recently conducted similar tests on samples from Tutankhamun's mummy.) The results showed that both the Samarian and Edomite remains were closely related, certainly from the same ethnic group. It seems, therefore, that the Edomites and the Israelites were both descendants of a Mari tribe who migrated south from Syria around 1750 BCE. The historical truth behind the biblical story of Jacob and Esau would therefore appear to be that one tribe – the ancient Hebrews – originally settled in the Shara mountains of Edom. Around fifty years later, with the growth of Hyksos power, some moved back to the north and made their home in the Samarian mountains. Jacob, it seems, represents the Hebrews who moved north and Esau represents the Hebrews who stayed in Edom.

From Egyptian records we know that when Tuthmosis III invaded Canaan and defeated the Hyksos tribes around 1500 BCE, the Edomites survived unconquered in their mountain strongholds. What is considered by Egyptologists to be a trustworthy account of Tuthmosis' campaigns is inscribed on a rock-cut sanctuary, dedicated to the goddess Hathor at Karnak. Discovered by the Swiss Egyptologist Edouard Naville in the nineteenth century, its walls are lavishly decorated with lengthy descriptions of the pharaoh's battles. Although many tribes, kingdoms and citadels are described as falling to Tuthmosis, not one is identifiable as being anywhere near the Shara mountains. Having survived in isolation while the other Hyksos were held captive in Egypt, the Edomites were apparently reunited under one kingdom with their Israelite cousins by the time of Solomon's reign. Archaeology shows that by the time of Solomon, the Edomites were not only a part of the kingdom of Israel, they shared the Hebrew religion. Excavations at the Edomite capital of Teman, beside the later city of Petra, carried out in the 1980s by Crystal Bennett, director of the British School of Archaeology in Jerusalem, have unearthed inscribed tablets dating from the ninth century BCE. Not only are they in Hebrew, but those containing prayers to God show that the Hebrew religion was being practised by the Edomites at this time.

When the Old Testament was committed to writing, however, the Jews of Judah considered the Edomites to be a blasphemous people who had strayed from the path of the Lord. Evidently they were considered adherents of the same tainted form of the Hebrew religion as was being practised throughout the rest of Israel. One of the Judean prophets who condemned the Edomites was Jeremiah, who preached in Jerusalem immediately before the Babylonian conquest. In the Old Testament Book of Jeremiah he launches repeatedly into a tirade against the Edomites: a people whom he does not portray as worshipping a pagan god, however, but a people who have forsaken the God of Israel. In one such passage we discover how Jeremiah believes that God will punish the Edomites for their sins:

> Concerning Edom, thus saith the Lord of hosts: Is wisdom no more in Teman? is counsel perished from the prudent? is their wisdom vanished? Flee ye, turn back, dwell deep, O inhabitants of Dedan; for I will bring the calamity of Esau upon him, the time that I will visit him. If grape-gatherers come to thee, would they not leave some gleaning grapes? if thieves by night, they will destroy till they have enough. But I have made Esau [the Edomite descendants of Esau] bare, I have uncovered his secret places, and he shall not be able to hide himself: his seed is spoiled, and his brethren, and his neighbours, and he is not. Leave thy fatherless

children, I will preserve them alive; and let thy widows trust in
me. For thus saith the Lord: Behold, they whose judgement was
not to drink of the cup have assuredly drunken; and art thou he
that shall altogether go unpunished? thou shalt not go unpunished, but thou shalt surely drink of it. For I have sworn by myself,
saith the Lord, that Bozrah shall become a desolation, a reproach,
a waste, and a curse . . . (JEREMIAH 49:7–13)

This last reference to the Edomite city of Bozrah is of particular
interest as it is here that we find direct evidence to link this
Edomite blasphemy with the Israelite cult of Baal. Bozrah was the
northernmost city of Edom, now identified as a flat-topped,
barren hill beside the village of present-day Buseirah, some sixty
kilometres north of Petra. This natural plateau would have been
easily defended in ancient times as it has steep ravines on three
sides. Between 1971 and 1974 Crystal Bennett excavated the site.
The city, she discovered, dated from the eighth century BCE and
seems to have been inhabited until well after the period of the
Babylonian Exile. It had been surrounded by walls several metres
thick and within these walls were numerous dwellings, a palace
and a temple. Although no statues or effigies were found to link
this temple with any particular sect, a discovery made in the 1930s
suggests that this had been a temple of what the Judeans called
Baal.

Excavations at the ancient Judean fort of Lachish, present-day
Tell el-Duweir, about forty-five kilometres south-west of Jerusalem, uncovered a remarkable collection of ancient letters. The
first dig at the site was conducted in the 1930s by the British
archaeologist James Starkey, but the project was terminated when
he was murdered by bandits in 1938. However, before he died
Starkey had uncovered the foundations of what turned out to be
an ancient guardhouse. Here, in the rubble, he found eighteen
clay tablets inscribed in Hebrew and dating from the period of
the Babylonian conquest. They were dispatches received by the

military commander of the fort: intelligence concerning the support the Judeans might expect from the various southern citadels that had not yet fallen to the Babylonians. One of the places mentioned is the Edomite city of Bozrah. According to one of the letters, the commander could not expect the support, even against this mutual foe, of their long-standing enemies the Edomites. The writer explains: 'Slack are the hands of the men of Edom, beguiled are they by the Chamarim.'

The Chamarim are mentioned in the Old Testament Book of Zephaniah. Zephaniah was a prophet who preached against the citizens of Judah who had been seduced by the cult of Baal, immediately before Josiah destroyed the sanctuary at Beth-el. He warns these blasphemers that God will forsake them:

> And I will stretch out mine hand upon Judah, and upon the inhabitants of Jerusalem; and I will cut off the remnants of Baal from this place, and the name of the Chamarims with the priests.
> (ZEPHANIAH 1:4)

From this verse it seems that the Chamarim were the Baal priests of Bozrah. It would appear, therefore, that the Edomites had wholly supported the brand of the Hebrew religion practised in the kingdom of Israel, and continued to do so well after Israel had ceased to exist. In fact, the Edomites might well have been the principal adherents. If the Mountain of God was in their land, then so it would seem was Beth-el. We have seen that II Kings 23:15–20 describes how, after he had destroyed Beth-el, Josiah slaughtered the chief servitors of the shrine who dwelt in a nearby city. The excavations of the Edomite capital at Teman reveal that it was indeed sacked by invaders some time in the late seventh century BCE, the very time that Josiah reigned.

It might have been because of this animosity between Judah and the Edomites that the Old Testament authors are often so vague concerning the Mountain of God's location – it was in

Edomite territory. It is with an Old Testament account of what appears to have been a confrontation between the Israelites and the Edomites that we find further confirmation that the Mountain of God was in Edom. The Book of Numbers tells us that while the Israelites were heading for the Mountain of God, after they had fled Egypt, they found themselves in the desert dying of thirst. God instructed Moses to strike his staff against a rock so that a miraculous spring might appear:

> And the Lord spake unto Moses saying, Take the rod, and gather thou the assembly together, thou and Aaron thy brother, and speak ye unto the rock before their eyes; and it shall give forth his water, and thou shalt bring forth to them water out of the rock: so thou shalt give the congregation and their beasts drink. And Moses took the rod from before the Lord, as he commanded him ... And Moses lifted up his hand, and with his rod he smote the rock twice: and water came out abundantly, and the congregation drank, and their beasts also. (NUMBERS 20:7–11)

The account goes on to tell us that this event occurred at a place called Kadesh, somewhere on the borders of Edom:

> And Moses sent messengers from Kadesh unto the king of Edom ... Let us pass, I pray thee, through thy country ... And Edom said unto him, Thou shalt not pass by me, lest I come out against thee with the sword ... Thus Edom refused to give Israel passage through his border: wherefore Israel turned away from him. And the children of Israel, even the whole congregation, journeyed from Kadesh, and came unto Mount Hor. (NUMBERS 20:14–22)

Here, the Israelites are refused passage through the Edomite kingdom so are forced to continue on to the sacred mountain by another route. This hostile reception by the Edomites might have been a later interpolation, as it goes unmentioned in a separate account of the same incident found in the Book of Exodus (EXODUS 17:8–16). It is in this separate account of the same incident that we find confirmation that the Mountain of God is in the land of Edom. According to the Exodus account, this same miraculous spring incident happens at Horeb – the Mountain of God.

> Behold I will stand before thee there upon the rock in Horeb; and thou shalt smite the rock, and there shall come water out of it, that the people may drink. And Moses did so in the sight of the elders of Israel. (EXODUS 17:6)

Taken together, these two separate accounts of the same incident tell us that Horeb, the Mountain of God, is at a now forgotten place called Kadesh on the borders of Edom.

If the God of Moses was principally associated with one of the Shara mountains of Edom, then this might reveal much about the origins of the Hebrew religion. The Edomites not only inhabited the Shara mountains at the time of the Exodus, they were already there when Moses – perhaps the first Moses – discovered God in the burning bush. This is not only demonstrated by the archaeological excavations of Teman, which have shown continuous Edomite occupation for over a thousand years from around 1700 BCE, it is also confirmed by the Bible itself. According to Genesis 36:8–9, well before the Exodus, Esau founded the kingdom of Edom: 'Thus dwelt Esau in mount Seir.' If Mount Seir was the Mountain of God, as we have speculated, and the first-century historian Josephus is right about 'the opinion men had that God dwelt there', then the men having this opinion are the local inhabitants: the Edomites.

So, was the God discovered by Moses originally an Edomite god? Was the Hebrew religion a religion that had already developed in Edom while the Israelites were held captive in Egypt? If so, then this would certainly be something that the later Judeans would be happy to forget. There is actually a compelling case that evidence of high Edomite status amongst the early Hebrews was deliberately expunged from the Bible.

The Old Testament authors go to considerable lengths to discredit the Edomites. The second Book of Kings suggests that the Edomites had rid themselves of Judean influence, even before Jeroboam and the ten tribes of Israel had done so. This occurred during the reign of David, evidently because they objected to the king's plans that his son should build the Jerusalem Temple:

> Yet the Lord would not destroy Judah for David his servant's sake, as he promised him to give him alway a light, and to his children. In his days Edom revolted from under the hand of Judah and made a king over themselves. (II KINGS 8:19–20)

By Josiah's time the Edomites had evidently come to be detested by the Judeans. The prophet Amos sums up perfectly how the kingdom of Judah regarded Edom in the mid-eighth century BCE:

> Thus saith the Lord; For three transgressions of Edom, and for four, I will not turn away the punishment thereof; because he did pursue his brother with the sword, and did cast off all pity, and his anger did tear perpetually, and he kept his wrath for ever: But I will send a fire upon Teman, which shall devour the palaces of Bozrah. (AMOS 1:11–12)

During the Babylonian Exile, the Jews even blamed the Edomites for their misfortunes. This is typified by one of Ezekiel's tirades:

> Therefore thus saith the Lord God; I will also stretch out mine hand upon Edom, and will cut off man and beast from it; and I will make it desolate from Teman ... And I will lay my vengeance upon Edom by the hand of my people Israel: and they shall do in Edom according to mine anger and according to my fury; and they shall know my vengeance, saith the Lord God.
> (EZEKIEL 25:13–14)

The Edomites cannot have been so badly thought of at the time of the Exodus, however. Indeed, such hostility between the Israelites and the Edomites would not have permitted Moses and his followers to spend so much time at the Mountain of God if it was in Edomite territory. If we look again at the story of Jacob and Esau we find indications that the Edomites were once as highly esteemed as any Hebrew tribe. In fact, it seems that they were originally regarded as true Israelites.

Like many ancient peoples, the Israelites required an ancestral founder – in their case Jacob. According to Genesis, it is he who is renamed Israel and his descendants, the children of Israel, are the Israelites. Why, then, is there the need to include Abraham in the Genesis narrative? According to Genesis 17:7–8, God picked Abraham to be the father of his chosen nation.

> And I will establish my covenant between me and thee and thy seed after thee in their generations for an everlasting covenant, to be a God unto thee, and to thy seed after thee. And I will give unto thee, and to thy seed after thee, the land wherein thou art a stranger, all the land of Canaan, for ever lasting possession; and I will be their God.

This passage makes it quite clear that, in God's own words, all of Abraham's offspring were the chosen people – Esau included. However, later in Genesis, it is Abraham's grandson Jacob who becomes the father of God's chosen nation. Abraham's other grandson Esau and his descendants are divinely disinherited. If this was in the original story, why bring Abraham into the narrative at all? The genealogy would only need to begin with Jacob. We are left with the suspicion that the story of Esau's disinheritance was added later to ostracize the Edomites.

It was only after Josiah's religious purge that the Exodus account was finally committed to writing, making the surviving narrative very much the Judean version of events. When he destroyed Beth-el, Josiah mercilessly slaughtered its devotees. He and the Judean priests would surely have had little compunction in eradicating any indication of past Edomite influence in the Hebrew world. There is even evidence in the Bible itself to suggest that certain Old Testament episodes had been reworked in Josiah's time, once Israel had ceased to exist. For example, the account of Josiah's sacking of the shrine at Beth-el in the second Book of Kings (II KINGS 23: 15–20) is referenced in an earlier passage in the first Book of Kings. According to I Kings 13:1–3, a prophet had visited Beth-el in Jeroboam's day and foretold its eventual destruction:

> And, behold, there came a man of God out of Judah by the word of the Lord unto Beth-el: and Jeroboam stood by the altar to burn incense. And he cried against the altar in the word of the Lord, and said, O, altar, altar, thus saith the Lord; Behold, a child shall be born unto the house of David, Josiah by name; and upon thee shall he offer the priests of the high places that burn incense upon thee, and men's bones shall be burnt upon thee. And he gave a sign the same day, saying, This is the sign which the Lord has spoken; Behold, the altar shall be rent, and the ashes that are upon it shall be poured out.

This passage is supposed to have been written three centuries before Josiah's time, yet it is a precise account of Josiah's eventual purge – Josiah is even included by name. The fundamentalist biblical scholar would see this, no doubt, as an example of the fulfilment of prophesy. From the historian's perspective, however, it would seem more reasonable to assume that the passage was interpolated into the narrative to justify Josiah's actions. There is even evidence in the Bible to suggest that the entire first five books of the Old Testament had undergone a reworking at the time Josiah was on the throne. II Kings 22.8 refers to an intriguing event that took place in the Jerusalem Temple during Josiah's reign:

> Hilkiah the high priest said to Shaphan the secretary, I have found the book of the law in the house of the Lord.

The book of the law was the Torah, the first five books of the Hebrew Bible. From this verse we must assume that these scriptures had been lost for generations before they were discovered hidden somewhere in the Jerusalem Temple. It might even be inferred that whatever written or oral accounts concerning the period before the conquest of Canaan existed before Josiah's reign, they were preserved in some different form from the Torah as it now survives. In the words of the eminent Israeli historian Dr Mordechai Snyder of the Hebrew University in Jerusalem:

> The book of law [found in the temple] may reflect the Torah's eventual composition during Josiah's reign, perhaps from a variety of existing sources.

Other biblical commentators, such as Dr Robert Mason of Brigham Young University, Utah, take this passage as evidence of amendments to Hebrew history by Josiah's scribes. According to Dr Mason:

> Considering his uncompromising nature, it is not beyond possibility that Josiah should arrange for new scriptures to be compiled to reflect Hebrew history in favour of Judaism as it existed at the time.

Even though Josiah and his followers might have attempted to defame the Edomites, evidence of their high status within Hebrew society may survive in the Old Testament. The Edomites might have been the mysterious people referred to as the Lord's Host. Each Hebrew tribe had an army that the Bible calls a host and a commanding officer to whom the Bible refers as a captain. The second chapter in the Book of Numbers lists all of them serving under Moses in the early days in the wilderness. There is

Nahshon, the captain of the host of Judah, Eliab, the captain of the host of Zebulun, Eliasaph, the captain of the host of Gad and so forth. There was, however, another host who seem to have been the Hebrew warrior élite – the Lord's Host. They are referred to only once in the Book of Joshua when they join with the Israelites as they march on Jericho. Incredibly, their captain outranks even Joshua.

> And it came to pass that when Joshua was by Jericho, that he lifted up his eyes and looked and behold, there stood a man over against him with his sword drawn in his hand: and Joshua went unto him, and said unto him, Art thou for us or for our adversaries? And he said, Nay; but as captain of the host of the Lord am I now come. And Joshua fell on his face to the earth ... And the captain of the Lord's host said unto Joshua, Loose thy shoe from thy foot; for the place whereon thou standest is holy. And Joshua did so. (JOSHUA 5:13–15)

Who is this mysterious character? According to the Old Testament, Joshua was Moses' successor and undisputed leader of the Israelites, yet this man so outranks Joshua that he grovels before him. Furthermore, he not only has military authority, he has priestly authority for he can declare a site to be holy. He is clearly a flesh-and-blood human being and no angel, as elsewhere in the Bible angels are always identified as such. Similarly, armies of angels are always described as hosts of angels or hosts of heaven.

There is compelling indication that a section has been erased from the Book of Joshua concerning this captain and his Lord's Host. After his dramatic appearance, the chapter ends abruptly and the account is taken up some time later. We have not been told who this man is, why the ground is holy or what he has come to say. All we can gather is that he has brought his host to aid Joshua in the coming battle. If the episode ever made sense, then something must have been removed. The reason, it now seems, was that this man was the leader of the Edomites. An ancient Hebrew text dating from before the Babylonian occupation of Judah, recently rediscovered by an American historian, throws a completely new light on Hebrew history. It seems that this was not the only reference to this man and his host to have been erased from the Old Testament. An entire book appears to have been removed – a book that identifies the Lord's Host as the army of the Edomites.

The Bible actually contains evidence that there was once a fortieth book of the Old Testament. Called the Book of Jasher, it is mentioned twice. Joshua refers to it: 'Is this not written in the Book of Jasher' (JOSHUA 10:13). So does King David: 'Behold it is written in the Book of Jasher' (II SAMUEL 1:18). This book, which seems to have been important to the early Israelites, was lost to history until the twentieth century. A number of different copies of the Book of Jasher appeared during the nineteenth century and were used by various offshoot Christian sects as a template to support their religious convictions. However, none was supported by any reliable provenance. Finally, a sixteenth-century English copy was rediscovered in the archives of Rouen Cathedral in 1929 and obtained by the Bibliothèque Nationale in Paris. It remained tucked away and forgotten in the vaults of the library until it was examined by the American historian Michael Martin of Philadelphia University in 1993. Martin studied the manuscript's provenance in great detail and was convinced of its authenticity before publishing it in 1995.

Martin's research traced the Book of Jasher back to ancient Judah. An original scroll containing it had been acquired by the Babylonian king Nebuchadnezzar when he captured Jerusalem in 597 BCE. With other booty it was returned to Babylon where it remained until it was looted by the Persian king Cyrus II when he conquered the city in 539 BCE. It then remained in Persia, in the great library of Gazna, until it was bought by Alucin, the abbot of Canterbury, when he visited the country during a pilgrimage around 800 CE. It was returned to Canterbury, where it was copied into Latin in the 1140s. This, in turn, was copied into English during the sixteenth century. Along with the medieval manuscript, the original scroll perished before the dissolution of the monasteries, but the manuscript containing the English copy was taken along with other documents to Rouen Cathedral in France, where it remained until it was acquired by the Bibliothèque Nationale.

The Book of Jasher, as it now survives, has no chapters or verses, which is how the Books of the Old Testament originally appeared. Like the books of Numbers, Leviticus and Deuteronomy, it covers the period the Israelites spent in the wilderness, but contains commentaries on events during and preceding the bondage in Egypt. However, where these other books have Joshua succeeding Moses, here Moses is succeeded by Jasher, after whom the book is named. Jasher is both a priest and a warrior, although he appoints Joshua as field commander of the Israelite armies. One reason why this book seems to have been removed from the Old Testament is that Jasher was the high priest of Beth-el. According to the Book of Jasher, Moses had appointed him and his select tribe of Hebrews to guard the holy sanctuary. More importantly, the Book of Jasher tells us that Jasher and his tribe are the Edomites.

In its opening passages, the Book of Jasher covers the period of Abraham just as it is outlined in the Genesis account. However, when it comes to Jacob there is no mention whatsoever of the disinheritance of Esau. In fact, the name Esau does not appear anywhere in the narrative. The Edomites are said to have descended from Jacob's brother Edom. This is undoubtedly the same person as Esau, however, as Genesis 36:8 tells us that Esau was also called Edom, after whom his descendants were named. According to the Book of Jasher, when Jacob and his family move into Egypt, Edom and his family remain behind in Mount Seir.

Jasher introduces himself into the story by explaining how he knows of the Hebrews early days:

All these things which I Jasher have written, received I from Caleb my father, yea even from Hezron my father's father, of the tribe of Edom, the son of Isaac, the son of Abraham who is Israel.

Here, it is not Jacob who is called Israel, but Abraham, which, as we have seen, would have made far more sense in the Genesis narrative. It is doubtful whether Jasher himself really did write the extant work, any more than Moses wrote the Torah, but whoever the author was, he clearly believed that the tribe of Edom was a legitimate tribe of Israel.

The Book of Jasher goes on to describe the high estate that the Edomites hold amongst the Israelites. To begin with, its author makes no attempt to hide the fact that the Mountain of God is in Edom. When Moses flees Egypt, he marries the daughter of the priest of Midian and finally comes to the Mountain of God. Although its location is not named, it has to be somewhere in Edom as on the Mountain of God Moses is greeted by Jasher's grandfather, Hezron the Edomite. For a while Moses lives amongst Hezron's people. In fact, Moses is not alone and seems to have escaped Egypt with other Israelites. Hezron, we are told, 'taught the children of Israel to shoot with the bow: he learnt his brethren to prepare themselves for battle'. We are not told specifically how Moses discovers God – the burning bush goes unmentioned – but, once again, it was clearly in Edom. When he returns to Egypt he tells the people: 'While I was in the land of our brethren [Hezron's people, the Edomites], I heard a voice saying unto me: Arise, go unto thy brethren, for I will by thy hand bring back the children of Israel.'

As in the Exodus account, the Israelites in captivity are ignorant of this new God: 'And the elders of the children of Jacob knew not Moses: neither regarded they the words of his mouth.' Eventually they are persuaded: 'And it came to pass, when the people saw all the signs and wonders which Moses wrought in the sight of all Israel, in the presence of the congregation, that they believed.' When they finally escape Egypt, the Israelites head directly for Edom where they are met at Kadesh by Hezron's delegation. They are made welcome and pass through Kadesh to arrive at the Mountain of God.

The narrative then follows pretty much the Exodus version of events concerning the Covenant, the Ten Commandments and the Ark of the Covenant. Like the Exodus story, the Hebrews make the golden calves and God decrees that they should wander in the wilderness for forty years before they can enter Canaan. However, when the Israelites leave Edom, Jasher and the Edomites remain behind: 'And I Jasher, did remain at the altar of the Lord that Moses did build.' As a previous passage describes Moses building an altar on the Mountain of God after he receives the Ten Commandments, Jasher is presumably being left as priest and guardian of the sacred site.

Moses finally returns to the mountain just before his death and appoints Jasher as his successor: 'And Moses said, The son of Caleb [Jasher] take the rod of my brother Aaron so that ye may lead the children of Israel into the land of Canaan.' Although it is actually Joshua who does most of the fighting, Jasher directs operations from his base in Edom. When Canaan is finally conquered, Jasher summons the conquered kings to Beth-el, in order to make peace. Here, Jasher is portrayed as the highest of all Israel's judges:

And in those days, the kings and princes of the sea coasts, the kings of the mountains, and the kings of the valleys, assembled themselves together, nigh unto Beth-el . . . And Jasher, the priests

of Edom, and all the elders of the tribes of Israel, came there also
... Then answered all the kings of the sea-coasts, the kings of the
mountains, and the kings of the valleys, and they said: What thou,
O Jasher, judge of all Israel.

So, according to the Book of Jasher, the Edomites are the priests
of Beth-el, the guardians of the Mountain of God and the chief
tribe of Israel. It is understandable then that by Josiah's time,
when the tribe of Judah were the ascendant Hebrew tribe and the
Jerusalem Temple was the 'house of God', such a book would
need to be omitted from the Hebrew Bible.

In conclusion, regardless of the Book of Jasher, from the Bible
itself it would seem that the Mountain of God was in Edom: a
mountain at a place called Kadesh, somewhere at the edge of the
Shara range. It was here that Moses found God and returned to
receive his laws. Or, as we previously surmised, the original
Moses found God and the second Moses returned to receive
God's laws. As the Edomites were already there and the mountain
was theirs, then so presumably was the God Moses discovered. If
we are right, then some time between the Edomites first settling
in the Shara mountains, around 1750 BCE, and the time of the
enslavement of their Israelite cousins, around 1500 BCE, a radical
religious concept had somehow developed. What, then, do we
find at the Mountain of God? Which one of the Shara mountains
might it have been?

Summary

- In the Old Testament, the most sacred site to the Hebrew God
  is the Mountain of God, often referred to as Mount Sinai. Find
  the Mountain of God and we may find the true origin of
  western religion. The different books of the Old Testament
  actually use different names for the Mountain of God. Exodus

usually refers to it as Mount Sinai, while Deuteronomy refers to it mainly as Horeb and the Book of Numbers as Hor.

- The true location of the Mountain of God is now a mystery as the Bible does not say directly where it is. All we are told is that it was somewhere in the Sinai wilderness. At the time the Bible was committed to writing – around 620 CE – the area known as the Sinai wilderness covered a large area including the desert lands of Paran, Midian and Edom – the modern-day Sinai Peninsula in eastern Egypt and a large part of southern Jordan. The Mountain of God could have been anywhere in this expanse.

- According to the Book of Exodus, Moses first discovered the Mountain of God on the far side of the Sinai wilderness from the land of Midian, which would place it in the land of Edom. This is confirmed by the Book of Numbers, which tells us that Aaron was buried on the Mountain of God in Edom. The first-century Jewish historian Josephus confirms the place of Aaron's death as the valley of Edom. According to the Book of Numbers, the Israelites have to pass through Kadesh to arrive at the Mountain of God, which was apparently on the borders of Edom.

- This might explain why the Bible is so vague about the actual location of the Mountain of God. At the time the first books of the Old Testament were committed to writing in their present form, Edom was considered to be the land of a blasphemous people – the Edomites, a thirteenth Hebrew tribe who had strayed from the path of the Lord.

- An entire book appears to have been removed from the Bible. Called the Book of Jasher, it is mentioned twice. Joshua refers to it: 'Is this not written in the Book of Jasher' (JOSHUA 10:13). So does King David: 'Behold it is written in the Book of Jasher' (II SAMUEL 1:18). The Book of Jasher was not rediscovered until 1993 in the Bibliothèque Nationale, Paris. It tells us not only that the Edomites are a legitimate tribe of Israel, but also that the Mountain of God is in their kingdom. Moreover, the Edomites are its priesthood and guardians.

8 MOUNTAIN OF GOD

Northern Israel was a bountiful land: a gentle hill country, lush with sub-tropical vegetation. Judah had highly fertile soil in which palms, olive and fig trees grew in abundance. This was Canaan, the Promised Land that God told Moses he would give to the Israelites:

> I am come down to deliver them out of the hand of the Egyptians, and bring them up out of that land unto a good land and a large, unto a land flowing with milk and honey. (EXODUS 3:8)

By contrast, southern Israel was a land of harsh extreme. Here was the Negev: a parched and arid wasteland. It remains unchanged today. As far as the eye can see, the sun beats down mercilessly upon dusty white rocks and searing, lifeless sand. Day after day, year after year, the ground bakes in the shimmering heat. In this dry, stony desert, two hundred kilometres long and two hundred kilometres wide, temperatures can rise to over forty degrees in the shade. At night, however, the temperature plummets close to zero and a bitter chill descends over this barren country.

In biblical times, the Negev formed the northern, and least hospitable, part of the Sinai wilderness, though at its heart there stood an oasis island of rock. This ring of mountains, rising to over a thousand metres above the desert floor, completely encircled the valley of Edom. Nourished by cool mountain streams and shaded by towering cliffs, it was a haven for life in this otherwise hostile terrain. Today, although the valley is far more life-bearing than the surrounding desert, it is nowhere near as fertile as it was three thousand years ago when rainfall was higher and numerous streams fed the valley floor. This, then, was the home of the Edomites.

Today, the Edom valley falls twenty kilometres inside Jordanian territory. It runs approximately north–south and is around a kilometre wide and five kilometres long. The mountains that surround it are in stark contrast to the desert beyond. The rocks are multi-coloured: golden brown, yellow, orange and red. The only way to enter the Edom valley, avoiding the gruelling haul over the mountains, is a long, narrow cleft at its southern end that winds its way through one and a half kilometres of solid rock. Called the Siq, it was created millions of years ago when some gigantic geological upheaval literally tore a mountain in two.

At its entrance the Siq is around five metres wide, but the further we progress inside, the narrower it becomes until sunlight can no longer shine down between the sheer walls to either side. Finally, after trudging for what seems for ever, when the deep, dark corridor seems about to close completely, it turns abruptly and opens out on to one of the most spectacular sites of the ancient world. Rising high above us in the facing cliff is the forty-metre edifice of a gigantic monument. Two tiers of towering Corinthian columns, colossal pediments, statue niches and carved urns are all cut from the living rock. It is the entrance to a vast hall, leading off into dark empty chambers deep inside the mountain. So awe-inspiring is this enigmatic monument that Steven Spielberg chose it for the location of the lost repository for the Holy Grail in his movie *Indiana Jones and the Last Crusade*. Now called the Treasury, its original function is something of a mystery, but it is thought to be the remains of a 2000-year-old tomb.

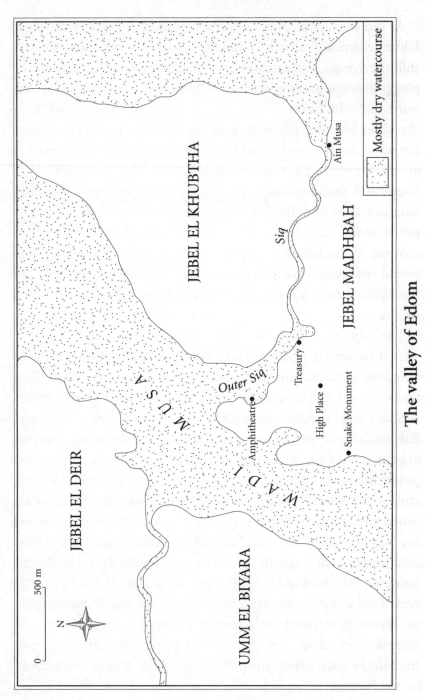

The valley of Edom

As old as it may be, the Treasury would not have been here in Edomite times. It is one of the many Nabatean monuments that still survive in this haunting place. Beyond the Treasury is a gorge, averaging some seventy metres wide, which leads downwards into the Edom valley, a further kilometre to the north. In the valley itself we find the ruins of Nabatean Petra. On a broad flat plain, set between the craggy mountains, the ruins seemed to go on for ever. They are classical constructions, influenced by Greek and Roman design: an amphitheatre, the walls of homes, administrative buildings and temples, all set around a series of paved roads. Either side of these straight avenues, stone pillars, colonnades and broken statues line the ways, which long ago would have been the thoroughfares of the ancient city. Cut into the cliffs, surrounding Petra, are hundreds of ornate and lavish tombs.

The city of Petra dates from the time well after Edom was sacked by Josiah, around 620 BCE. Following their defeat by the kingdom of Judah, the Edomites fell into decline and the Nabateans arrived in the area. The Nabateans originated around the Arabian Gulf but had been forced westwards by the expanding Babylonian empire. At first they were compelled to a nomadic existence in the Arabian desert until the collapse of Edomite power allowed them to move into the Shara mountains. By the end of the fourth century BCE, Alexander the Great had established Greek influence throughout the eastern Mediterranean and the Nabateans quickly took control of new trade routes that came into existence through the Shara range. Standing on a crossroads between the lands of the Mediterranean and the lands of the Near East and Asia, the Nabateans became rich and powerful and the great new cosmopolitan city of Petra grew up over the Edomite capital of Teman. One of the most important cities of the Middle East, Petra remained independent until it was annexed by the Romans in CE 106.

The previous Edomite city of Teman might have been less elaborate, but it was a formidable site for its time. Excavations at the Edomite level of occupation have unearthed sophisticated pottery, inscribed clay tablets with Hebrew inscriptions and many ornate artefacts, revealing a prosperous and well-defended settlement. One find from a building on the mountain of Umm el Biyara, which overlooked the main city, demonstrates that around 700 BCE, following the destruction of the kingdom of Israel, the Edomites not only remained free from Assyrian conquest they also had their own king. A seal-impression, which would have been attached to a letter or proclamation, was found to bear the name of King Qaush-gaber. An inscription from Nineveh records this same man ruling the only part of the kingdom of Israel that remained beyond the control of the Assyrian king Esarhaddron in 681 BCE.

By the time the Assyrian Empire fell and Josiah came to the throne of Judah, some of the Old Testament authors attempted to portray the Edomites as a foreign people. Certain passages present them as a Gentile kingdom against which Judah had waged triumphant holy wars. David is said to have enslaved them (I KINGS 11:15), and Joram of Judah (848–841 BCE) is said to have smashed their kingdom:

> So Joram went over to Zair [Seir] and all the chariots with him: and he rose by night, and smote the Edomites. (II KINGS 8:20)

Again, under Amaziah (796–767 BCE), Judah is said to have decisively defeated the Edomite army:

> And Amaziah strengthened himself, and led forth his people, and went to the valley of Salt [the Negev], and smote of the children of Seir ten thousand. (II CHRONICLES 25:11)

Both of these assertions seem most improbable. Not only do the excavations at Teman show the Edomites of this time to have been enjoying a period of considerable prosperity, with no sign of foreign aggression, but elsewhere the Old Testament itself suggests that these two accounts were fictitious. Chapter nine of the second Book of Kings tells us that Joram was such a weak and ineffectual king that Jehu of Israel attacked his country and had him killed. Jerusalem only held out because Israel became preoccupied with Syria. As for Amaziah: according to chapter twenty-five of the second Book of Chronicles, he was even weaker. We are told he was an inept character who almost lost Jerusalem to Jehoash of Israel. The capital only survived because Amaziah plundered the temple coffers to pay him off and gave up much of Judah's territory. If true, then neither king had the strength to lead a successful campaign against the well-defended Edom valley. In fact, the inscription on the Moabite Stone, dating from less than a decade before Joram's reign began, tells us that Edom was not only a part of Israel but that its army formed a formidable part of Israel's forces.

Returning to the time of the Exodus, around 1360 BCE, the city of Teman was a Bronze Age settlement of simple mud-brick houses. There was, however, a central palace complex from which the leaders of the Edomites controlled their valley kingdom. The approach to the valley was the gorge in which the Treasury now stands. Now called the Outer Siq, this gorge runs between two mountains: Jebel el Khubtha to the east and Jebel Madhbah to the west. Was this the Kadesh spoken of in Numbers 20:14–22? In this account of Moses and the miraculous spring, Kadesh, where the event took place, is on the borders of Edom whence Moses sends a message to the Edomite king to ask his permission to enter his land. It is also where the Edomite king greets the Israelites in the Book of Jasher. At the time the story appears to be set, the kingdom of Edom was centred on the valley beyond the Outer Siq, which formed the only accessible approach to the kingdom for any large number of people laden with all their belongings. If this was Kadesh, then the Mountain of God must be one of the two mountains that rise above the gorge. Exodus 17:6 tells us that the miraculous spring incident occurred at 'the rock in Horeb'. As we have seen, Horeb *was* the Mountain of God.

Amazingly, this gorge is known by the local Bedouin as Wadi Musa – the 'Valley of Moses'. Is this just a remarkable coincidence? Seemingly not. It was here, in the early nineteenth century, that an intrepid explorer made a chance discovery of immense significance in the search for the Mountain of God.

The city of Petra declined with the Roman Empire and by the time of the conversion of the Arabs of the area to Islam in the seventh century it was abandoned altogether. The Crusaders returned briefly and built a series of forts but, thereafter, the ancient city became forgotten to Europeans. It was eventually rediscovered by John Burckhardt in 1812.

Having been educated at Göttingen University, the Swiss-born Burckhardt travelled to London in 1806 to meet with Sir Joseph Banks, a man of wealth and influence whose obsession was to discover the source of the Nile. Burckhardt immediately hit it off with Sir Joseph and soon volunteered for the job. The reason why no European had previously attempted such an expedition was the great animosity that existed between the Muslims and the Christian Europeans. To travel through northern Africa at the time would have been suicidal. For the next three years, therefore, Burckhardt read Arabic and Islamic Studies at Cambridge University, in order that he might pass himself off as a Muslim trader. His studies completed, and assuming the name Ibrahim ibn Abdallah, he took a boat to Turkey where he began his arduous journey south along the eastern Mediterranean coast, keeping a secret diary as he went. Burckhardt's appearance aroused no suspicion amongst his fellow travellers – a caravan of Muslim traders – as he had a naturally dark complexion and black hair. However, although he spoke Arabic fluently, his accent was strange.

Burckhardt records that when he was questioned about his curious accent, he told his companions that he was from India and that his first language was Hindi: a language which, incidentally, he did not speak. He hoped to God that no one else did either. When asked for a sample of his native tongue, he would recite Shakespeare in German. Luckily for him, it seemed to satisfy all concerned. The explorer spent three years in Syria, perfecting his Arabic and studying Koranic law, before finally setting off with another caravan bound for Cairo, from where he intended to launch his expedition to find the Nile's source.

As Burckhardt passed through the Negev desert, he began to hear tales of the ruins of a magnificent ancient city hidden away in the Shara mountains. His curiosity aroused, he sought to find a pretext to visit the site. He could not openly declare a desire to do so, for the local Bedouin might easily interpret his motives as spying. The fear and suspicion engendered by centuries of isolation had made these desert peoples suspicious of any motive they could not understand. Hearing that there was an Islamic shrine in the vicinity of the ruins, he told the Bedouin he wished to worship there. No one would object to a religious motive so he was allowed to pass. It was thus that in the August of 1812 John Burckhardt became the first westerner for over half a millennium to enter the valley of Edom.

Accompanied by a guide from the Bedouin Lyathene tribe, Burckhardt rode through the Siq and towards the Wadi Musa gorge. When he stopped at a spring to water his donkey, his companion started shouting and pointed his gun at him. The spring, he was told, was too sacred for a beast to drink from. It was called Ain Musa – the 'Spring of Moses'. It was here, the Bedouin told him, that Moses had struck his staff against the

rock to create the miraculous spring after the Israelites had left
Egypt. Almost as an afterthought, Burckhardt made a note of the
incident in his diary and included it in his book *Travels in Syria
and the Holy Land* published in London in 1822. Although
Burckhardt's original work still survives in the Griffith Institute
at Oxford University, biblical scholars, archaeologists and historians alike, who have attempted to search for the Mountain of
God, seem to have overlooked his find.

The Ain Musa tradition was indeed ancient. It is attested to by
the medieval Arab chronicler Numairi. Numairi was an Egyptian
and his chronicle, dating from around CE 1300, still survives at
the Dar el Kutub in Cairo. Referring to the approach to Petra,
Numairi writes:

> At the foot of a mountain in the ravine there is a spring, which
> is said never to run dry. The people thereabouts say that Moses,
> Prophet of God, peace upon him, did bring it forth with his
> staff.

In light of what we have examined in the previous chapter, surely
it is beyond coincidence that in all the Sinai wilderness a local
tradition places the miraculous spring incident exactly where we
reasoned it should have occurred. Even today the spring is still
called Ain Musa and local people continue to revere the site,
which is now covered by a small domed shrine. It is located on
the west side of the gorge. If the Bedouin tradition is correct,
then the Mountain of God must be the mountain that rises above
it – Jebel Madhbah.

When we examine Numairi's work further we discover another
ancient tradition that suggests that the local Bedouin unwittingly
knew that the Mountain of God was in their land. Numairi
writes:

> On this mountain is the tomb of Aaron, Prophet of God, the
> brother of Moses, peace upon them.

As we have seen, the Old Testament tells us that Aaron had died on the sacred mountain. Numbers 20:26 also makes it clear that Aaron was buried on top of it: 'Aaron shall be gathered unto his people, and shall die there'. The phrase 'gathered unto his people' is used often in the Bible when referring to burial or entombment. The mountain Numairi mentions, however, is not Jebel Madhbah, but one to the north-west of the valley. It is still called Jebel Haroun – 'Aaron's Mountain'.

Like the spring of Moses, the local inhabitants still venerate Jebel Haroun as the site of Aaron's tomb. Just below the summit, on a flat ridge overlooking a sheer cliff, there perches the little whitewashed mosque that stands over a cave where the prophet is said to have been laid to rest. It is a simple square building with a dome on top, and an Arabic inscription above the door tells us that it was erected by 'Muhammad, son of Calaon, Sultan of Egypt in the year 739 of the Hegira' – which is the mid-thirteenth century.

So we do not have one but two mountains overlooking the valley of Edom that local traditions associate with the Mountain of God: one at each end. Although this second tradition is a positive indication concerning the area as the location of the Mountain of God, it also confuses matters. Which of the two mountains was the sacred mount?

There is some indication in the Bible that the entire ring of mountains around the Edom valley was sometimes referred to as the Mountain of God. There seems to be confusion between the single mountain and the range. As we have seen, the Hebrew word for the Shara range was Seir, which was also the name for a specific mountain in it: Mount Seir, seemingly the Mountain of God. For example: 'That day on his way unto Seir' (GENESIS 33:16). 'Five hundred men, went to mount Seir' (1 CHRONICLES 4:42). The same is true when referring to the sacred mountain as Sinai: 'The Lord came from Sinai' (DEUTERONOMY 32:2). 'The

Lord spake with Moses in mount Sinai' (NUMBERS 3:1). And again when referring to it as Horeb: 'And when he departed from Horeb' (DEUTERONOMY 1:19). 'By the mount Horeb' (EXODUS 33:6). It seems that there is occasional confusion between the sacred mountain and the range it is in: both might be referred to as Seir, Sinai or Horeb.

The same may also apply when the Book of Numbers speaks of Aaron's death and burial on the Mountain of God as occurring at Mount Hor. Numbers 20:23 refers to Aaron's death occurring '*in* mount Hor', which is a strange way to refer to a specific mountain. Why does the author not say '*on* mount Hor'? The oldest surviving complete Hebrew Bible dates from the third century CE and is now preserved in the National Library of Israel on the campus of the Hebrew University in west Jerusalem. It seems to have remained unchanged from before Christian times as a number of its books were found amongst the Dead Sea Scrolls, the relevant texts dating from around 100 BCE. It was from just such a manuscript that the Greek and later Christian Old Testaments were translated. If we consult this Hebrew Bible we find that the word used during the Mount Hor episode is *bethud*, which indeed translates directly as 'in'. The Exodus account of Moses' spring also uses the word 'in': 'the rock *in* Horeb' (EXODUS 17:6). However, unlike the modern Bible's Book of Numbers account of Aaron's death, the Hebrew original uses the word *bayal*, which actually translates as 'at'. Of the two, the second is the more specific: Aaron's burial is being referred to as *in* the area of Hor or Horeb, whereas the spring is being referred to specifically as *at* the sacred mountain itself. If we consult the Exodus account of the miraculous spring again, we are left in no doubt that the mountain on which God gave Moses the Covenant and the Ten Commandments was the same mountain where he made the spring appear. After Moses performs the miracle, the Israelites: 'camped before the mount. And Moses went up unto God, and the Lord called unto him out of the mountain.' On balance, therefore, it seems more likely that the sacred mountain is Jebel Madhbah.

If we climb Jebel Madhbah we find compelling evidence that we really have discovered the place where Moses found God. On a natural plateau, known as Attuf Ridge, just below its summit, at a height of 1035 metres above sea level, are the remains of an ancient centre of worship. Cut into the rock, to a depth of about forty centimetres, there is a large rectangular depression, known as the courtyard, measuring approximately fourteen metres by six. Around it are the remains of rock-cut benches where a congregation would once have sat. Near the centre of the courtyard there is a small raised platform of stone, fifteen centimetres high, two metres long and one metre wide, which was probably used for offerings. The courtyard itself is aligned on a north–south axis and is set lengthways against a stone altar. The altar, measuring approximately a metre high, two metres wide and three metres long, stands above the courtyard at the top of a flight of steps to the immediate west.

As the entire site is constructed from stone, it cannot be radiocarbon dated. The age of stone buildings is usually determined by dating items such as tools and pottery found in their foundations. However, because the structure is cut from solid bedrock, no such dating is possible with the Attuf Ridge site. Earlier last century the site was taken to be a Nabatean creation, from the same period as the Petra ruins, but the lack of any Nabatean inscriptions and statues of their gods, which lavishly adorn the temples and shrines in the valley below, has made many modern investigators question this notion. Archaeologist Dr Samuel Colby, of the University of Maryland, made a detailed examination of the site in 1992, and is among those who are convinced that it is an Israelite High Place dating from the Edomite period. Interviewed in May 2000, he said:

The sunken courtyard, with its length set against the altar, and its slightly raised platform set perpendicular to the courtyard are unique features of an Israelite High Place.

The raised stone platform, set before the altar in the sunken courtyard, is of particular interest to Dr Colby. He believes that it was a shewbread table, on which offerings were laid in Israelite temples:

> This is without a doubt a shewbread table, typical of such Hebrew sites. All High Places have these before the altar.

Dr Colby also notes with interest:

> The term High Place is unique to early Hebrew temples. Jebel Madhbah translates directly from the Arabic as 'Mountain of the High Place'.

If Jebel Madhbah is the Mountain of God then the Attuf Ridge site might be the biblical Beth-el – the house of God. One unusual feature of the altar strongly supports this possibility. A number of other High Places have been excavated throughout Israel and Jordan and in each of them the altar is a plain, raised stone block with no ornamentation other than four corner turrets. The Jebel Madhbah altar differs in one significant respect. To either side it has slight protrusions where appendages appear to have broken off.

In 1996 students from the British School of Archaeology in Jerusalem were excavating the scree on a ledge just below the site to the east. Here they discovered two large stone appendages in the shape of horns, each about thirty centimetres long. Their bases were found to match precisely the diameters of the truncated protrusions on the altar. It seems that these two stone horns were originally fixed to it. The Old Testament Book of Amos mentions such horns when it prophesies the destruction of Beth-el:

> That in the day that I shall visit the transgressions of Israel upon him I will also visit the altars of Beth-el: and the horns of the altar shall be cut off, and fall to the ground. (AMOS 3:14)

Amos was the prophet from Judah who preached against Beth-el during the reign of Jeroboam II (782–47 BCE). One thing he found particularly abhorrent were these horns. Like others in Judah, he found them to be a form of pagan idolatry, seemingly associated with the continued veneration of the bull. Even though Amos and other Judean prophets in the Old Testament preached against the practices at other High Places, not once are such horns mentioned in connection with their particular altars. The horned altar design seems to have been employed by Moses in the tabernacle in the wilderness (EXODUS 29:12) but for a fixed site it seems to have been special to Beth-el.

From the archaeological perspective, the altar on Jebel Madh-bah is also unique for such a site. Archaeologists have found other early Hebrew altars, such as those at Schechem and Dan, which have raised appendages sometimes referred to as horns. However, in each case there have been four such appendages, attached to the corners of the altar surface like the turrets of a castle. They are always straight and rise vertically. In no way do they resemble the two curved horns of a bull that protrude horizontally from the animal's head. As the horned altar at the High Place on Jebel Madhbah appears to be unique for such a site, there is a persuasive case that this and Beth-el are one and the same. The horns might have been broken off and thrown from the plateau when Josiah sacked the site around 620 BCE.

When we begin the ascent of Jebel Madhbah from the Outer Siq, we find a number of other fascinating features that reflect biblical references to Beth-el and the Mountain of God. About half-way along the Wadi Musa, at the foot of the mountain, is a Roman-style amphitheatre from the Nabatean period. Immediately behind it, a long flight of steps is cut into the cliff face, seemingly by the same people who created the High Place. They lead all the way up the mountain, joining a series of ever-higher ledges, eventually to bring the traveller to the sacred site. About a third of the way up, the steps become a pathway running around the cliff. Here, carved into the rock-face, is a four-and-a-half-metre relief depicting a lion. Now somewhat weathered, the creature is shown side on with its head turned to face the visitor. The style and the extent of weathering led Dr Colby to believe that it dates from Edomite times:

> Nabatean artisans were highly skilled, employing the classical disciplines from Greece and Rome. This particular relief is inconsistent with other Nabatean works and is far cruder in design.

What it represents is a mystery but it may be associated with a story in the first Book of Kings. According to chapter thirteen of I Kings, a peculiar episode concerning a lion occurred at Beth-el during the reign of Jeroboam I, shortly after the kingdoms of Israel and Judah divided. A nameless Judean prophet, described only as 'a man of God', comes and preaches against Jeroboam and the shrine at Beth-el, foretelling that one day the shrine will be destroyed. Eventually he is chased away by the priesthood. Another nameless prophet, whose sympathies lie with the man of God, hears what has happened:

> Now there dwelt an old prophet in Beth-el; and his sons came and told him all the works that the man of God had done that day in Beth-el: the word which he had spoken unto the king, them they told also to their father . . . And he went after the man of God, and found him sitting under an oak: and he said unto him, Art thou the man of God that camest from Judah? And he

said, I am. Then he said unto him, Come home with me, and eat bread ... So he went back with him, and did eat bread in his house, and drank water. (I KINGS 13:11–18)

However, when he leaves the house at Beth-el, the man of God is killed by a lion:

And it came to pass, after he had eaten bread, and after he had drunk, that he saddled for him an ass, to wit, for the prophet whom he had brought back. And when he was gone, a lion met him by the way, and slew him: and his carcass was cast in the way, and the ass stood by it, the lion also stood by the carcass. And, behold, men passed by, and saw the carcass cast in the way, and the lion standing by the carcass ... (I KINGS 13:23–25)

When the prophet hears of the man's death he returns to collect the body:

And he went and found the carcass cast in the way, and the ass and the lion standing by the carcass: the lion had not eaten the carcass, nor torn the ass ... And the prophet took the carcass of the man of God, and laid it upon the ass, and brought it back ... (I KINGS 13:28–9)

Back at Beth-el, the prophet buries the man of God in his own tomb:

And he laid his carcass in his own grave; and they mourned over him, saying, Alas, my brother! And it came to pass, after he had buried him, that he spake to his sons, saying, When I am dead, then bury me in the sepulchre wherein the man of God is buried; lay my bones beside his bones. For the saying which he cried by the word of the Lord against the altar in Beth-el.
(I KINGS 13:31–2)

The significance of the lion in the narrative is unclear. However, as it stands there beside the body doing no harm to anyone else who passes by, it is clearly an allegorical motif. Lions are frequently used in the Old Testament narrative as symbols of God acting in judgement. They also represent the power of Judah. Might the lion carving at Jebel Madhbah have been inspired by this story, perhaps during the time of Josiah?

According to the second Book of Kings, when Josiah sacks Beth-el and desecrates its surrounding tombs, he leaves one tomb intact – the tomb that contains the man of God and the old prophet:

> And as Josiah turned himself, he spied the sepulchres that were there in the mount, and sent, and took the bones out of the sepulchres, and burned them upon the altar, and polluted it, according to the word of the Lord which the man of God proclaimed, who proclaimed these words. Then he said, What title is that that I see? And the men in the city told him, It is the sepulchre of the man of God, which came from Judah, and proclaimed these things that thou hast done against the altar of Beth-el. And he said, Let him alone; let no man move his bones. So they let his bones alone, with the bones of the prophet that came out of Samaria. (II KINGS 23:16–18)

The reason Josiah leaves this tomb intact is that the man of God had foretold that a righteous man would one day destroy the Beth-el shrine. A passage in the first Book of Kings tells us that after he plundered Beth-el Josiah made a sign that the prophecy had been fulfilled:

> And he gave a sign the same day, saying, 'This is the sign which the Lord hath spoken . . .' (I KINGS 13:3)

We are not told what Josiah's sign is but it might have been the carved lion. Not only was the lion specifically associated with the man of God's prophecy concerning Beth-el's destruction, and also with God's judgement, it was the symbol for the kings of Judah. According to Genesis 49:8–9, Judah, the father of the tribe, is told by Jacob that he will be the lion of Israel:

Judah, thou art whom my brethren shall praise: thy hand shall be in the neck of thine enemies; thy father's children shall bow down before thee. Judah is a lion whelp: from the prey, my son, thou art gone up: he stooped down and crouched as a lion . . .

The use of the lion to symbolize the kings of Judah was verified during excavations at the Judean town of Hebron in 1960. Here a gold seal was unearthed, dating from the seventh century BCE – precisely the time that Josiah was on the throne. It is inscribed with the royal seal of the Judean kings – a lion. It would certainly make sense for Josiah to commission such a carving on the approach to Beth-el: a warning to all those who visited the site and a reminder that, by the words of God's own prophet, the shrine had been ravaged.

Interestingly, just around the mountain from the carved lion, an artificial cave is cut into the rocks. It is about three metres deep and two metres high and wide. Although now empty, it is thought by Dr Colby to have been used as a tomb. Might this have been the sepulchre Josiah left intact?

Further along the path we come to another cave, this time a natural formation created millennia ago by an ancient water-course. It is by far the largest on Jebel Madhbah. According to the Old Testament there is a sacred cave on the Mountain of God. An account in the first Book of Kings tells how the prophet Elijah, disturbed by the worship of Baal at Samaria, travels to the Mountain of God to commune with the Lord:

And he arose, and did eat and drink, and went in the strength of that meat forty days and forty nights unto Horeb the mount of God. And he came thither unto a cave, and lodged there; and behold, the word of the Lord came unto him . . . (I KINGS 19:8)

When we finally reach the top of the path, we are confronted with an awesome piece of ancient engineering. A final flight of steps leads up on to a terrace just below Attuf Ridge. It is joined to the shrine by a narrow ridge about two hundred metres long. This terrace, about sixty metres by thirty metres, is quite literally the gateway to the High Place. Rising from it, about thirty metres apart, are two towering obelisks, each over six metres high. The work necessary to create these giant structures is even more impressive than one might at first imagine. Like the High Place itself, they have been sculpted from the mountain bedrock. To create these obelisks, the Edomites had to have hacked away six metres of rock from all around them. The entire terrace is therefore an artificial construction: almost certainly a sacred approach to the shrine on Attuf Ridge.

Although Dr Colby does not link the Jebel Madhbah site with Beth-el, he does believe that such High Places were the primitive prototypes for the Jerusalem Temple.

> The Jebel Madhbah site may have been the direct precursor to Solomon's temple. It is unique for a High Place, having the pair of obelisks flanking its approach ... The Jerusalem Temple had two free-standing pillars flanking its entrance.

There are two accounts of the construction of Solomon's temple in the Old Testament:

> And he set up the pillars in the porch of the temple: and he set up the right pillar, and called the name thereof Jachin: and he set up the left pillar, and called the name thereof Boaz.
> (I KINGS 7:21)

> Also he made before the house two pillars of thirty and five cubits high ... And he reared up the pillars before the temple, one on the right hand, and the other on the left; and called the name of that on the right Jachin, and the name of that on the left Boaz.
> (II CHRONICLES 3:15–17)

(Jachin means 'Yahweh will establish' and Boaz means 'In the strength'.)

These pillars served no structural purpose: they did not support the porch roof but were free-standing in front of the entrance. Their meaning is a mystery, but they obviously held an important religious significance. If Dr Colby is right, then the two obelisks on Jebel Madhbah fulfilled a similar role. Perhaps, when he constructed his new house of God, Solomon hoped to re-create this awe-inspiring aspect of the shrine at Beth-el.

If we are right then the Edomites had already established their unique religion by the time their Israelite cousins left Egypt. As such, the High Place on Jebel Madhbah might already have been there. The split level of the Jebel Madhbah site – the obelisk terrace below the shrine plateau – certainly fits well with what we are told of the Israelites' first encounter with God on the Mountain of God. After Moses has produced the spring, and the Israelites make camp at the foot of the mountain and prepare to meet with God himself:

> The Lord will come down in the sight of all the people upon Mount Sinai ... And Moses brought forth the people out of the camp to meet with God; and they stood at the nether part of the mount. (EXODUS 19:11 AND 17)

The implication here is that there are two levels to the sacred site. As 'nether' means lower, then the people are standing on some lower precinct to God's holy shrine. This is precisely what would have happened if they had ascended Jebel Madhbah to arrive at the obelisk terrace, looking up to Attuf Ridge, two hundred metres to the north.

On another occasion the elders of Israel are invited up into the nether part of the mountain:

> And he said unto Moses, Come up unto the Lord, thou and Aaron, Nadab, and Abihu, and seventy of the elders of Israel; and worship ye afar off. And Moses alone shall come near the Lord: but they shall not come nigh; neither shall the people go up with

him ... And went up Moses, and Aaron, Nadab, and Abihu, and
seventy of the elders of Israel: And they saw the God of Israel:
and there was under his feet as it were a paved work of a sapphire
stone. (EXODUS 24:1–10)

Once again, this might well have been the obelisk terrace. The
students from the British School of Archaeology in Jerusalem,
who discovered the horns of the shrine altar, also discovered
large broken slabs of worked slate in the scree around the obelisk
terrace. They concluded that the slate, which was not indigenous
to the area, had been used to form a paved area around the
obelisks. The slate, samples of which can still be found in the
ravine between the terrace and Attuf Ridge, is of a greenish hue,
and if polished might have shone in the sunlight to have produced an effect, 'as it were a paved work of a sapphire stone'.
The 'feet' of God might even have referred to the obelisks
themselves. Often in the Old Testament landmarks are described
or named as appendages of God. For example, the hill on which
the city of Samaria stood was called the 'fist of God', and there is
Penuel, the 'face of God' – a cliff in the valley of Jordan (JUDGES
8:8).

Moving finally across to the High Place, once more we find
something that fits with what the Old Testament narrative tells
us concerning the Mountain of God. According to the Exodus
account, before Moses again ascends to the top of the mountain,
he asks for ox blood to take with him:

And he sent young men of the children of Israel, which offered
burnt offerings, and sacrificed peace offerings of oxen unto the
Lord. And Moses took half the blood, and put it in the basins;
and half the blood he sprinkled on the altar ... (EXODUS 24:5–6)

Although the passage does not specifically say where this altar
is, it could be interpreted to mean that the altar was already on
the mountain's summit. The Attuf Ridge altar does have beside it

what could be described as basins. When she examined the site in the early 1980s, archaeologist Crystal Bennett concluded that they had been used in the ritual of animal sacrifice. To the immediate south of the altar there is a round stone block, the same height as the altar and about a metre and a half in diameter, with an unusual round basin carved into the top. A channel runs from the basin that Bennett suggested had been used to collect the blood from sacrificial animals. Another depressed stone, on the other side of the altar platform, she believed to have served a similar function.

Not only are these basins evidence of animal sacrifices, the altar horns suggest cattle sacrifice in particular. In the above passage Moses specifically requests that oxen be sacrificed. The Book of Leviticus begins by referring to God instructions concerning the sacrifice of cattle:

> And the Lord called unto Moses ... saying, Speak unto the children of Israel, and say unto them, If any man of you bring an offering unto the Lord, ye shall bring your offering of the cattle ... And he shall kill the bullock before the Lord: and the priests, Aaron's sons, shall bring the blood, and sprinkle the blood round about upon the altar. (LEVITICUS 1:1–5)

This ritual was still being practised at Beth-el in Jeroboam's time, much to the annoyance of the priests of the Jerusalem Temple:

> And Jeroboam ordained a feast in the eighth month, on the fifteenth day of the month, like unto the feast that is in Judah, and he offered upon the altar. So did he in Beth-el, sacrificing unto the calves ... (I KINGS 12:32)

So there is much the Bible tells us about Beth-el and the Mountain of God that can be found here on Jebel Madhbah. But what about God himself? To begin with, we have the awesome circumstances surrounding God's appearance on the mountain:

> There were thunders and lightnings, and a thick cloud upon the mount, and the voice of the trumpet exceeding loud; so that all the people that was in the camp trembled. (EXODUS 19:16)

If we interpret the description objectively, then it would seem that a violent electrical storm has descended on the mountain. Such storms are a rarity in the area, although when it does rain it can be torrential. It might have been no coincidence that such a storm was raging when the Israelites first arrived. After an eruption like Thera, the volcanic dust contaminating the atmosphere would have played havoc with the short-term climate throughout much of the world. After the Krakatau eruption of 1883 freak weather conditions were reported around the globe: it snowed in Florida, there were tornadoes in England and it rained in the Sahara.

It is the description of a trumpet, however, that tallies specifically with Jebel Madhbah. When there is a strong wind from the east, the Siq and Wadi Musa below act together to create a most unusual phenomenon. The wind howls down the narrow cleft to trumpet, quite literally, through the Wadi Musa gorge. The noise it makes is not only eerie: if you happen to be in the gorge itself it is deafening. The sound can only be described as a bizarre cacophony of Buddhist prayer horns being blown in unison. Add this to the raging storm, and it would not be surprising if 'the people that was in the camp trembled'.

Have we at last rediscovered the lost Mountain of God? Many of Jebel Madhbah's features certainly match the biblical accounts. Not only do we have the local traditions placing the tomb of Aaron and the spring of Moses in the area, we also have the Attuf Ridge sanctuary that uniquely matches what we know of Beth-el in a number of ways. The typography of Jebel Madhbah also matches exactly the descriptions of the Mountain of God as they appear in Exodus. Most indicative of all, however, there is a tomb on Jebel Madhbah that might have belonged to Moses himself.

Summary

• The approach to the Edom valley is now called the Outer Siq. This gorge runs between two mountains: Jebel-ash-Shara to the east and Jebel Madhbah to the west. This appears to have been the Kadesh spoken of in Numbers 20:14–22. In this account of Moses and the miraculous spring, Kadesh is at the approach to Edom where the incident occurs. Exodus 17:6, however, tells us this same event occurred at 'the rock in Horeb'. As Horeb was the Mountain of God, then one of these two mountains that rise above the gorge must have been the sacred mount.

• This gorge is known by the local Bedouin as Wadi Musa – the 'Valley of Moses'. In the gorge there is a shrine called Ain Musa – the 'Spring of Moses' – that local tradition cites as the place where Moses made the miraculous spring appear. As the Bible tells us that this was at the foot of the Mountain of God, then the mountain that rises above this spring has to have been the sacred mount – Jebel Madhbah.

• At the summit of Jebel Madhbah we find compelling evidence that we really have discovered the place where Moses found God. On a natural plateau known as Attuf Ridge, there are the remains of an ancient Hebrew centre of worship. Called a High Place, it dates from around the fifteenth century BCE. This seems to be Beth-el – the house of God – which stood on the Mountain of God. A number of other High Places have been excavated throughout Israel and Jordan and each of them is built to the same plan. The Attuf Ridge site differs in one significant respect: its altar had stone horns attached to it. The Book of Amos tells us that the Beth-el altar was unique in that it, too, had horns attached to its altar.

• The Book of Exodus, 24:10, tells us that when Moses communed with God on the sacred mountain the Israelites stood just below the summit where they, 'saw the God of Israel: and there was under his feet as it were a paved work of a sapphire stone'. Just below Attuf Ridge there is another plateau where there stand two giant six-metre obelisks, dating from the same period as the High Place. Recent archaeology has shown that the area around the obelisks was once paved with green slate slabs. The 'feet' of God may have been a reference to the obelisks and, if polished, the paved terrace might well have shone in the sunlight to produce the effect described in the Exodus verse.

• Exodus 19:16 says that when the Israelites first ascended the Mountain of God they heard 'the voice of the trumpet exceeding loud'. This tallies with an unusual phenomenon that still occurs on Jebel Madhbah. When there is a strong wind from the east, the Siq and Wadi Musa below act together to create a most unusual phenomenon: the wind howls down the narrow cleft to trumpet, quite literally, through the Wadi Musa gorge. From these and other similar descriptions in the Bible that link with Jebel Madhbah, it seems that this was the Mountain of God.

9 THE SACRED STAFF

In 1839 an enigmatic rocky chamber was discovered beneath a stone monument on Jebel Madhbah. Although it no longer contained a body, the excavators concluded that it had once been used as a tomb. In light of our current investigation, this chamber might have been the final resting place of one of the two historical figures that seem to have combined to form the biblical Moses. To begin with, it seems that Moses was originally thought to have been buried on the Mountain of God.

The whereabouts of the tombs of Prince Tuthmosis and chief steward Kamose, our two Moses candidates, are unknown. So also is the tomb of Moses as he is portrayed in the Bible. Even when the Old Testament was committed to writing, the whereabouts of Moses' tomb seem to have been forgotten. According to Deuteronomy 34:1: 'No man knoweth of his sepulchre unto this day.'

According to the Old Testament, Moses did not live to enter the Promised Land of Canaan, but died shortly before Joshua began his campaign of conquest. If we are right, then this would have been the second Moses: Prince Tuthmose.

> And Moses went from the plains of Moab unto the mountain of Nebo, to the top of Pisgah, that is over against Jericho ... So Moses the servant of the Lord died there in the land of Moab, according to the word of the Lord. And he buried him in a valley in the land of Moab, over against Beth-peor ...
> (DEUTERONOMY 34:1–5)

According to Deuteronomy, then, Moses is buried at a place called Beth-peor, although the precise location of his tomb is unknown. There are two extra-biblical accounts of Moses' demise that might tell us more. The first is found in the Book of Jasher:

And when Moses had made an end of blessing the children of Israel, he went up out of the plains of Moab, unto the mount and was taken unto his forefathers . . . And I Jasher, with each of the elders of the tribes of Israel, did take him and laid him beside Peor . . . And upon his sepulchre was made an altar to the Lord.

The Book of Jasher seems to add little to Deuteronomy, other than to say that there was an altar on top of Moses' tomb. We can assume that it was a tomb, rather than a simple grave, as the word sepulchre is used in both accounts. One interesting point concerning this account is that Jasher, Moses' successor, was responsible for the funerary proceedings. This might account for why Deuteronomy fails to name the 'he' who buried Moses. The name might have been removed at the same time that the Book of Jasher was removed from the Hebrew Bible. The second extra-biblical account of Moses demise appears in the work of Josephus:

When Moses had spoken thus at the end of his life, and had told what would befall to every one of their tribes afterwards, with the addition of a blessing to them, the multitude fell into tears, insomuch that even the women, by beating their breasts, made manifest the deep concern they had when he was about to die . . . Now one may make a guess at the excess of this sorrow and lamentation of the multitude, from what happened to the legislator himself; for although he was always persuaded that he ought not to be cast down at the approach of death, since the undergoing it was agreeable to the will of God and the law of nature, yet what the people did so overbore him that he wept himself. Now as he went thence to the place where he was to vanish out of their sight, they all followed after him weeping; but Moses beckoned with his hand to those that were remote from him, and bade them stay behind in quiet, while he exhorted those that were near him that they would not render his departure so lamentable ... All those who accompanied him were the senate, and Eleazar the high priest, and Joshua their commander. Now as soon as they were come to the mountain called Abarim he dismissed the senate; and as he was going to embrace Eleazar and Joshua, and was still discoursing with them, a cloud stood over him on the sudden, and he disappeared in a certain valley, although he wrote in the holy books that he died, which was done out of fear, lest they should venture to say that, because of his extraordinary virtue, he went to God. (*ANTIQUITIES IV* 8:48)

In this longer version of events Moses would seem to have ascended bodily into heaven, which would seem to have been the popular story of Moses' demise by the first century CE. This was probably a late interpolation to affirm Moses as the greatest of God's prophets. The Old Testament has the prophet Elijah ascending bodily to heaven. Accordingly, the more important prophet Moses had to have done likewise.

All three accounts place the death or ascension of Moses on a mountain in the land of Moab: a kingdom that lay to the immediate east of the river Jordan and the Dead Sea. The Book of Jasher fails to name the mountain, whereas Deuteronomy and Josephus give two different names. In fact, they provide us with two separate locations. Deuteronomy calls it Nebo, which is the modern Jebel en Neba, sixteen kilometres east of the north end of the Dead Sea. Josephus, on the other hand, calls it Abarim, which is the modern Jebel el Hamra, some thirty-five kilometres to the south.

The confusion over which of these mountains Moses died on seems to have existed at the time Deuteronomy was committed to writing. Earlier in the narrative, when God commands Moses to go to the mountain, the author includes both sites:

> Get thee up unto this mountain Abarim, unto mount Nebo,
> which is in the land of Moab ... And die in the mount whither
> thou goest up, and be gathered unto thy people ...
> (DEUTERONOMY 32:49–50)

It seems that the writer was unfamiliar with the geography of
ancient Canaan. He not only wrongly assumes that Abarim and
Nebo were the same mountain, he also believes that it was next
to Jericho: 'And Moses went from the plains of Moab unto the
mountain of Nebo, to the top of Pisgah, that is over against
Jericho ...'(DEUTERONOMY 34:1). Jericho, however, was thirty
kilometres to the north-west of Nebo and almost fifty kilometres
north-north-west of Abarim. The Book of Numbers also makes
reference to Moses' death and, like Josephus, the author links it
with Mount Abarim:

> And the Lord said unto Moses, get thee up unto this Mount
> Abarim, and see the land which I have given unto the children of
> Israel. And when thou hast seen it, thou also shall be gathered
> unto thy people, as Aaron thy brother was gathered.'
> (NUMBERS 27:12–13)

So we have three different locations for Moses' death. Mount
Nebo, Mount Abarim and a nameless mountain near Jericho.
The latter would seem to be the most unlikely of the three as
Jericho was on the other side of the Jordan from Moab, in the
land of Canaan. The Old Testament is quite specific that Moses
never crossed the Jordan, as God had forbidden it: 'and behold it
[Canaan] with thine eyes: for thou shalt not go over this Jor-
dan'(DEUTERONOMY 3:27).

It seems, then, that by the time all these verses were finally
written down some confusion had occurred. The true location of
Beth-peor seems to have been forgotten, which is implied by the
words, 'No man knoweth of his sepulchre unto this day.' The
Book of Jasher, although it does not tell us where Moses was

buried, other than by something called Peor, suggests that Moses went to another mount after he left the plains of Moab: 'He went up out of the plains of Moab, unto the mount and was taken unto his forefathers.' Perhaps a mix-up arose between the mountain where Moses blessed the Israelites before their crossing into Canaan and the mountain where he eventually died. Indeed, if we cross-reference certain verses in the Old Testament narrative, it seems that the mountain of Moses' death and burial was actually the Mountain of God.

If we compare a verse from the Book of Numbers with one from the Book of Leviticus, we find that the mountain in Moab, where Moses blessed the Israelites, was thought by at least one author to have been the Mountain of God. According to Numbers, Moses received the Ten Commandments and the laws of God on this mountain in Moab:

> These are the commandments and the judgements, which the Lord commanded by the hand of Moses unto the children of Israel in the plains of Moab by Jordan near Jericho.
> (NUMBERS 36:13)

These are the last words of the Book of Numbers, where the author is summarizing all that has been written. There can be no doubt that he believes that this is Mount Sinai as he has paraphrased the last words of Leviticus:

> These are the commandments, which the Lord commanded Moses for the children of Israel in Mount Sinai. (LEVITICUS 27:34)

However, the Mountain of God could certainly not have been in Moab as it was nowhere near the Sinai wilderness. We can tell that the Numbers' author is uncertain as to precise locations as he has mistakenly placed Jericho in Moab. Although there is no reference to another such city in the Bible, there might have been more than one Jericho. However, the Jericho in question must have been the place where Joshua's battle would soon be fought, as this is the last verse of Numbers, referring to the moment just before the invasion of Canaan. As the Jericho where the battle is fought is the other side of the Jordan from Moab, then the author has to have been mistaken about its location.

Perhaps, then, the original tradition placed Moses' death and burial on Mount Sinai, but confusion arose later between this and the location of the blessing of the Israelites. It would make more sense for Moses to have been buried on the Mountain of God, the place where he met the Lord face to face and received the divine laws, rather than in enemy territory. Indeed, when we look at Deuteronomy 32:50 we find a suggestion that Moses indeed died where Aaron had died: on Hor – the Mountain of God.

> And die in the mount whither thou goest up, and be gathered unto thy people; as Aaron thy brother died in Mount Hor, and was gathered unto his people.

The Book of Numbers also seems to reflect a tradition that Moses died on Mount Hor:

> And when thou hast seen it, thou also shall be gathered unto thy people, as Aaron thy brother was gathered. (NUMBERS 27:13)

According to Deuteronomy Moses was buried next to Beth-peor and the Book of Jasher tells us he was buried beside Peor. When we investigate the origin of the word Peor, we have further evidence that Moses was buried on the Mountain of God. Beth-peor actually means 'house of Peor', suggesting that Peor was either a person or a deity. In fact, the name Peor appears else-where in the Old Testament, as Baal-Peor, a title the Judeans sometimes used to refer to the god worshipped in Israel.

> And they called the people unto the sacrifice of their gods: and the people did eat and bowed down to their gods. And Israel joined himself unto Baal-peor. (NUMBERS 25:1–3)

> Your eyes have seen what the Lord did because of Baal-peor: for all the men that followed Baal-peor, the Lord God hath destroyed them from among you. (DEUTERONOMY 4:3)

As we have seen, Baal simply means Lord, so Baal-Peor is Lord Peor. It seems, therefore, that Beth-Peor, the 'house of Peor', was a sanctuary to the god that was later worshipped in Israel. As we have seen, many of the High Places were thought by the Judeans to have been consecrated to Baal. Only one that we know of, however, was in territory under Hebrew control at the time of Moses' death, around 1320 BCE – Beth-el on the Mountain of God.

If Moses was buried on Jebel Madhbah, then where might his tomb be found? Deuteronomy tells us that Moses was buried in a valley beside Beth-peor (DEUTERONOMY 34:5). Elsewhere in the Bible Beth-peor appears simply as Peor, as it does in the Book of Jasher. Although we are not told where it is, on these occasions it is not in a valley but on a high mountain.

> And Balak brought Balaam unto the top of Peor, that looketh towards Jeshimon. And Balaam said unto Balak, Build me here seven altars. (NUMBERS 23:28–9)

The Deuteronomy reference 'against Beth-peor' might be taken to mean that it was at the bottom of Peor. However, the Deuteronomy reference to Pisgah as the place on the mountain where Moses died, leads us to another intriguing possibility as to what Beth-peor actually was. The word *pisgah* is a common Hebrew noun denoting a high ridge on a mountain or hill. Three ridges run from Jebel Madhbah: Attuf Ridge, which connects to the obelisk terrace, and the longest that runs in a crescent around the extreme south-west of the Edom Valley. It is on the southwest ridge that we find the Edomite burial site and a curious feature that may have been the Peor in question.

This site, overlooking the entire Edom Valley, is one of the most colourful in the Shara range. The rocks here are a mixture of all the shades of red, blue, orange and yellow. Just before the path from Attuf Ridge reaches another plateau, there are two artificial columns of rock, about a metre and a half high, which mark the entrance to an area known as the Southern Graves. Excavations carried out here by Crystal Bennett's team in 1985 revealed that this was the original Edomite necropolis. Interestingly, although distinctive pre-Nabatean Edomite pottery was found here, there were few human remains. This might have been the cemetery desecrated by Josiah when he pulverized the bones and spread them over the altar of Beth-el. Could one of these graves have been the sepulchre 'against Beth-peor' where Moses was said to have been laid to rest?

The Book of Jasher tells us specifically that Moses was buried 'beside Peor'. What was this Peor? We know that this was a word by which the Judeans referred to the god worshipped by the Israelites. However, Peor was not a Hebrew word, but Akkadian: the language of ancient Babylon. In Akkadian *peor* means serpent or snake. We have seen earlier how the snake was revered by Israel, and particularly how it was associated with Moses. The Judeans saw the snake as an emblem of Baal or, more accurately, the god that the kingdom of Israel was venerating. Back in Moses' time, however, the snake was a symbol of Moses' authority to speak for God. So Peor was seemingly a snake. Moses was buried next to a snake. Dominating the Southern Graves is one of Petra's most curious and enigmatic monuments: the Snake Monument. It is what remains of a gigantic stone carving of a snake, coiled around a stone block that once stood almost ten metres high. Could this have been the Peor in the Book of Jasher?

In the 1960s American tourists began to visit the site of the Southern Graves in their droves and the local Bedouin took the sudden interest as evidence of pagan worship. A group of hippies set up camp at the Snake Monument and began to cover it with flowers. In response, the Bedouin set charges of dynamite around the monument and blew it to bits. All that remains now of the monument is its base on which can be seen the lower coils of the snake.

In 1818, six years after Burckhardt's discovery of Petra, two British explorers, Charles Irby and James Mangles, visited the area and became the first westerners to describe the Snake Monument. It was, Mangles wrote, 'a singular monument hewn from the rock ... an obtuse cone, produced by the coils of a spiral ... standing on a vast square pedestal or altar'. In 1924 the American archaeologist Henry Pike made a full survey of the monument as it then survived:

> The great Snake Monument must once have encircled a towering cone of rock some 30 feet high which at some point must have been the focal point of some ancient sect.

It seems that this huge carved monolith was an Edomite construction. Interviewed in April 2000, John Murrow, a member of Crystal Bennett's team who excavated the graves in 1985, said:

> As there are no depictions of snakes in the Nabatean ruins, it is doubtful that it was a Nabatean deity ... The ceramics from the Southern Graves are Edomite, dating from as early as the fourteenth century BC ... It would seem that the great Snake Monument is contemporary with them. It was probably here, dominating the ridge, well before the Nabateans arrived.

The Snake Monument might, therefore, have been old enough to be the Peor referred to in the Book of Jasher. But what about the Beth-peor, the 'house of Peor', referred to in Deuteronomy? There is an ancient construction right next to the Snake Monument that is a possible contender. Just below the Snake Monument, cut into the cliffs overlooking the ruins of Petra, there is another structure carved out of the rocks: a cave dwelling of some kind with a door opening and an oval window to either side. Inside, it consists of a single chamber, some five metres square and two metres high. John Murrow examined the structure in 1985 and believes that it was an early shrine built to honour the snake depicted in the monument:

> The crudeness of the carving indicates an early date for the structure, which was probably contemporary with the Snake Monument.

The Book of Deuteronomy tells us that Moses was buried 'against Beth-peor' – presumably right next to it. Immediately above and behind the shrine there is a single stone altar, some three metres high and one metre wide, with the remains of steps still visible to the side. According to the Book of Jasher, an altar was built over Moses' tomb.

Interestingly, this altar was one of the first monuments to be excavated in or around the Edom Valley. In 1839 the Royal Academician David Roberts was the first visitor to attempt some archaeological work in the area. In March of that year his party came to Petra under the protection of Sheikh Hussein of the Alaween tribe, who had acquired from the Pasha of Egypt (who controlled the area at the time) the exclusive rights to escort foreign travellers in the district. This brought him into contention with the Bdoul sheikh, Abu Zeitun, who wanted to strike his own deal with the travellers.

Left alone on the Southern Graves ridge, Roberts and his team were free to dig in the area around the Snake Monument. It was directly beneath the altar stone that they found something of particular interest. A large boulder blocked what seemed to be some kind of artificial passage. After a day's backbreaking work, they finally removed the stone. Beyond it, the passage continued two metres further down into the rock to open into a small chamber. The chamber was approximately two metres long, half a metre wide and half a metre high. Roberts was sure they had found the tomb of some high-status individual but, as there were no human remains inside, he concluded that it had been desecrated in antiquity. However, in rubble to the rear of the chamber they discovered four artefacts that appeared to have been missed by the desecrators: a black painted wooden staff; a broken clay vessel, thought to be a water pitcher; a piece of cord made from spun silver strands; and, the most valuable find, a solid gold bowl around 14 centimetres wide and deep.

It was this last artefact that almost cost Roberts and his party their lives. John Kinnear, who travelled with Roberts, described what happened:

> We heard shouts behind us; and looking back, found that we had been pursued by a party of Arabs all armed with guns . . .

The angry Bedouin were members of the Bdoul tribe, led by Abu Zeitun himself. Seeing the golden bowl, the sheikh demanded they hand it over. According to Kinnear,

> On this he seized the bowl and the silver cord, but seeing that there were Egyptian writings on the staff, he snapped it and threw it into the shrub.

The party only escaped with their lives when members of the Alaween tribe returned in the nick of time and the sheikh and his men fled.

The mention of the bowl, pitcher and cord is interesting, for it seems to identify the grave as early Hebrew. Although the Bible suggests that after the Exodus the Israelites no longer buried grave goods with their dead, the bronze bulls unearthed at Schechem have shown that historically such practices continued until at least the eleventh century BCE. There is a reference in the Old Testament Book of Ecclesiastes to these three items being associated with death:

Or ever the silver cord be loosed, or the golden bowl be broken,
or the pitcher be broken ... Then the dust shall return to earth
as it was: and the spirit shall return unto God who gave it.
(ECCLESIASTES 12:6–7)

The Book of Ecclesiastes looks at life in terms of a fleeting
journey of the soul and reflects on the possibility of life both
before and after death. Because of this apparent speculation on
reincarnation, which was so at odds with Judean thinking at the
time the Old Testament was committed to writing, many biblical
scholars have pondered over how the book came to be included
in the Hebrew Bible. The author only identifies himself as
Qohelet – 'the one who gathers' – which was a term used for a
preacher in earliest Hebrew times. For this reason it is thought
that Ecclesiastes is one of the earliest books in the Old Testament.
The unusual collection of objects found in this grave might
therefore have been of very early Hebrew origin.

It is, however, the staff that is of greatest interest. Kinnear does
not tell us how long it was, but he does say that it was painted
black with Egyptian writing on it. It was the writing that made
the sheikh break it and throw it away, believing that it was
somehow cursed. In fact, it is doubtful that the local Bedouin
chieftain would have recognized Egyptian hieroglyphics and
probably he threw the stick into the bushes as he thought the
writing was some manner of magical text. It was probably
Kinnear who recognized it as Egyptian. Whether or not he could
read hieroglyphics, Kinnear would certainly have recognized them
as such. He had been in Egypt, as guest of the Pasha, only a few
weeks earlier, and taken on a trip around the temple of Luxor. If
this grave really was Moses' tomb, then might the staff have been
the biblical staff of Moses?

A sacred staff is associated with Moses throughout the Exodus
story. Moses has a staff with him when he first encounters God
in the burning bush. God imbues it with great power:

> And thou shalt take this rod in thine hand, wherewith thou shalt do signs. (EXODUS 4:17)

It is even described as the rod of God, suggesting that, like the Ten Commandments, it was fashioned by God himself:

> And Moses took the rod of God in his hand. And the Lord said unto Moses, When thou goest to return into Egypt, see that thou do all these wonders before Pharaoh, which I have put in thine hand. (EXODUS 4:20–21)

The staff's miraculous properties are said to bring about the plagues of Egypt:

> I will smite with the rod that is in mine hand upon the waters which are in the river, and they shall be turned to blood. (EXODUS 7:17)

It is not only deemed responsible for creating the plagues, it can control the very forces of nature:

> And Moses stretched forth his rod towards heaven: and the Lord sent thunder and hail... (EXODUS 9:23). And Moses stretched forth his rod over the land of Egypt, and the Lord brought an east wind upon the land all that day. (EXODUS 10.13)

When they leave Egypt, it is with this rod of God that Moses parts the sea and creates the miraculous spring:

> Lift up thy rod, and stretch out thine hand over the sea, and divide it. (EXODUS 14:16)

> And the Lord said unto Moses, Go on before the people, and take with thee of the elders of Israel; and thy rod wherewith thou smotest the river, take in thine hand, and go ... and thou shalt smite the rock, and there shall come water out of it. (EXODUS 17:5–6)

It even has the power to influence the course of battle:

And Moses said unto Joshua . . . I will stand on the top of the hill with the rod of God in my hand . . . And it came to pass, when Moses held up his hand, that Israel prevailed. (EXODUS 17:9–11)

Whether or not this rod really was responsible for all these miraculous feats, the ancient Israelites clearly believed it was. It is quite possible that at a time when the Hebrews were still being buried with grave goods, Moses would have been buried with his staff. The Bible does not tell us what happened to the staff after Moses' death, but the Book of Jasher tells us that no other man should ever possess it.

And with his mighty rod, and in all the wonders and terrors Moses shewed in the land of Egypt to Pharaoh and in the sight of all Israel . . . No other man should possess the rod of God, for wherewith the wind, the fire, the waters and the earth itself tremble and be obedient to he who holds it.

It seems that it was believed that any man might be able to use the staff. On four occasions in the Bible Aaron uses it:

Say unto Aaron, Take thy rod, and cast it before Pharaoh, and it shall become a serpent. (EXODUS 7:9)

And the Lord spake unto Moses, Say unto Aaron, Take thy rod, and stretch out thine hand upon the waters of Egypt . . . that they may become blood. (EXODUS 7:19)

And the Lord spake unto Moses, Say unto Aaron, Stretch forth thine hand with thy rod over the streams, over the rivers, and over the ponds, and cause frogs to come up over the land of Egypt. (EXODUS 7:5)

And the Lord said unto Aaron, Stretch out thy rod, and smite the dust of the land, that it may become lice over all the land of Egypt. (EXODUS 8:16)

For this reason alone, the ancient Israelite priesthood might have deemed it essential to bury the rod with Moses. It was a dangerous weapon of God with the power to manipulate the terrible forces of nature.

So what happened to the staff found by the Roberts team? Kinnear does not say, but it appears that once the sheikh had left, Roberts retrieved it from the thicket and it returned with him to England. A reference to it is found in the work of another English explorer, John Wilson, who dug in Petra in 1843. He excavated the remains of a Nabatean temple called Qasr el Bint on the west side of the Edom valley. Here he discovered the well-preserved remains of an Egyptian woman, still *in situ* in a wooden coffin of the Ptolemaic period, dating to around 50 BCE. Its lid bore a faded, but still discernible painting of the woman. There was nothing to identify who she was, but she was obviously wealthy and must have held a position of some importance in the city to have been buried in the temple. Writing of the find, Wilson makes reference to what must have been the staff found by Roberts:

> We cannot know how many Egyptians were in residence here, as no other items of Egyptian origin have been found, save that discovered by Mr Roberts and his party.

Wilson does not specifically refer to the item as the staff, but as this was the only Egyptian artefact mentioned in association with Roberts's excavations in Kinnear's account then it must have been the same. The item is mentioned again by Wilson when he sells the coffin in England. What happened to the mummy is unclear, but Wilson sold the coffin to Lord Devon for his private collection at Powderham Court near Exeter. According to Wilson: 'His Lordship purchased the coffin, already having obtained the aforementioned item acquired by Mr Roberts.'

The staff would therefore seem to have ended up in Powderham

Court. However, it was apparently passed on in early 1912. An item described as 'an Egyptian curiosity' is recorded in the Powderham accounts as having been sold along with the coffin to a Mr Stanley May, an American businessman and antiquities collector, who stayed with Lord Devon in March of that year. In fact, May had bought a number of items from the estate, which seems to have been enduring hard times. According to the diary of Lady Devon, after leaving Powderham Stanley May, his sister and other members of his family embarked on a ship bound from Southampton to New York on 10 April. Presumably both the coffin and the staff went with him.

By bizarre chance, the ship that the May party sailed on was the *Titanic*. May, his sister Lily, his brother Richard and his nephew Jack are all registered in the *Titanic* passenger list for the legendary ships ill-fated first and last voyage. Along with the coffin, did the staff found at the tomb beside the Snake Monument finally end up at the bottom of the Atlantic when *Titanic* sank on 14 April 1912?

When we examine the accounts of the *Titanic*'s voyage we discover that Stanley May was incredibly lucky. He and his party disembarked when the ship anchored for the last time off Ireland, just two days before the sinking. At the last minute they had decided to go on a motor tour of Ireland before continuing their journey home on another ship the following week. The mummy case survived with them. May originally intended to sell the coffin to the Metropolitan Museum in New York, but instead he sold it the following year to the British archaeologist and explorer Edward Ayrton. The staff, or any item that might have been the staff, is not recorded again in inventories of the May family, so was it sold along with the coffin to Edward Ayrton?

The coffin finally ended up in the Metropolitan Museum in New York – it was Edward Ayrton who went to a watery grave. He fell overboard mysteriously from a fishing cruiser while on

A preserved fragment of one of the Lachish letters discovered at
Tell el-Duweir in the 1930s. These ancient military dispatches dating from
the early sixth century BCE reveal that the Edomites were still worshipping
the Hebrew God well after the collapse of Israel. (*British Library.*)

A scene on the Triumphal Arch, erected by the emperor Vespasian in Rome,
shows the menorah being looted from the temple of Jerusalem in 70 CE.
(*Simon Donnelly Picture Library.*)

The Siq at Petra. This long narrow gorge formed an easily guarded entrance to the valley of Edom. (*Sandi Sorrel.*)

The Outer Siq at Petra. Was this the 'rock in Horeb' where Moses created the miraculous spring? (*Sandi Sorrel.*)

OPPOSITE: The Outer Siq, showing the Treasury and Jebel Madhbah. (*Jane Taylor.*)

The long flight of ancient carved steps that leads up to the High Place on Jebel Madhbah. Was this the Mountain of God? (*Sandi Sorrel.*)

One of the two stone obelisks on Attuf Ridge. Where these the 'feet of God' described in the book of Exodus? (*John Murrow.*)

The Southern Graves at Jebel Madhbah. The mysterious building that may be the Beth-peor of the Old Testament is in the middle ground and just above it stood the Snake Monument and the rock chamber discovered by David Roberts and John Kinnear in 1839. Was this the tomb of Moses? (*John Murrow.*)

The Treasury at Petra.
Carved from solid rock, its original
purpose remains a mystery.
(*Simon Donnelly Picture Library.*)

The Sabean Stone found below
Jebel Madhbah. Carved with
a crescent moon mounted over a
truncated triangle, it appears to
represent the sacred mountain
and the ancient Edomite deity
worshipped there.
(*British Institute at Amman.*)

A seal of the Israelite king Jeroboam II.
Found at Megiddo and dating from
the ninth century BCE, it shows
that the ancient kings of Israel were
represented by the lion.
(*Hebrew University, Jerusalem.*)

The ivory brooch discovered during the excavations of Teman.
Dating from the twelfth century BCE, it appears to depict the horned pole
used during early Hebrew ceremonies performed at the Attuf Ridge shrine.
(*British Institute at Amman.*)

The sanctuary on Attuf Ridge showing the shewbread table
before the altar complex. Carved from solid rock, is this the biblical
Beth-el – the 'house of God'? (*John Murrow.*)

ABOVE AND BELOW: These houses of ancient Akrotiri were uncovered from beneath 36 metres of solid lava rock after almost 3500 years. This thriving Minoan city was completely covered by volcanic fallout when Thera erupted around 1360 BCE. (*Museum of Prehistoric Thera.*)

OVERLEAF: The Obelisk Terrace, with the High Place above it. (*Jane Taylor.*)

Lake Tissa in Ceylon on 18 May 1914. His estate in England was handled by the solicitors Hamish & Hunter of the Strand in London, and their records show that the coffin, along with larger Egyptian artefacts, ended up in the New York Museum. Other items referred to as 'small Egyptian antiquities' were donated, along with a collection of photographs and drawings of Egyptian monuments, to the Municipal Museum in Birmingham by Ayrton's cousin Anna McClatchie in 1927. They included three rings from Akhenaten's reign, a decorated scarab from the reign of Amonhotep I and 'a priestly staff' from the reign of Tuthmosis III.

The staff seems to be one still on display in Birmingham Museum's Egyptian gallery. It is 1.35 metres long, two centimetres wide, made from cedar wood, painted black and inscribed with white hieroglyphics. It is certainly eighteenth dynasty and matches Kinnear's description. Moreover, it is partly snapped in two, only being held together by a thin strip of wood to one side, fitting with Kinnear's acount of the staff being broken by Abu Zeitun. Although there is no way to determine for sure whether this was the staff found by Roberts in 1839, it would seem beyond coincidence that it so closely corresponds with the one in Kinnear's account.

When we examine the staff we see a feature that Kinnear did not describe. Its handle is fashioned in the shape of a cobra head. This, in its own right, is nothing unusual, as all court officials of ancient Egypt carried staffs of office bearing cobra heads. However, it does mean that it was indeed a serpent staff. Remarkably, the inscription suggests that it may actually have belonged to Kamose, the man whom we have already identified as a prime candidate for the first Moses. Although the hieroglyphics identify the owner as 'Tuthmosis, butler to the princess', it may well be the same person. Like other royal officials, Kamose adopted the name affix of his pharaoh Tuthmosis III on becoming minister and he may earlier have served as the butler to his guardian the princess Termut.

If the grave beside the Snake Monument was the final resting place of Moses, referred to in the Books of Jasher and Deuteronomy, then the man buried there must have been the second Moses: Prince Tuthmose. Kamose had lived over a century before. Perhaps his staff, believed to have been blessed or even made by God, was handed down to the second Moses as a symbol of divine office. For whatever reason it was placed in the chamber, it is surely significant that a staff bearing the name of a man we have associated with the story of Moses should have been found in what we have otherwise reasoned might have been Moses' tomb.

With this confirmatory evidence to link Jebel Madhbah with the Mountain of God, we move now to Yahweh himself. Is there anything in the valley of Edom finally to reveal the earliest conceptions of the one God?

Summary

• The whereabouts of the tombs of Prince Tuthmosis and Kamose, the men who seem to have combined to form the Moses story, are not known. Neither is the tomb of Moses as he is portrayed in the Bible. According to the Old Testament, Moses did not live to enter the Promised Land of Canaan, but died on a mountain shortly before Joshua began his campaign of conquest. The location of his tomb is evidently forgotten.

• When we cross-reference certain verses in the Old Testament narrative, it seems that the mountain of Moses' death and burial was actually the Mountain of God. Deuteronomy 32:50 suggests that Moses died where Aaron died, on the sacred mountain: 'And die in the mount whither thou goest up, and be gathered unto thy people; as Aaron thy brother died in Mount Hor, and was gathered unto his people.' So also does the Book of Numbers: 'And when thou hast seen it, thou also shall be gathered unto thy people, as Aaron thy brother was gathered' (NUMBERS 27:13).

- According to Deuteronomy 34:5, Moses is buried at a mountain beside something it describes as Beth-peor – the 'house of Peor'. Peor was not a Hebrew word, but Akkadian: the language of ancient Babylon. In Akkadian *peor* means serpent or snake. The burial site of the ancient Edomites is on a ridge running south-west of Jebel Madhbah. Now called the Southern Graves, it is dominated by a giant carving of a coiled snake, originally ten metres high. Just below the Snake Monument is an ancient Edomite shrine: an artificial cave where it seems the snake was venerated. This might have been the house of Peor described in Deuteronomy.

- In 1839 the British archaeologist Edward Roberts excavated a rock-cut tomb next to the shrine. Although the body was gone and the tomb seems to have been robbed in antiquity, it still contained a number of artefacts that identify it is a Hebrew grave. The most interesting item was a staff, painted black and inscribed with Egyptian hieroglyphics. The artefact was returned to England, where it was donated eventually to the Municipal Museum in Birmingham.

- The staff is still on display in a case in the museum's Egyptian gallery. It is described as a staff of office, typical of those belonging to leading government officials. It is just over a metre long, two centimetres wide and made from cedarwood, painted black. It is inscribed with white hieroglyphics. Its handle is fashioned in the shape of a cobra head. In the Exodus story Moses has a staff associated with a serpent that is said to perform miracles. The hieroglyphics identify the owner as 'Tuthmosis, butler to the princess', but it may well be the same person.

10 THE GOD OF EDOM

The Hebrews split into two religious factions during the tenth century BCE, leading to the Israelites dividing into two separate kingdoms. The religious reformation, instigated by the tribe of Judah, modified the ancient rituals, proscribed the making of effigies and established a priesthood centred exclusively on the Jerusalem Temple. The kingdom of Israel continued to venerate God at the ancient High Places, and continued to represent aspects of God's power in the form of devotional images, chief amongst them the serpent and the bull. The Judeans came to regard such practices as pagan, and to separate God as he was worshipped in Israel from God as he was worshipped in Judah. They referred to Israel's God by the ancient and forbidden form of address: Baal. Nevertheless, the religion of Israel was the more fundamentalist – the earlier religion of the Hebrews. If we are to learn the true nature of the early Hebrew faith and discover the real origins of God, then it is the religion of the kingdom of Israel we must examine. Unfortunately, we have almost nothing but the Old Testament to go on and this, having been compiled by the Judeans, is distinctly biased. In Judah, the reformed faith survived to evolve into modern Judaism and Christianity, but the faith of the kingdom of Israel perished with the Assyrian invasion of the seventh century BCE. From the Judean perspective, the kingdom of Israel was wicked and blasphemous; its people worshipped idols and its deity was an antithesis of the true God. The Old Testament tells us next to nothing about how God was really perceived in Israel, how he was worshipped or how the religion influenced the daily lives of its practitioners.

This schism has much in common with the European Reformation of the sixteenth century, when the Protestants broke away from the Catholic Church and proscribed what they regarded as the superstitious rites of Rome. The Protestants abandoned the Mass, Confession and the apostolic succession; they gave up the lavish trappings of worship and making images of saints. If the Vatican and the Catholic countries had been wiped out in some terrible calamity similar to the eradication of Israel by the Assyrians, then we might now have only Protestant accounts from which to learn what the Mother Church had once been like. The observances of Mass, Confession and the Rosary might have been forgotten to history. So also might the adoration of saints, the veneration of relics, the monastic orders and the entire pageantry of the Roman Church. All we might learn from the writings of fervent Reformation Protestants is that the Catholic Church was headed by a corrupt pope, and that it practised rituals considered nothing less than profane. However, the Catholic Church survived and its devotional practices are alive throughout the world today. The ancient kingdom of Israel, however, ceased to exist over two and a half thousand years ago.

If Atenism was an offshoot of the Hebrew faith, Egyptian records might have told us much of this early religion. However, due to the persecutions that followed the restoration of traditional Egyptian religion after Akhenaten's reign, almost nothing survives other than the few tantalizing inscriptions we have previously examined. It is possible, though, that in the Edom valley, where the faith appears to have originated, we might discover something of the early religion of the Hebrews. Sadly, no written records have been discovered from this area predating the Nabatean era, apart from a few Hebrew inscriptions that tell us only that, in some way, the God of Israel was being worshipped here. The eradication of the kingdom of Israel might not, however, have seen the end of their religion. It seems to have survived in its homeland of Edom until at least the time of the Babylonian Exile.

Although the Old Testament does not tell us directly what happened to Edom after Josiah's time, it seems to have survived as an independent kingdom. We can gather that after he plundered the shrine at Beth-el and sacked the city of Teman Josiah returned to Jerusalem. Even if his forces occupied Edom for a while, they would certainly have been impelled to leave when Judah was defeated by the Egyptians in 609 BCE.

Not all the Jews condoned the actions of Josiah. One Old Testament author condemns Judah, complaining that Josiah and his followers had taken things too far. Writing around 605 BCE, shortly after the battle of Carchemish, when the Babylonians beat the Egyptians and took control of Judah, the prophet Habakkuk blames the downturn of events on the plundering of Beth-el and the sacking of Teman. There are a number of references in the short Book of Habakkuk that reflect his position:

> O Lord, how long shall I cry, and thou wilt not hear! even cry unto thee of violence ... (HABAKKUK 1:2). Woe to him that coveteth an evil covetousness to his house ... (HABAKKUK 2:9). Thou hath consulted shame to thy house ... (HABAKKUK 2:9). Thou art filled with shame for glory ... (HABAKKUK 2:16)

Habakkuk even believed that God's true house was still in the land of Edom: 'God came from Teman ... His glory covered the heavens, and the earth was full of his praise' (HABAKKUK 3:3). Nevertheless, whatever sympathies lay with Edom seem to have evaporated once the Edomites sided with the Babylonians.

Around 550 BCE, the prophet Obadiah preached against Edom from his captivity in Babylon. The Book of Obadiah is one of the shortest in the Bible, and is nothing less than a tirade against the kingdom of Edom. Nonetheless, it provides an important insight as to the status of the kingdom around seventy years after Josiah's carnage. As it is the last and most complete biblical narrative to concern the kingdom of Edom, it is included here in full:

The vision of Obadiah. Thus saith the Lord God concerning Edom; We have heard a rumour from the Lord, and an ambassador is sent among the heathen, Arise ye, and let us rise up against her in battle. Behold, I have made thee small among the heathen: thou art greatly despised. The pride of thine heart hath deceived thee, thou that dwellest in the clefts of the rock, whose habitation is high; that saith in his heart, Who shall bring me down to the ground? Though thou exalt thyself as the eagle, and though thou set thy nest among the stars, thence I will bring thee down saith the Lord. If thieves come to thee, if robbers by night (how art thou cut off!) would they not have stolen till they had enough? if the grape-gatherers came to thee, would they not leave some grapes? How are things of Esau searched out! how are his hidden things sought up! All the men of thy confederacy have brought thee even to the border: the men that were at peace with thee have deceived thee, and prevailed against thee; they that eat thy bread have laid a wound under thee: there is none understanding in him.

Shall I not in that day, saith the Lord, even destroy the wise men out of Edom, and understanding out of the mount of Esau? And thou mighty men, O Teman, shall be dismayed, to the end that every one of the mount of Esau may be cut off by slaughter. For thy violence against thy brother Jacob shame shall cover thee, and thou shalt be cut off for ever. In the day thou stoodest on the other side, in the day that the strangers carried away captive his forces, and foreigners entered into his gates, and cast lots upon Jerusalem, even thou wast as one of them. But thou shouldest not have looked on the day of thy brother in the day that he became a stranger; neither shouldest thou have rejoiced over the children in Judah in the day of their destruction; neither shouldest thou have spoken proudly in the day of distress. Thou shouldest not have entered into the gate of my people in the day of their calamity; yea, thou shouldest not have looked on their affliction in the day of their calamity, nor have laid hands on their substance in the day of their calamity; Neither shouldest thou have stood in the crossway, to cut off those of his that did escape; neither shouldest thou have delivered up those of his tent that did remain in the day of distress.

For the day of the Lord is upon all the heathen: as thou hast done, it shall be done unto thee: thy reward shall return upon thine own head. For as ye have drunk upon my holy mountain, so shall all the heathen drink continually, yea shall drink, and they shall swallow down, and they shall be as though they had not been. But upon Mount Zion shall be deliverance, and there shall be holiness; and the house of Jacob shall possess their possession. And the house of Jacob shall be a fire, and the house of Joseph a flame, and the house of Esau for stubble, and they shall kindle in them, and devour them; and there shall not be any remaining of the house of Esau; for the Lord hath spoken it. And they of the south shall possess the mount of Esau; and they of the plain the Philistines: and they shall possess the fields of Ephraim, and the fields of Samaria: and Benjamin shall possess Gilead. And the captivity of this host of the children of Israel shall possess that of the Canaanites, even unto Zarephath; and the captivity of Jerusalem, which is in Sepharad, shall possess the cities of the south. And saviours shall come up on Mount Zion to judge the mount of Esau; and the kingdom shall be the Lord's.

The first and most obvious fact we can infer from Obadiah is that hostility towards Edom had reached fever pitch by the middle of the sixth century BCE. Second, we gather that Edom had sided with the Babylonians and pillaged Jerusalem. The Edomites had 'entered into the gate of my people in the day of their calamity ... and laid hands on their substance'. In fact, it seems that they actually helped the Babylonians round up the Jews who attempted to flee: 'Neither shouldest thou have stood in the crossway, to cut off those of his that did escape.' We can also assume that the Edomite religion was still going strong and that the Edomites were back worshipping at Beth-el: 'For as ye have drunk upon my holy mountain, so shall all the heathen drink continually.' Although Obadiah still seems to have some respect for the Mountain of God, to him the new house of the Lord is Mount Zion: the hill on which the Jerusalem Temple stood.

This is the end of Edomite history so far as the Bible is concerned. It leaves off with them doing quite well for themselves and free from Babylonian rule. They must also have survived as an independent country through Persian rule in Judah, as they do not appear in the lists of vassal states of that empire. Indeed, we can assume that the Edomite kingdom remained intact for another two hundred years as the Greeks, who occupied the area in the late fourth century BCE, actually named the entire region after them. They called it Idumea – land of the Edomites. However, by this time another people had come and settled alongside them in the Shara mountains: the Nabateans.

The Nabateans who first arrived in the Shara mountains were no military force, simply a stream of dispossessed peoples who gradually arrived from Arabia in small groups. It seems likely, therefore, that the Nabatean movement into the Edom valley was not so much an invasion but a migration. In all probability, the two cultures peacefully coexisted. In fact, even when the Nabateans became the dominant culture and amassed the wealth to build the city of Petra, the Edomites appear to have continued as a kingdom within a kingdom. Few Nabatean writings have survived but the works of Greek and Roman visitors to the city of Petra still exist. One, by the classical author Diodorus Siculus, writing in the first century BCE, speaks of a clan amongst the Nabateans who lived outside mainstream society in the surrounding mountains:

These people are ruled by their own king, but all are equal in his sight and he is called by them 'brother'. They are exceedingly learned and there are many philosophers amongst them. The women are treated as equals . . . Although they welcome travellers, they do not permit their sons and daughters to marry outside their caste, believing their blood belongs to their god . . . They do not keep slaves and are much inclined to share their possessions . . . They are forbidden to consume the blood of animals and must first prepare the carcass by ritual draining . . .

As they are described as having their own king, it would seem that these people were not the Nabateans so must presumably have been the Edomites. When Diodorus speaks of 'their god', we can assume that they only had one: another indication that they were the Edomites. Their position on slavery is equally indicative: state slavery had been restricted in Israel. David used foreign captives for forced labour as, it seems, did Solomon. However, because of their own experiences in Egypt, slavery was not an accepted Israelite practice. Certainly, in both Israel and Judah, the economy was never based substantially on slavery, unlike Greek and Roman society, which could not survive without it. As the Egyptians kept slaves and the Nabateans were slave traders, then just about the only non-slaving peoples whom Diodorus' clan could have been were a Hebrew tribe. Proscribing the consumption of blood was also very much a Hebrew concept and still remains central to orthodox Jewish belief. According to the Book of Leviticus: 'Ye shall not eat any thing with the blood . . .'(LEVITICUS 19:26).

Another foreigner to visit Petra also describes a Nabatean clan who appear to be the Edomites. Athenodorus, a one-time tutor to the emperor Augustus, spent some time in Petra during the late first century BCE. His writings survive, second-hand, in the work of the Roman writer Strabo. According to him:

They prepare common meals together in groups of thirteen persons . . . The king is so democratic that, in addition to serving himself, he even serves the rest himself in turn. He often renders an account of his kingship in the popular assembly; and sometimes his mode of life is examined . . .

This sounds very much like the manner in which the contemporary Jewish Passover was celebrated. Jesus, for example, in Palestine just a few years later, personally served his disciples at the Last Supper. Moreover, there were thirteen at the meal. Both Diodorus and Athenodorus refer to this clan as having their own king. It would seem, therefore, that their autonomy was still respected by the Nabatean rulers.

Returning to Diodorus, he tells us about the clan's god:

> Their god is Dhu-esh-Shera, but of his likeness, none is found . . . They will, on occasion, erect a pillar or stone block and anoint it with sacred oil . . .

Here we have three unique Hebrew conventions: one god, no images of him and the venerated stone pillar. The Old Testament refers repeatedly to single stone pillars being erected to honour God. A succession of Hebrew leaders erect pillars to God, including Jacob, Joshua and Samuel:

> And Jacob took a stone, and set it up for a pillar . . . (GENESIS 31:45)

> And Joshua wrote these words in the Book of the law of God, and took a great stone, and set it up there under an oak, that was by the sanctuary of the Lord. (JOSHUA 24:26)

> Then Samuel took a stone, and set it between Mizpeh and Shen, and called the name of it Eben-ezer, saying, Hitherto hath the Lord helped us. (1 SAMUEL 7:12)

With reference to Jacob, Genesis tells us that, like the people mentioned by Diodorus, he actually anoints the pillar with oil:

And Jacob rose up early in the morning, and took the stone that he had put for his pillow, and set it up for a pillar, and poured oil upon the top of it. (GENESIS 28:18)

The name of the deity, Dhu-esh-Shera, is also reminiscent of the God of Israel: like the Hebrew names for God, it is a title. It translates from Nabatean as 'Lord of Shera'. Shera was the Nabatean name for what the Greeks called the Shara mountains. We have seen how the word Seir, the Hebrew name for the range, could also pertain to the specific Mountain of God. Dhu-esh-Shera might therefore have been the Lord of the sacred mountain – 'Lord of Seir'. Remarkably, this is exactly how one enigmatic passage in the Bible describes God. Genesis 33:14 has Jacob referring to God as 'Lord unto Seir'.

In conclusion, there can be little doubt that this particular clan were the Edomites, continuing to live a semi-autonomous existence within Nabatean society in the first century BCE. Furthermore, they were still worshipping the God of Israel in their own way six hundred years after Josiah had attempted to eradicate their religion once and for all.

This, then would seem to be the order of events:

- In 931 BCE the united Hebrew kingdom divides into Israel and Judah. The Hebrew religion also divides into two separate denominations.

- The Judean sect develops into Judaism. Its adherents, the Jews, accept the Jerusalem Temple as the new 'house of God', and proscribe the making of certain effigies that were previously acceptable to the Hebrew religion.

- The sect in Israel is more fundamentalist. They continue to venerate God at his traditional seat of power, and with similar customs to those that existed at the time of the Exodus.

- Edom is a part of the kingdom of Israel and its High Place at Beth-el is the chief centre of worship in the kingdom. After Israel is conquered by the Assyrians in 722 BCE, Edom remains independent.

- When the Nabateans migrate into the Edom valley and establish their own kingdom, by 300 BCE, the Edomites retain an autonomous existence. Thereafter, the Edomites still practise the religion they had practised when they were part of the kingdom of Israel.

Interestingly, if the Edomite religion survived until Roman times, this might explain how the traditions of Moses' spring and the tomb of Aaron survived to be remembered by the local Bedouin. Our best chance of peering back in time to rediscover the original Hebrew religion is therefore to examine the Edomite religion as it existed in Nabatean times. It is with an artefact from the Nabatean period that we discover more about the enigmatic Edomite god.

In 1982 a carved block of stone, measuring 48 x 20 x 20 centimetres, was found in the Wadi Musa close to the amphitheatre. It was inscribed with Sabean writing – the language spoken by the peoples of northern Arabia: close relatives of the Nabateans – and commemorates the death of one Mukharib, a priest with whom the maker had traded. Known as the Sabean Stone, it can be dated to around the time of the birth of Christ as it names the Nabatean king Aretas IV, who reigned from 8 BCE to CE 40. Above the inscription a symbol is carved in stark relief: a crescent moon with the sun between its horns. Beneath the sun and moon there is another symbol, an elongated triangle.

The archaeologist Crystal Bennett reasoned that the triangle depicted the sacred mountain of Jebel Madhbah and that the sun and moon symbolized the ancient Edomite deity who was worshipped there. As many early civilizations considered the moon to be feminine, because of the perceived link between the menstruation and lunar cycles, and the sun to be masculine, Bennett reasoned that the Edomite god was an androgynous deity, having both male and female attributes.

One intriguing Old Testament passage makes reference to the Baal at Beth-el as being associated with the sun and the moon.

> And he [Josiah] put down the idolatrous priests ... them that burned incense unto Baal, to the sun and the moon ...
> (II KINGS 23:5)

The importance of the bull or calf to both the kingdom of Israel, and the earlier Hebrews as a whole, might have been that its horns were shaped like the crescent moon. As the animal was male, it personified both male and female aspects.

Was the god of the Edomites and the original God of Israel partly female – a genderless, universal god? In the Bible God is a male divinity. But had God always been perceived as such?

Judean society was misogynistic. It was a patriarchal society where family lines were male-based and polygamy was accepted. Women had few legal rights, and were excluded from the ranks of religious officialdom. They were highly vulnerable without the protection of a male relative. The Judean Old Testament authors portray early Hebrew society in much the same way. However, this cannot have been so. Although the Hebrew Bible, as it now survives, defines the role of women in Judean terms, contradictory references to a few seem to have escaped the censor's pen. Aaron and Moses' sister Miriam, for example, is not only responsible for saving Moses' life as a baby, but she leads the congregation of Israel in prayer after they have escaped Egypt. Moreover, she is actually described as a prophetess:

> And Miriam the prophetess, the sister of Aaron, took a timbrel in her hand; and all the women went out after her with timbrels and

with dances. And Miriam answered them, Sing ye to the Lord, for
he hath triumphed gloriously. (EXODUS 15:20–21)

The prophetess Hannah, the mother of Samuel, seems to have
been a warrior leader, which would have been inconceivable in
later Judah:

And Hannah prayed, and said, My heart rejoiceth in the Lord,
mine horn is exalted in the Lord: my mouth is enlarged over
mine enemies; because I rejoice in thy salvation ... The bows of
mighty men are broken, and they that stumbled are girded with
strength. (I SAMUEL 2:1–4)

The most intriguing, however, is Deborah, the greatest of the
Israelite judges from the period immediately after the conquest
of Canaan. The Book of Judges praises her leadership, which
united the tribes of Israel as none had since Joshua. In fact, the
only other person ever to do so again was King David. She is not
only described as a prophetess and a warrior but as the 'mother
of Israel'. It seems that Deborah's exploits were just too familiar
to be expunged from the Hebrew Bible. Nevertheless, the scribes
who committed the extant Book of Judges to writing evidently
attempted to diminish her importance in Israelite history as far
as they could.

To begin with, the Old Testament is strangely silent about
Deborah's parentage:

And twenty years he [the king of the Canaanites] mightily
oppressed the children of Israel. And Deborah, a prophetess, the
wife of Lapidoth, she judged Israel at that time. (JUDGES 4:3–4)

Whereas nearly every important figure in Israelite history is given
a family tree and named as son of or daughter of someone, she is
only referred to as the wife of Lapidoth. As this man appears
nowhere else in the Bible and we are given no inkling as to who
he might have been, he was presumably someone of little conse-

quence. He was certainly no chieftain or prophet. It was evidently not through him that she became chief judge and mother of Israel. How did she rise to such an exalted position? An explanation is found in the Book of Jasher, where she is portrayed as Jasher's daughter. Here Jasher succeeds Moses, outlives the army commander Joshua and names Deborah as his heir.

This would explain much about the omission of Deborah's parentage in the Old Testament. Because of his Edomite origins, Jasher and his book, which revealed so much at odds with Judean thought, were expunged from the Hebrew Bible. It is not surprising that he is not named as Deborah's father. Indirectly, though, the Bible links Deborah's seat of power with the land of Edom:

> Lord, when thou wentest out of Seir, when thou marchedst out of the field of Edom, the earth trembled, and the heavens dropped, the clouds also dropped water. The mountains melted from before the Lord, even that Sinai from before the Lord God of Israel . . . the inhabitants of the villages ceased, they ceased in Israel, until that I Deborah arose . . . (JUDGES 5:4–7)

What is most significant about Deborah in the Book of Jasher is that she is depicted as Moses' spiritual successor: Moses chooses Jasher, Jasher chooses his daughter. As such, she is not merely one of the Hebrew tribes' judges: she is, in effect, divine queen of Israel. This was something the later Judeans could never have accepted.

It is clear from all this that the early Israelites, during and immediately after the Exodus, were a people who held women in high esteem. If the Edomites who survived in Petra in the first century BCE are any indication, then women were still being revered in the kingdom of Israel throughout its existence. Diodorus tells us that amongst the Edomite sect 'the women are treated as equals' (see page 244). This is further supported by evidence found on the Sabean Stone that refers to Edomite priestesses. The priesthood of the deity symbolized by the sun and moon seems to have been represented by both genders. The inscription on the stone is basically an obituary to the priest whom it commemorates and listed on it are a number of his fellow servitors. Called the *lauwa* – 'servants of the temple' – they might even have been the servitors of the shrine on Attuf Ridge. Interestingly, there are as many women included in the list as there are men.

If the cult of the Aten in Egypt was inspired by the Israelite religion, as we have reasoned, then once again we find evidence that God was originally considered both male and female. Although often described in the masculine, the Aten is clearly envisaged as having both male and female characteristics. In addressing the Aten, the 'Hymn to the Aten' refers to the pharaoh Akhenaten as 'your son who came forth from your body': the god is seen as not only siring a child, as would a man, but actually giving birth, as would a woman.

Akhenaten, the chief prophet and spokesman for the god, also had himself represented in a bisexual manner, seemingly to personify the divine attributes of the Aten. In most of the statues and carvings of the king his physique is distinctly feminine, with heavy breasts, swelling hips and ample thighs. Since he occasionally wears a long clinging robe similar to a woman's gown, some representations of the king were at first confused with those of his queen. In many of the reliefs, without accompanying inscriptions, there is no way of telling if Akhenaten is a man or a woman.

We know from Diodorus that the Edomite deity was called Dhu-esh-Shera by the Nabateans. Interestingly, although this translates as Lord of Shara, the Nabatean word *Dhu* could actually be applied to either a male or female. The nearest equivalent in modern English would be the word monarch. King is male, queen is female, but a monarch can be either. The Judeans called the

God of the kingdom of Israel Baal, which again has the same unisexual meaning. *Baal* was the original form of address used for both men and women of standing. In the Bible women are very much associated with Baal. In the divided monarchy period, the two most important queens were, from the Judean perspective, corrupt, evil and responsible for the continuation of the cult of Baal. Not only was there Jezebel, who is portrayed as sanctioning the cult in Israel, but Queen Athaliah who, after seizing the throne by killing all her family around 853 BCE, brought the cult of Baal into Judah.

If the Edomite god is any indication then it seems that the God of Israel was not originally a he at all, but an androgynous deity. Moreover, the early religion of the Hebrews was free from sexual discrimination. How, though, was this early Hebrew God worshipped, and how was it perceived to influence the daily lives of the devotees?

On the Sabean Stone we find a second glyph: a tree design consisting of a central stem with three branches to either side. Around its trunk is wrapped a serpent. Although no accompanying inscription explains this design, it is identical to later depictions of the Kabbalah, an ancient Jewish symbol that represented the soul's path to enlightenment. Also called the Tree of Life, the base, the top and the six branches each represented one of the eight *sefiroth* or aspects of the mind. The serpent wrapped around it represented the knowledge one would eventually acquire after its mysteries were properly understood. Kabbalism, the use of the Kabbalah for meditation purposes, was practised amongst a few Jews during the time of the Greek occupation of Judah. It is referenced by a number of Greeks who say that it was frowned upon by the orthodox Jewish authorities. The existence of this symbol on a memorial to a high priest of the Edomite god implies that the Edomites' religion practised Kabbalism. As this appears to be the oldest surviving representation of the Kabbalah, and Edomite religion seems to have remained insular, then Kabbalism might have been an intrinsic element of early Hebrew religion. As such, Kabbalism may not only reveal something of Edomite mysticism but the very nature of early Israelite faith.

Although Kabbalism is referenced in pre-Christian times, the oldest surviving Kabbalistic work dates only to the thirteenth century CE. Nevertheless, it provides an important insight as to how this form of mysticism was practised. The oldest surviving treatise on the Kabbalah is called *The Zohar* ('The Book of Splendour'), written about 1275 by the Spanish Jew Moses of Leon. According to *The Zohar*, Kabbalism taught that the soul could ascend temporarily into heaven during life on earth. This was done by practising a form of mediation through which the different parts of the mind were understood, brought under control of the will and balanced one against another. In this way the soul could elevate itself into the realm of *Kavod* – 'glory'. The Kabbalists viewed the soul as a series of spheres or *sefiroth*, one successively around the other like the layers of an onion. The outermost sphere was *Kether*, the realm of God, and the inner-most was *Malkuth*, the physical body. Between these were the eight spheres, which each corresponded with an aspect of the human mind. By moving the will progressively outwards through these spheres, one could join directly with the divine spark.

For meditation purposes, the soul's journey between the physical and the Godhead was represented by the Tree of Life. The roots of the tree were called *Yesod* (foundation) and corresponded with the imagination. By controlling the imagination one could rise to the sphere represented by the lower left branch, *Hod* (majesty). *Hod* was the logical, reasoning part of the mind, and to bring it under the control of the will it needed to be balanced with its opposite branch, *Netsah* (endurance), human emotion. In the same way the next two branches, *Din* (power) and *Hesed* (mercy), had to be balanced to work in harmony, before the last

two *Hokhmah* (wisdom) and *Binah* (understanding) finally
worked as one. In this way the awareness reached the top of the
trunk, *Rahamin* (compassion). Once one had truly mastered the
mind and learned real compassion for all God's creations, one
could enter *Kether* and experience *Kavod* – the glory of the Lord.

If the Edomites were the original Kabbalists, then above all else
they valued compassion. This is certainly something that strikes
us about the Edomite religion. They treated men and women
as equals, they lived a communal life of sharing, their king was
addressed as brother and they refused to keep slaves. If the Atenists
in Egypt are any indication, they were an exceptionally gentle
people. Akhenaten stood down the army because he abhored
violence, and the killing of animals for sport was outlawed in his
kingdom. Why, then, do the ancient Israelites appear to be so
brutal, merciless and warlike?

In the Old Testament, once they begin the invasion of Canaan
the Israelites behave like barbarians. In Jericho they not only
burn down the town senselessly but they loot it of its treasures to
adorn Beth-el:

> And they burnt the city with fire, and all that was therein: only
> the silver, and the gold, and the vessels of brass and of iron, they
> put into the treasury of the house of the Lord. (JOSHUA 6:24)

Joshua's forces then move north to the city of Ai, where they
systematically slaughter everyone within its walls, women and
children included:

> And so it was, that all that fell that day, both of men and women,
> were twelve thousand, even all the men of Ai. For Joshua drew
> not his hand back, wherewith he stretched out the spear, until he
> had utterly destroyed all the inhabitants of Ai. Only the cattle and
> the spoils of that city Israel took for a prey unto themselves ...
> (JOSHUA 8:25–7)

Continuing their march of destruction, the Israelites push on northward until they reach Makkedah:

> And that day Joshua took Makkedah, and smote it with the edge of the sword, and the king thereof he utterly destroyed, them, and all the souls that were therein; he let none remain: and he did to the king of Makkedah as he did unto the king of Jericho. (JOSHUA 10:28)

This merciless campaign of slaughter and plunder continues until Hazor finally falls to them:

> And Joshua at the time turned back, and took Hazor, and smote the king thereof with the sword: for Hazor beforetime was the head of all those kingdoms. And they smote all the souls that were therein with the edge of the sword, utterly destroying them: there was not any left to breathe: and he burnt Hazor with fire. And all the cities of those kings, and all the kings of them, did Joshua take, and smote them with the edge of the sword, and he utterly destroyed them ... (JOSHUA 11:10–12)

Perhaps, as they believed that Canaan was their homeland, taken from them by the Egyptians and given to the chieftains of these city states, the Israelites felt justified in conquering the country. But, if the narrative is to be believed, they plundered, looted and slaughtered senselessly. Not only this, but the author takes great pride in repeatedly describing the atrocities in detail. The reason, it seems, is that God had commanded the carnage. For instance, before the battle for Ai, God tells Joshua to kill and steal without compunction:

> And the Lord said unto Joshua, Fear not, neither be thou dismayed: take all the people of war with thee, and arise, go up to Ai: see, I have given into thy hand the king of Ai, and his people, and his city, and his land: And thou shalt do to Ai and her king as thou didst unto Jericho and her king: only the spoil thereof,

and the cattle thereof, shall ye take for prey unto yourselves: lay thee an ambush for the city behind it. (JOSHUA 8:1–2)

Here God has apparently ordered the Israelites to break two of his own Ten Commandments: 'Thou shalt not kill' (EXODUS 20:13); 'Thou shalt not steal' (EXODUS 20:15). But this was not the first time he had ordered his Commandments to be broken. He began the moment he had written them. When Moses comes down from the Mountain of God with the Ten Commandments – on two stone tablets inscribed by God's own hand – he discovers the Israelites worshipping the golden calf:

> And when Moses turned and went down from the mount, and the two tablets of the testimony were in his hand: the tablets were written on both their sides ... And the tablets were the work of God, and the writing was the writing of God, graven unto the tablets. And when Joshua heard the noise of the people as they shouted, he said unto Moses, There is a noise of war in the camp. And he said, It is not the voice of them that shout for mastery, neither is it the voice of them that cry for being overcome: but the noise of them that sing do I hear. And it came to pass, as soon as he came nigh unto the camp, that he saw the calf, and the dancing: and Moses' anger waxed hot, and he cast the tablets out of his hands, and brake them beneath the mount. And he took the calf which they had made, and burnt it in the fire ...
> (EXODUS 32:15–20)

Moses is furious that the Israelites should have broken the first two Commandments: 'Thou shalt have no other gods before me. Thou shalt not make unto thee any graven image ...'(EXODUS 20:1–2). But how can he be so incensed? The people do not yet know what these Commandments are. Moses, according to God's instructions, then goes on to break a Commandment himself. He orders the death of all those who danced before the calf:

> Then Moses stood in the gate of the camp, and said, Who is on the Lord's side? let him come unto me. And the sons of Levi [the

tribe of Levi] gathered themselves unto him. And he said unto them, Thus saith the Lord God of Israel, Put every man his sword by his side, and go in and out from gate to gate throughout the camp, and slay every man his brother, and every man his companion, and every man his neighbour. And the children of Levi did according to the word of Moses: and there fell of the people that day about three thousand men. (EXODUS 32:26–27)

In fact, God is so pleased with the Levites for their murderous rampage that he makes them the Israelite priesthood:

At that time the Lord separated the tribe of Levi, to bear the ark of the covenant of the Lord, to stand before the Lord to minister unto him, and to bless his name, unto this day. Wherefore Levi hath no part, nor inheritance with his brethren; the Lord is his inheritance, according as the Lord thy God promised him. And I stayed in the mount, according to the first time, forty days and forty nights... (DEUTERONOMY 10:8–10)

Surely this entire episode is so blatantly contradictory and hypocritical that it could not have been in the original account. Once again we have what has to have been a later interpolation. We can see from this passage that these particular words are supposed to have been written by Moses himself: 'I stayed in the mount.' Why then does it refer to the Levites holding the priest-hood 'unto this day', implying a time after the Levites had been appointed the priests of the Jerusalem Temple by Solomon? Once again, we are surely looking at a Judean version of events, at a time when the kingdom was fighting a precarious existence against a series of foreign invaders: a time when they were desperately trying to rid themselves of foreign and pagan influence. Indeed, this episode not only justifies Josiah's similar actions against Edom and Beth-el, it also exonerates his priesthood who endorsed the atrocities.

A more balanced perspective of the entire episode is found in the Book of Jasher. In its account, Moses orders the Levites to slay three thousand men, but it has nothing to do with a golden calf or idolatry. Here, it is to quash a rebellion – Aaron has tried to seize control in Moses' absence:

> And as they descended [the mount], Joshua spake unto Moses, and said, Lo, Nadab and Abihu have joined themselves unto the people: and the voice of the people seemeth as the voice of the rebellion. And it was told unto Moses, and unto Joshua, saying, The voice of the people is the voice of shouting, and of great joy: lo, Aaron, Hur, Nadab, and Abihu stand up before the people.

Three thousand of Aaron's followers are then killed in a skirmish between Moses' bodyguard, the Levites, and Aaron's followers. The only reason Aaron survives is because he reaffirms his oath of loyalty to Moses. God, speaking through Jasher, far from condoning the slaying, rebukes Moses and condemns all the Israelites for warring amongst themselves:

> For as thou hast done this thing, and as the children of Israel stood witness to the sword, so shall all the children of Israel wander in the wilderness forty years, and bear your whoredoms, until your carcasses be wasted in the wilderness.

In the Old Testament account God punishes the Israelites for worshipping the golden calf by condemning them to wander for forty years in the wilderness until an entire generation has expired. Here, however, the same punishment is more reasonably inflicted because of Israelite disunity.

The Book of Jasher also provides another side to the conquest of Canaan story. Here, Joshua conquers Canaan in very much the same bloodthirsty way but, after the battle of Jericho, when Jasher sees the carnage, he opposes Joshua. However, when many of the Israelites continue to follow Joshua's lead, Jasher and his followers return to Edom where they remain in seclusion until

Joshua's death. It is then that the Israelites return and seek Jasher's leadership. By this time he is old, so his daughter Deborah takes command and seeks a peace treaty with the remaining Canaanites. She is eventually forced to fight them but only after the Israelites are themselves attacked.

It seems, then, that the Edomite religion was fundamentally pacifist. Indeed, if Diodorus is right, it seemed to have remained so until Roman times. He tells us of their altruistic beliefs:

> They have no poor amongst their kind, they honour the meek and dispossessed, and value mercy, peace and forgiveness of transgressions.

Here we have a remarkable similarity to the beliefs of another Hebrew sect – the followers of Jesus. In the Gospel of Matthew, Jesus's words on the Sermon on the Mount are very similar:

> Blessed are the poor in spirit: for theirs is the kingdom of heaven. Blessed are they that mourn: for they shall be comforted. Blessed are the meek: for they shall inherit the earth. Blessed are they which do hunger and thirst after righteousness: for they shall be filled. Blessed are the merciful: for they shall obtain mercy. Blessed are the pure in heart: for they shall see God. Blessed are the peacemakers: for they shall be called the children of God. Blessed are they that are persecuted for righteousness' sake: for theirs is the kingdom of heaven. (MATTHEW 5:1–11)

Could it be that the Edomite religion influenced the teachings of Jesus Christ? Two of the New Testament gospels fail to say where Jesus was before he began his ministry: the two that do have a mysterious gap in Christ's life between the ages of twelve and thirty. A number of historians have suggested that Jesus spent these missing years as an Essene, as there are many similarities between his teachings and those of the Essene sect.

The Essenes began in the second century BCE, shortly after the Maccabaean revolt against Seleucid rule. In 169 BCE the Seleucid king Antiochus IV, fearing the spread of Judaism, decided to reverse the trend and attempted to Hellenize the Jews. Jewish practices were forbidden and scriptures were destroyed. This so angered the Jews that in 167 BCE Judas Maccabaeus led a mass revolt against Seleucid rule. After a lengthy guerrilla campaign a new and tolerant administration was established in Palestine: the Hasmonean dynasty who, although Greek, put an end to the continual fighting by converting to Judaism. The two chief Jewish sects, the Sadducees and the Pharisees, both accepted Greek influence, but a third sect was formed at this time to advocate a purer, fundamentalist form of Judaism: the Essenes.

The Essenes withdrew into the seclusion of the Judean wilderness where they founded various communities. A considerable amount is known of their religion as it is outlined in the Dead Sea Scrolls. Since the chance discovery of the first of these scrolls in a cave near what had been the Essene monastery of Qumran in 1947, ten further caves have been excavated in the cliffs overlooking the Dead Sea to reveal an extensive collection of over eight hundred Essene manuscripts. It has taken half a century for the ancient library to be gradually reassembled from thousands of delicate fragments and, even though there is still much work to be done, an informative outline of Essene doctrine has been recovered. Although traditional Jewish scriptures were found amongst the manuscripts, such as extracts from the Old Testament, there were specific Essene scripts, such as *The Manual of Discipline* and *The Community Rule*, which detailed the convictions and daily rituals of the community at Qumran.

From the scrolls we learn that they differed from most other Jewish sects in their belief in a communal Judaism in which each community lived as a co-operative, with collective ownership of property, collective organization of work and communal housing. Every member of the community would live for the general good of the others: something like a modern kibbutz. They were pacifists, they taught forgiveness and they were deeply spiritual, which is why it has been suggested that Jesus had once been an Essene.

Whether or not Jesus was inspired by Essene teachings, it is quite possible that the Essenes had been inspired by the Edomites. The work of the Roman historian Strabo suggests that the Essenes were in Petra around the time that Jesus was born. He records that somewhere about the year 10 BCE, the Nabatean king Obodas II tried to over-tax his people. There were many groups in Petra who opposed the king. Of one of these, Strabo writes:

> The Esser sect of the Jews, who were treated better here than they were by Herod in Judea, were most incensed. For they claimed to have no belongings, being sworn to poverty in such matters.

Although he calls them Essers, the similarity of the name and their customs suggests that they were the Essenes. There are no known sects in Judaism with such a similar name. If there were Essenes in Petra at this time, then they might well have been influenced by the contemporary Edomite sect mentioned by Diodorus.

In conclusion, it seems that the Edomite religion was truly unique and much to be admired. It treated women as equals, it valued peace and harmony and appears to have been fairly democratic. It had a highly refined form of mysticism, in which anyone who was willing to undergo the training could experience the glory of God. The reason it developed along lines so different from the cultic practices of the surrounding peoples was probably the same reason it survived for so long: its isolation. The valley of Edom was an oasis, protected by impassable mountains and a vast, hostile desert. It developed isolation in Edom between 1700 and 1500 BCE, while the other Hebrews were in Egypt and Canaan with the Hyksos. Indeed, it evolved in a similar fashion to Tibetan Buddhism, with which it has much in common. In Tibet, the isolation afforded by the Himalayan mountains allowed a religion of peace and harmony to develop. The isolation afforded by both desert and mountain allowed the compassionate religion of the Edomites to bloom. This, it seems, is the religion that so inspired Moses.

But why one God as opposed to many? Once more, isolation was probably responsible for this unique concept. For two centuries the Edomites lived beyond the influence of other cultures. All ancient communities had their local protector deity. For example, in Egypt Ra was originally the god of Heliopolis, but he became a part of the national pantheon of gods when Egypt became a kingdom. In later Greece, Athena was originally the goddess of Athens, but she became just one of the gods of Olympus once the city became the hub of the Greek empire. As the Edomite deity was so associated with the sacred mountain, it probably began as a mountain god, venerated as protector of the kingdom. For two centuries, however, this was the only god the Edomites knew. This was plenty of time for the deity to come to be regarded as the god of the whole world.

How, though, did this God come to be accepted by the Israelites as a whole during the time of the Exodus? It seems that, unlike in the surrounding nations where the gods spoke only to the ruling élite, the God of Israel spoke to all the people. It is when we examine how this tradition began that we may at last find the very origin of the western God.

Summary

• From the writings of Greek and Roman visitors to the city of Petra, such as Diodorus Siculus and Athenodorus, we can determine that the original Hebrew religion was still being practised by the Edomites as late as the first century BCE. They speak of clan who live outside mainstream society in the surrounding mountains. As they are described as having their own king, it would seem that these people were not the Nabateans so must presumably have been the Edomites. The fact that they are also described as having only one god is another indication that they were the Edomites.

- These same people had many customs in common with the ancient Hebrews. They proscribed the consumption of blood and rejected slavery, both Hebrew traditions. Moreover, they celebrated a feast that sounds very much like the Jewish Passover. Diodorus tells us that: 'Their god is Dhu-esh-Shera, but of his likeness, none is found ... They will, on occasion, erect a pillar or stone block and anoint it with sacred oil ...' Here we have three unique Hebrew conventions: one god, no images of him and the venerated stone pillar. The Old Testament refers repeatedly to single stone pillars being erected to honour God.

- The name of the deity, Dhu-esh-Shera, is also reminiscent of the God of Israel: like the Hebrew names for God, it is a title. It translates from Nabatean as 'Lord of Shera'. 'Shera' was the Nabatean name for what the Greeks called the Shara mountains. Dhu-esh-Shera might therefore have been the Lord of the sacred mountain of Jebal Madhbah. Remarkably, this is exactly how one enigmatic passage in the Bible describes God. Genesis 33:14 has Jacob referring to God as 'Lord unto Seir', and Seir was the Hebrew name for a mountain in the Shara range.

- In 1982 a block of carved stone was found in Petra. Known as the Sabean Stone, it can be dated to around the time of the birth of Christ. On it is a symbol carved in stark relief: a crescent moon with the sun between its horns. Beneath the sun and moon there is another symbol, an elongated triangle. The archaeologist Crystal Bennett reasoned that the triangle depicted the sacred mountain of Jebel Madhbah and that the sun and moon symbolized the ancient Edomite deity who was worshipped there. As many early civilizations considered the moon to be feminine, because of the perceived link between the menstruation and lunar cycles, and the sun to be masculine, Bennett reasoned that the Edomite god was an androgynous deity, having both male and female attributes.

• On the Sabean Stone we find a second glyph: a tree design consisting of a central stem with three branches to either side. Around its truck is coiled serpent. It is identical to later depictions of the Kabbalah, an ancient Jewish symbol that represented the soul's path to enlightenment. The existence of this symbol on a memorial to a high priest of the Edomite god implies that the Edomites practised Kabbalism. If the Edomites were the original Kabbalists, then above all else they were pacifists. Indeed, the Edomites might even have influenced early Christianity. The Roman writer Strabo suggests that the Jewish Essene cult was centred on Petra at this time and their practices are very similar to those of the Edomites. As many writers have seen a link between Essene teachings and the teachings of Jesus, it is possible that the Edomite religion even influenced the development of Christianity.

11 THE FORBIDDEN FRUIT

The Hebrew religion is exceptional in the ancient world regarding the personal relationship it advocates between the Israelites and their God. The Old Testament portrays many Hebrews from humble backgrounds communing directly with their deity. Unlike other ancient cultures where it was only the king or a high-born oracle who spoke for the gods, few of the Hebrew prophets were of noble birth. Indeed, it was not only the priests and prophets: many episodes in the Hebrew Bible involve ordinary people speaking personally to God. This might, of course, have been simple invention or mere fantasy. Yet even if it was, an intriguing question still remains: how did such a unique tradition arise? The solution to this enigma begins with a mysterious Israelite artefact.

Strangely, considering the Judean stance on idolatry, the Old Testament refers to something as 'the Lord' that is clearly an object. During the forty years in the wilderness, when the Israelites were away from the Mountain of God, they worshipped in a holy tent known as the tabernacle. It is during a ceremony in the tabernacle that the object is first mentioned:

> And they brought that which Moses commanded before the tabernacle of the congregation: and all the congregation drew near and stood before the Lord. (LEVITICUS 9:5)

What exactly is being referred to as 'the Lord'? Biblical scholars have long puzzled over what this enigmatic artefact might have been. All we can gather is that Moses had told the congregation to bring it with them. Although, on many subsequent occasions, the Israelites are described as standing before 'the Lord', we are never told what this representation of God actually is.

Whatever 'the Lord' was, we can assume that it was placed on the tabernacle altar. The later Israelites used an artefact to symbolize God's presence on the high altar of the Jerusalem Temple. Just as in today's synagogues, God's presence was represented in the form of the menorah – the seven-branched candelabrum. Might 'the Lord' have been the menorah? According to the Bible, the menorah has been used since the time of the Exodus and is first described when God talks to Moses on the sacred mountain.

> And thou shalt make a candlestick of pure gold ... And six branches shall come out of the sides of it; three branches of the candlestick out of the one side, and three branches of the candlestick out of the other side ... And thou shalt make the seven lamps thereof: and they shall light the lamps thereof, that they may give light over it ... And look that thou make them after their pattern, which was shewn thee in the mount.
> (EXODUS 25: 31–40)

Interestingly, we are told here that Moses made the menorah after the pattern he saw 'in the mount' – the Mountain of God. If we are right, then the Moses in question is the second Moses: the one who brought the Israelites back to Edom around 1360 BCE. If he saw something on Jebel Madhbah from which the menorah design came, then it must presumably have been on the high altar at the Edomite shrine on Attuf Ridge. After all, this appears to have been the biblical Beth-el, the house of God, and it is here that Moses seems to have communed with God. Is there anything about this particular altar that might provide a clue to what it was?

The high altar stone at the Attuf Ridge shrine has a curious feature that has mystified archaeologists for years: a peculiar hole cut into the top to a depth of about ten centimetres. It is evidently a socket into which something was slotted: the question is, what? By a remarkable stroke of luck, an ancient depiction of the altar was found during Crystal Bennett's excavations of Teman just below Jebel Madhbah. In the foundation rubble of a complex of domestic buildings, dating to the twelfth century BCE, an ivory disc of six centimetres in diameter was discovered. Thought to be a brooch, it is inscribed with the picture of an altar, just like the one at Attuf Ridge. The illustration depicts a pole rising from the altar, near the top of which is a pair of upturned horns. Between the horns there is an asterisk-like symbol that appears to represent the sun.

This, it seems, is what fitted into the slot in the High Place altar all those years ago. The Attuf Ridge altar is the only one found anywhere in the Edom Valley to have this curious socket feature. Accordingly, it would appear that the disc illustration depicts the altar at this specific site. If the illustration were to scale, then the pole would have been about a metre high (plus the section in the slot) and the horns around a metre wide. As it was placed at the most hallowed part of the shrine, then the artefact must in some way have symbolized the god being revered on Jebel Madhbah.

This curious artefact would appear to have represented the same god being venerated by the Edomites well over a thousand years later. The horns – which would appear to represent the crescent moon – with the sun shining between them is exactly the same as the symbol for the Edomite deity represented on the Sabean Stone. The Sabean Stone shows the lunar horns and sun symbols above a triangle. Crystal Bennett suggested that the sun and moon represented the deity and the triangle represented the mountain where it was worshipped. On the disc, however, the lunar horns appear to be attached to the pole, together forming a totem or devotional artefact with the sun rising above it. The similarity of the symbolism suggests that the Edomites of the twelfth century BCE, the time from which the disc dates, were worshipping the same god as their descendants worshipped over a thousand years later when the Sabean Stone was made. As this seems to have been the Hebrew God then the pole depicted on the disc might be the earliest Hebrew religious symbol yet discovered. If the disc found at Teman shows an accurate representation of what had been placed into the altar, then just such an artefact might have been there for Moses to see.

When we compare the shape of the horned pole with the traditional shape of the menorah we see that they are strikingly similar. The oldest surviving depiction of the menorah is on a coin dating from the reign of Herod the Great. It shows the sacred candelabrum with three branches to either side of the central stem, arcing upwards and outwards in exactly the same way that the horns spread out from either side of the pole. The central, and seventh, branch is formed from the stem, which continues up to become a candle-holder of an equal height to the other six. Likewise, the shaft of the horned pole continues through the horns to end level with the horn points. Furthermore, the size of both artefacts seems to have been the same.

A scene on the Triumphal Arch, erected by the emperor Vespasian in Rome, shows the menorah being looted from the Jerusalem Temple in 70 CE. Judging by the height of the figures carrying it, it seems to have had the same dimensions as the horned pole. Interestingly, both artefacts also appear to have been specifically fashioned to stand as high as they were wide. This meant that the menorah required a heavy, broad base to prevent it falling over and the horned pole had to be slotted into the altar.

Such a horned pole to represent the presence of God might have developed into the more elaborate menorah design in Judea by the time the Exodus account was committed to writing. The disc can be dated to around 1150 BCE, thanks to datable ceramic fragments found in the same layer of debris. This means that the sanctuary is at least that old, and that it was already in existence no less than a hundred years before the Jerusalem Temple was built. As we have seen, Beth-el appears to have been the prototype for Solomon's temple: the Attuf Ridge site has the obelisks flanking the sacred approach, as the free-standing pillars flanked the entrance to the Jerusalem Temple; stone benches were set around the courtyard, precisely matching the seating arrangements in the holy precinct; and there is the low-set table, before the altar, just as the shewbread table was placed before the high altar in Jerusalem. Now we have another remarkable similarity. At the Attuf Ridge site the horned pole adorned the altar, whereas in Jerusalem the menorah was placed on the high altar to symbolize God's presence.

If this horned pole was the object referred to in the Old Testament as 'the Lord', then it seems to perform an awesome miracle. After Moses tells his people to bring the object into the tabernacle and they stood before 'the Lord' he tells them:

> This is the thing which the Lord commanded that ye do: and the glory of the Lord shall appear unto you. (LEVITICUS 9:6)

Here we have another mystery. What exactly is the glory of the Lord? In later Christian times the term 'glory of the Lord' came to be associated with the invisible presence of God: the holy spirit that inspired the pure in heart. However, this notion of an invisible God appears to have been more of a Greek concept. There are only three references in the Bible to God being invisible and they are all in the New Testament:

> Who is the image of the invisible God. (COLOSSIANS 1:15)

> Him who is invisible. (HEBREWS 11:27)

The King eternal, immortal, invisible. (I TIMOTHY 1:17)

All three are by St Paul who seems to have been a Greek convert to Christianity. Confirmation of Paul's Gentile background comes from both historical sources and literary research. According to Epiphanius, a fourth-century bishop of Salamis, Paul was the son of Greek parents and adopted Judaism only after spending time in Jerusalem and marrying a Jewish woman. Paul's Greek origins are also confirmed by linguistic studies of his biblical letters, which reveal that all his Old Testament quotations are from the Greek translation, the Septuagint, even where its text wrongly diverges from the Hebrew original. Paul, therefore, must have consulted the Greek Old Testament rather than the Hebrew version, which would not have been the case if he was born a Jew and had understood the Hebrew language.

Paul's home city of Tarsus was a centre of Stoicism, a Greek philosophy that taught self-control in adversity and the acceptance of a universal law; it emphasized the equality of men and women, denounced slavery and advocated a world-wide human brotherhood, devoid of national frontiers. Most importantly, however, it taught the existence of an all-encompassing spirit of nature: a kind of universal, invisible God. Paul might have seen Judaic teaching in terms of Stoicism and perhaps it was originally through his influence that the notion of an invisible God found its way into Christian theology. In the Leviticus account, however, the glory of the Lord physically manifests itself to be seen by the Israelites:

> And Moses and Aaron went into the tabernacle of the congregation, and came out, and blessed the people: and the glory of the Lord appeared unto all the people. (LEVITICUS 9:23)

This is no one-off event. It seems that each time the Israelites do whatever it is they do, the glory of the Lord appears. For example, in Numbers 20:6:

> And Moses and Aaron went from before the presence of the assembly unto the door of the tabernacle of the congregation, and they fell upon their faces: and the glory of the Lord appeared unto them.

The Leviticus account goes on to describe exactly what is seen:

> And there came a fire out from before the Lord, and consumed upon the altar the burnt offerings ... (LEVITICUS 9:24)

So the glory of the Lord, which is like fire, literally comes out of whatever it is that is described as 'the Lord'. Some biblical commentators, following Israeli historian Martin Buber's influential *Moses* published in 1956, have suggested that this is the Ark of the Covenant. However, this seems unlikely for two reasons. The ark is mentioned almost two hundred times in the Bible, so why not mention it here? More importantly, the first time this glory of the Lord is seen the ark has not yet been made. It is when the Israelites first arrive at the Mountain of God, before Moses goes up and receives instructions on how to make the ark:

> And the glory of the Lord abode above mount Sinai ... And the sight of the glory of the Lord was like devouring fire on the top of the mount in the eyes of the children of Israel.
> (EXODUS 24:15–17)

Some biblical commentators have suggested that this particular reference to fire implies that the Mountain of God was a volcano. However, if the Mountain of God was in the Sinai wilderness it was no volcano. Geologists know of no active volcanoes in the area in recent geological time. Moreover, the phenomenon is also said to take place in the tabernacle and seems to be associated with the object we have identified as the horned pole. There would indeed have been one of these on top of the sacred mountain at the Attuf Ridge shrine. A fascinating insight into what the glory of the Lord might really have been survives in the writings of a later Christian scholar.

By the year 500 CE the city of Petra had all but been abandoned. Nevertheless, a people did survive in the Shara mountains who seem to have continued to practise a form of the Edomite religion. The sixth-century writer Stephen of Byzantium includes them in his *Ethnica*, which was a mammoth attempt to document all the cultures and religions of the world. In this work he describes an unusual sect who still dwelt in the Edom Valley:

> Many of these people have made their homes in caves and cliff dwellings [presumably, the Nabatean rock tombs] ... They are a heathen people who worship the sun. Each dawn they position a polished bronze dish in the windows to these dwellings to reflect the first rays of sunlight inside. They say that in this way the sun god himself enters their shrines.

This practice is remarkably similar to one observed by the Atenists in Egypt. In Akhenaten's capital of Amarna, they built what Egyptologists refer to as sun kiosks: shrines whose main window was orientated to receive the first rays of the morning sun. In this window, called the 'window of appearance', there was placed a polished gold or silver disc that reflected the sun's rays on to an altar where a ritual meal was laid. In this way the Aten was seen to have blessed the food that the devotees would eat.

Does the practice described by Stephen of Byzantium mean that the earlier Edomites had once done something similar? Is this how the horned pole was used? If the lunar horns on top of the pole were flat and made of polished metal, such as bronze, then the sunlight might have been reflected from them on to the shewbread table where offerings were laid. Leviticus 9:24 actually tells us that the glory of the Lord, 'consumed upon the altar the burnt offerings' (see page 270). The high altar at the Attuf Ridge sanctuary is due east of the courtyard and is orientated perfectly for such a device to work. If the horned pole was placed into the high altar, the polished crescent could reflect the first rays of the morning sun directly down on to the lower altar.

That the glory of the Lord blessed, or was seen somehow to empower, the offerings with God's presence, is confirmed by the Leviticus narrative. Moses directs Aaron to place the offerings on the shewbread altar:

> And Moses said unto Aaron, Go unto the altar, and offer thy sin offering . . . and offer the offerings of the people . . .
> (LEVITICUS 9:7)

> And Aaron lifted up his hand toward the people, and blessed them, and came down from the offerings . . . (LEVITICUS 9:23)

> And there came a fire out from before the Lord, and consumed upon the altar the burnt offerings . . . (LEVITICUS 9:24)

This last verse is a perfect description of the sun's rays being reflected from the device on the high altar to shine down on to the shewbread table. Such sunlight might indeed have been seen as divine fire. After all, God's first words in the Old Testament are 'Let there be light' (GENESIS 1:3). It would certainly make sense for the horned pole to have been used in this way. The Edomite deity was seen as embodying both solar and lunar – male and female – aspects. To reflect the sun's rays from the lunar horns would literally bring both of these facets together. Indeed, the lunar horns are doing what the moon itself does, reflecting sunlight. Concentrating the sun's rays on the offerings would be seen as imbuing them with God's power as the Atenists imbued their ritual meal with the glory of the Aten.

The Old Testament describes various offerings being made to God and they always consist of edible items. They included not only various forms of meat, but unleavened bread (after which the altar was named) and fruits. A passage in Deuteronomy even confirms that the early Hebrew offerings were associated with the sun and the moon. Referring to the fruit offerings on the shew-bread table, the Deuteronomy author writes:

> And for the precious fruits brought forth from the sun, and for the precious things brought forth from the moon.
> (DEUTERONOMY 33:14)

He even goes on to associate the glory of God that radiates upon them with the horns:

> His glory is like the firstling of his bullock, and his horns are like the horns of unicorns. (DEUTERONOMY 33:17)

'The firstling of the bullock' is the bull's first-born: the first calf it sired before its ritual castration. This is clearly a reference to the divine spark of life. As we have seen, the calf was considered to represent God's presence. 'His horns' specifically refers to God's horns: presumably the lunar horns. This is implied by the reference to the unicorn: the mythical beast with a single horn. Unlike cattle horns, the lunar horns are a single, unbroken horn.

The significance of these offerings being imbued with God's glory is that they are consumed by the priesthood. When Moses decrees that Aaron and his descendants are to be the high priests, they are told that they, and only they, are permitted to eat the food that is brought to the tabernacle as offerings:

> And thou shalt take the ram of the congregation, and seethe [cook] his flesh in the holy place. And Aaron and his sons shall eat the flesh of the ram, and the bread that is in the basket, by the door of the tabernacle of the congregation. And they shall eat those things wherewith the atonement was made, to consecrate and to sanctify them: but a stranger shall not eat thereof, because they are holy. And if ought of the flesh of the congregation, or of the bread, remain unto the morning, then thou shalt burn the

remainder with fire: it shall not be eaten, because it is holy.
(EXODUS 29:31–4)

But what was the significance of eating this holy food? It seems
that it enabled the Israelites to hear God's words. Each time the
food is consumed the glory of the Lord appears and God speaks:

And ye said, Behold, the Lord our God hath shewed us his glory
and his greatness and we have heard his voice out of the midst of
the fire: we have seen this day that God doth talk with man, and
he liveth. (DEUTERONOMY 5:24)

How, exactly, was God speaking? Often in the Old Testament
narrative we are told simply that 'the Lord said . . .' However, it
seems that God's words are transmitted through an oracle.
During the period of the Exodus this appears to have been Moses
himself. For example, in Leviticus, immediately after the account
of the glory of the Lord falling upon the offerings altar, God
speaks to the people:

And Nadab and Abihu, the sons of Aaron, took either of them his
censer, and put fire therein, and put incense thereon, and offered
strange fire before the Lord, which he commanded them not . . .
Then Moses said unto Aaron, This is that the Lord spake, saying,
I will be sanctified in them that come nigh me, and before all the
people I will be glorified. And Aaron held his peace.
(LEVITICUS 10:1–3)

In this particular passage the commandments of the Lord are
clearly those given by Moses. Nearly every chapter of Leviticus
begins with the words: 'And the Lord spake unto Moses, saying . . .' Thereafter, it simply says: 'And the Lord said . . .' A
strong indication that it was Moses doing the talking comes with
the Exodus account of his confrontations with the pharaoh. At
the burning bush, when God tells Moses to demand that the
pharaoh release the Israelite slaves, he is told that he must use his

staff to perform 'signs', such as the one he was shown when his staff became a serpent. When Moses visits the pharaoh, however, it is Aaron who uses the staff:

> And Moses and Aaron went in unto Pharaoh, and they did as the Lord commanded: and Aaron cast down his rod before Pharaoh, and before his servants, and it became a serpent. (EXODUS 7:10)

The reason why Moses has not performed the miracle himself is that he is communing with God:

> And the Lord said unto Moses, Pharaoh's heart is hardened, he refuseth to let the people go. (EXODUS 7:14)

Nearly every time that Moses and Aaron visit the pharaoh with their demand, it is Aaron who performs the miracles while Moses does the talking:

> And the Lord spake unto Moses, Say unto Aaron, Stretch forth thy rod over the streams, over the rivers, and over the ponds, and cause frogs to come up upon the land of Egypt. And Aaron stretched out his hand over the waters of Egypt; and the frogs came up, and covered the land of Egypt ... And Moses said unto Pharaoh, Glory over me: when shall I intreat for thee, and for thy servants, and for thy people, to destroy the frogs from thee and thy houses, that they may remain in the river only?
> (EXODUS 8:5–9)

Once Moses is dead, God speaks though Joshua. Interestingly, once Joshua has died, God appears to speak directly to all of the people of Israel:

> Now after the death of Joshua it came to pass, that the children of Israel asked the Lord, saying, Who shall go up for us against the Canaanites first, to fight against them? And the Lord said, Judah shall go up: behold I have delivered the land into his hands.
> (JUDGES 1:1–2)

Once more, however, it seems that someone is speaking for God. The Book of Jasher tells us that Jasher speaks for God after Joshua is dead, which would explain why the speaker is not named in the above passage. Throughout much of the early Israelite period God speaks through the descendants of Aaron, the high priests, such as his son Eleazar and his grandson Phinehas. As with Moses, the glory of the Lord appears over the offerings table before they speak the words of God. It seems, then, that the importance of the ritual feast was this: the glory of the Lord imbued the offerings that, on being consumed, passed the holy presence into the oracle, enabling him to speak for God.

The practice of the sacrificial and other food offerings being eaten by the priesthood continued throughout ancient Hebrew history and still survived in Judea in Roman times. It was even adopted by the Christians, although to them it was the consumption of the bread and wine, representing the body and blood of Christ, which filled them with God's Holy Spirit. For the early Hebrews' priests, however, the eating of the food that had been imbued with the glory of the Lord, allowed them literally to talk as God.

When we examine how this practice appears to have originated we discover an intriguing possibility to explain how Moses first discovered God. The ancient Edomites appear to have used a sacred fruit that grew on Jebel Madhbah to induce visions. Writing of the sect who appear to have been the Edomites (see Chapter X), the Greek historian Diodorus Siculus refers to this fruit:

> Being eaten, it has the power to effect fantasy. Their priests will sometimes use the fruit to bring on such fantasy, which they say is the voice of their God.

Having spent many years researching the use of medicinal plants in the classical world, American botanist Dr Karen Varbles of Brigham Young University, Utah, believes that the plant to which Diodorus refers is a hardy desert shrub called *Datura stramonium*. Commonly known as the thorn apple, it is a thorny shrub with white, lily-like flowers and a spiny black fruit. The fruit is the hallucinogenic. In fact, it might well have been this variety of bush that was the burning bush in the Exodus story. The summit of Jebel Madhbah is a harsh and rocky environment for vegetation. Only a handful of small bushes can be seen dotted here and there. One or two grow around the shrine at Attuf Ridge – and they are all thorn apples.

If we look at the full passage from Deuteronomy concerning the fruits of the sun and moon, we see that they were originally associated with both mountains and the burning bush from which God had spoken to Moses:

> And for the precious fruits brought forth from the sun, and for the precious things brought forth from the moon. And for the chief things of the ancient mountains, and for the precious things of the lasting hills. And for the precious things of the earth and the fullness thereof, and for the good will of him that dwelt in the bush ... (DEUTERONOMY 33: 14–17)

This is how the Book of Exodus describes Moses' encounter with the burning bush:

> And the angel of the Lord appeared unto him in a flame of fire out of the midst of a bush: and he looked, and, behold, the bush burned with fire, and the bush was not consumed ... God called to him out of the midst of the bush ... (EXODUS 3:2–4)

The modern translation of the Bible simply uses the word bush when talking of Moses' encounter. However, the original Hebrew version uses the words *mikvah seneh*, which actually means 'bush that burns'. In this context the words do not mean a bush that itself burns – that would be written *kiy seneh* – but a bush that is burning someone or something else. There is clear evidence of an early misunderstanding here. Like all languages, there were regional variations of the Hebrew tongue. The enigmatic burning bush story might have resulted from a simple mistranslation as the Exodus account was copied and recopied into its present form. At some point someone might wrongly have assumed that the bush itself had been burning and embellished the account to make sense of the narrative.

So what was the bush originally supposed to have burnt? Perhaps the original story had Moses himself being burnt without being consumed. Indeed, this is exactly what the fruit of the thorn apple does. Apart from being an hallucinogenic, it has a fiery, hot taste and causes sweating and burning sensations throughout the body.

So the thorn apple might have originated the practice of empowering food with the glory of the Lord. At first it was only the thorn apple itself that was thought to enable communion with God, but later the power of God was considered infused into any sacred food by the ceremony of the reflected sun.

It might not only have been the story of the burning bush that originated with the thorn apple, but the oldest tradition of them all: the forbidden fruit of the Garden of Eden. We have seen how the Kabbalah – the Tree of Life – was a sacred symbol for the ancient Edomites. It represented the way in which one could seek union with God through meditation. Why, though, was it depicted in the form of a tree? In earlier times might the Kabbalah simply have represented the thorn apple bush, the union with God being achieved through its fruit alone? The Kabbalah was itself considered a forbidden practice by the ancient Judeans and seems to have been behind one of the two forbidden trees of the Garden of Eden story – it is actually referred to in Genesis as 'the tree of life'.

And the Lord God said, Behold, the man is become as one of us, to know good and evil: and now, lest he put forth his hand, and take also of the tree of life, and eat, and live for ever: Therefore the Lord God sent him forth from the garden of Eden, to till the ground from whence he was taken. So he drove out the man; and he placed at the east of the garden of Eden Cherubims, and a flaming sword which turned every way, to keep the way of the tree of life. (GENESIS 3:22–24)

It is not only the Tree of Life that links the Garden of Eden story to the Kabbalah but also the serpent. On the Sabean Stone the Kabbalah is shown with the serpent coiled around its trunk. The ancient Greeks described the Kabbalistic serpent as representing divine knowledge (see Chapter X). It is the guardian of the Tree of Life. In ancient Judea the serpent came to represent evil, and in such a guise the devil tempts Adam and Eve to eat the forbidden fruit:

Now the serpent was more subtil than any beast of the field which the Lord God had made. And he said unto the woman, Yea, hath God said, Ye shall not eat of every tree of the garden? And the woman said unto the serpent, We may eat of the fruit of the trees of the garden: But of the fruit of the tree which is in the midst of the garden, God hath said, Ye shall not eat of it, neither shall ye touch it, lest ye die. And the serpent said unto the woman, Ye shall not surely die: For God doth know that in the day ye eat thereof, then your eyes shall be opened, and ye shall be as gods . . . (GENESIS 3:1–5)

Here humanity's fall from grace is attributed to Adam and Eve eating the forbidden fruit. The fall from grace theme was taken from the Babylonian Garden of Dilmun legend. However, in the Babylonian version there is no tree and no snake. The serpent and tree motifs were therefore seemingly of Hebrew origin. If the serpent and the forbidden tree were an attempt to discredit the Kabbalah and the Kabbalah originated with the thorn apple, then it is understandable that the Judeans should associate the fruit with mankind's original sin. By the time the Old Testament was written the Judeans would have considered the thorn apple as blasphemous as other aspects of the Edomite religion. In fact, it might have been considered the most profane as it represented the origins of a religion that had become the antithesis of Judaism. There is actually a passage in the Old Testament that specifically links the forbidden fruit of the Garden of Eden with the Mountain of God.

We have seen how the serpent was originally a symbol for God's authority and power. By the time of the Babylonian Exile the serpent had become associated with Satan, and the prophet Ezekiel makes reference to Satan being cast out of Eden after he has beguiled Adam and Eve:

> Thou hast been in Eden the garden of God ... Thou art the anointed cherub that covereth; and I have set thee so: thou wast upon the holy Mountain of God; thou hast walked up and down in the midst of the stones of fire. Thou wast perfect in thy ways from the day that thou wast created, till iniquity was found in thee. By the multitude of thy merchandise they have filled the midst of thee with violence, and thou hast sinned: therefore I will cast thee as profane out of the Mountain of God ... (EZEKIEL 28:13–16)

Here we have a reference to the Garden of Eden story, clearly equating it with the Mountain of God. If Jebel Madhbah was the Mountain of God then its sacred Edomite fruit, the thorn apple, was the same as Eden's forbidden fruit. The garden itself was taken from Babylonian legend but the fruit and the snake were, it seems, associated with the land of Edom.

Regardless of whether or not the thorn apple was behind the story of the forbidden fruit of the Garden of Eden, it seems that we have finally discovered where, when and how Moses first discovered God. The religion that would ultimately develop into the manifold faiths of the western world began as the religion of a mountain god with whom its devotees sought spiritual communion via the narcotic properties of the thorn apple. Sometime around 1364 BCE, the renegade Egyptian priest Kamose might have stood high on Jebel Madhbah and eaten the sacred fruit. The experience that followed changed his life. It convinced him that here in this remote place he had discovered the one and only God.

Summary

- The Old Testament refers to something as 'the Lord' that is clearly an object. Whatever 'the Lord' was, we can assume that it was placed on the tabernacle altar. The later Israelites used the menorah to symbolize God's presence on the high altar of the Jerusalem Temple, so the object might have been the prototype for this design. Exodus tells us that Moses first made the menorah after the pattern he saw on the Mountain of God. If he saw something on Jebel Madhbah from which the menorah design came, then it must presumably have been on the high altar at the Edomite shrine on Attuf Ridge. This appears to have been the biblical Beth-el, the house of God, and it is here where Moses seems to have communed with God.

- The high altar at the Attuf Ridge shrine has a peculiar hole cut into the top to a depth of about ten centimetres. It is evidently a socket into which something was slotted. An ancient depiction of the altar was found on an ivory disc discovered during the excavations of the Edomite city of Teman. Thought to be a brooch, it is inscribed with the picture of a pole rising from the altar, near the top of which is a pair of horns. This, it seems, was what fitted into the slot in the High Place altar all those years ago.

- If the horned pole was 'the Lord' then it seems to have performed an awesome miracle. The Old Testament describes the 'glory of the Lord' coming from it as divine fire, which descends upon the food offerings on the shewbread altar. The lunar crescent on the horned pole seems to have been made of polished bronze and was used by the Edomites to reflect the first rays of the morning sun on to the offerings table below the high altar in order to bless the food with the power of God. The high altar at the Attuf Ridge sanctuary is due east of the courtyard and is orientated perfectly for such a device to work. It would seem that this might account for the descriptions of the glory of the Lord.

- The practice of eating a meal imbued with the glory of God might have originated with the ancient Edomite custom of using the hallucinogenic fruit of the thorn apple to induce visions. Indeed, this might be the origin of the burning bush story. The thorn apple is the only bush to grow on Jebel Madhbah. Accordingly, if this was the Mountain of God where the Bible tells us the episode occurred, the bush must have been one of these. As well as being an hallucinogenic, the thorn apple has a fiery, hot taste and causes sweating and burning sensations throughout the body.

- The illustration on the Sabean Stone depicts what appears to be the Kabbalah – the Tree of Life – with a serpent coiled around it. As this is found on the same stone that depicts the god of Jebel Madhbah then this design might have originated with its sacred thorn apple bush. One of the forbidden trees in the Garden of Eden story is called the Tree of Life and it is a serpent that tempts Adam and Eve to eat the forbidden fruit.

The Book of Ezekiel even links the Garden of Eden story to the Mountain of God. The Jebel Madhbah thorn apple might, therefore, have given rise to the story of the forbidden fruit of the Garden of Eden.

APPENDIX ONE

The Books of the Old Testament

These are the books of the Old Testament as they now appear in the King James I English translation of the Bible. After the second Book of Chronicles there is no chronological order to the arrangement of the texts. They are set out in the order that they first appeared in the Septuagint, the Greek translation made by Greek-speaking Jews during the third century BC.

GENESIS Genesis, *Bereshith*, in the Hebrew Bible, meaning 'in the beginning'. It tells the story from the creation to the time of the Israelite sojourn in Egypt.

EXODUS Exodus tells the story of the Israelites' bondage in Egypt, their eventual escape under the leadership of Moses – the Exodus after which the book is named – and their wandering in the great wilderness to the east of Egypt for forty years where they receive God's laws.

LEVITICUS Leviticus, meaning 'the priestly book', is named after the tribe of Levi who have become the priestly caste amongst the Hebrews. Its Hebrew name is *Vayyiqra*, meaning 'and he summoned'. It consists mainly of legislation, dealing with priesthood, rituals, feasts, fasts, purity and holiness.

NUMBERS Numbers relates events during the Israelites' journey through the desert from Mount Sinai to the borders of Canaan. Numbers is its Latin name, so-called because it begins with a census numbering the Israelites: its Hebrew name *Be-midbar* simply means 'in the wilderness'.

DEUTERONOMY Deuteronomy comes from a Greek word meaning 'the second law': its Hebrew title *Debarim* comes from the first word of the line, 'these are the words that Moses spoke'. Deuteronomy continues the wilderness story from Sinai to the death of Moses. As well as laws, it contains prophesies and commentaries on the relationship between God and the people of Israel.

JOSHUA The Book of Joshua is named after the leader of the Israelites following Moses' death. It covers the period when the Israelites conquer Canaan, beginning with the siege of Jericho and ending with the sacking of Hazor.

JUDGES The Book of Judges is named after a series of Israelite leaders referred to as judges, such as Gideon, Jephthah and Samson. Its Hebrew title, *Shophetim*, translates directly as 'judges'. The book covers a period of some ten generations, in which the twelve tribes of Israel fight a precarious existence in Canaan, opposed by a series of surrounding peoples.

RUTH The Book of Ruth is set during the period of the judges and tells the story of a widow whose faith and integrity in the face of adversity are recognized and rewarded by God.

SAMUEL I AND II The two Books of Samuel are named after the prophet Samuel, God's chosen spokesman who brings together the tribes of Israel under one monarchy. In the Hebrew Bible, they were originally one book but the translators of the Septuagint divided it into two parts. The prophet Samuel is instructed to unite the tribes of Israel under one king. He first chooses Saul, who ultimately fails to keep the country together, and then chooses Israel's greatest king, David.

KINGS I AND II The two Books of Kings are so-called because they deal with the succession of Hebrew kings from David's son Solomon until their destruction by the empires of Assyria and Babylon.

CHRONICLES I & II Originally one book, the *Dibre hayyamin* – 'accounts of the days' – in the Hebrew Bible, the first and second Books of Chronicles cover the same period as the Books of Samuel and Kings with additional religious commentaries on the Jerusalem Temple, its priests and the Hebrews' responsibilities to God.

EZRA Named after the prophet Ezra, it tells how the Jews must pick up their lives after the exile in Babylon, through the rebuilding of the Temple and the leadership of Ezra himself.

NEHEMIAH Originally joined to the Book of Ezra, it is written in the first person by Nehemiah, the last native governor of Judah under Persian rule. It concerns the return to Jerusalem, the rebuilding of the walls of Jerusalem and the Jews' religious obligations.

ESTHER Named after a Jewish queen of Persia, the wife of King Xerxes, it is a story of intrigue set in the Persian court: a plot to discredit the Jews which Esther uncovers by risking her life.

JOB The story of Job, an entirely just and righteous man, and his continued faith in God despite terrible misfortune. It is set in some unspecified period in the distant past.

PSALMS The Book of Psalms, meaning hymns, contains songs and laments of ancient Israel, seventy-three of which have been attributed to King David. They appear to have been a part of the formal worship in the Jerusalem Temple, originally set to music.

PROVERBS The Book of Proverbs is a collection of proverbs and instructions on religious themes. They are attributed to Solomon as their Hebrew title *Mishle Shelomoh* literally means 'The Proverbs of Solomon'.

ECCLESIASTES In the Hebrew Bible, the Book of *Qohelet*, it is attributed to David's son and is a commentary on the search for the key to life's meaning.

SONG OF SONGS Also called the Song of Solomon, it is a love poem attributed to King Solomon. It is thought to be an allegory concerning God's dealings with Israel.

ISAIAH The Book of Isaiah concerns the prophesies of the prophet Isaiah, whom the Old Testament portrays as living around the time of Hezekiah.

JEREMIAH This book concerns the teachings of the prophet Jeremiah who preaches in the years immediately before the Babylonian conquest, during which he warns the Jews of the consequences of forsaking God.

LAMENTATIONS An anonymous collection of five poems lamenting the destruction of the Jerusalem Temple by the Babylonians.

EZEKIEL Named after a prophet of the Babylonian Exile, it relates his teachings and visions concerning the Jews and their need to renew their relationship with God.

DANIEL A lively story concerning the faith of the prophet Daniel in slavery at the court of Nebuchadnezzar. He becomes an interpreter of dreams, survives being thrown into a lions' den by the intervention of God and has a series of visions concerning God's kingdom.

HOSEA The teachings of the prophet of that name who lived in the kingdom of Israel at the time it was being conquered by the Assyrians.

JOEL The teachings of the prophet Joel, concerning God's judgement and retribution. Joel lives during some unspecified period and goes unmentioned elsewhere in the Old Testament.

AMOS The teachings of a prophet of that name who preaches in the kingdom of Israel during the reign of Jeroboam II. Born in Judah, he speaks out against the priests of Beth-el.

OBADIAH A prophet of Babylonian Exile who denounces the kingdom of Edom. However, Obadiah is critical of the purges of Josiah against the shrine at Beth-el.

JONAH Set during the Assyrian ascendancy, it is the story of Jonah, a prophet who is told by God to preach in the enemy capital of Nineveh. On his voyage there he is shipwrecked and swallowed by a 'large fish' – usually depicted as a whale – only to be regurgitated on the shore.

MICAH It is named after a prophet during the age of Hezekiah who preached against injustice and corruption.

NAHUM A prophet from the period of the Assyrian decline who preaches against the enemy.

HABAKKUK A prophet from the period of the Assyrian decline who preaches against the lawlessness of Judah.

ZEPHANIAH A prophet from the reign of Josiah who preaches against the sins of Judah.

HAGGAI The work of a chief prophet during the rebuilding of the Temple after the exile in Babylon.

ZECHARIAH The work of another chief prophet at the time of the rebuilding of the Temple.

MALACHI This is the last Book of the Old Testament, written after the Jews returned from exile. The prophet Malachi calls upon the people to change their ways.

APPENDIX TWO

Ancient Israel and Judah
Approximate Chronology BCE

1000–972 David unifies the tribes of Israel. City of Jerusalem captured from the Jesubites and made the capital of the kingdom of Israel.

972–32 Solomon builds the Jerusalem Temple and establishes it as the chief centre of Hebrew worship.

932 Tribe of Judah splits from Israel and founds an independent kingdom around Jerusalem.

THE DIVIDED MONARCHY

ISRAEL	JUDAH
931–910 Jeroboam I	931–914 Rehoboam
New altar erected at Beth-el	Egypt besieges Jerusalem. Temple riches plundered
909–807 Nadab	914–911 Abijam
907–886 Baasha	910–871 Asa
885 Elah	
885 Zimri	
Four army commanders as succession of kings, following a series of assassinations and palace coups. Incursions by Syria.	Abijam attacks Israel and sacks Beth-el. Asa forced to withdraw by Baasha, who forms alliance with the Syrians. Peace pact made between Asa and Omri of Israel

885–874 Omri

Civil war, in which Omri triumphs and establishes a new dynasty. New capital built at Samaria. Syrians expelled. Peace with Judah

873–53 Ahab

Ahab and his queen Jezebel sanction the Baal cult. The cult opposed by the prophet Elijah

853: Ahaziah

Ahaziah continues to sanction the Baal cult. Elisha replaces Elijah as chief prophet to oppose the Baal cult

853–41 Jehoram

Erosion of Israel's territory by Syria. After Ramoth-gilead, rebel commander Jehu and his troops attack the depleted army and kill the king

841–13 Jehu
813–797 Jehoahaz

Under the influence of Elisha, Jehu overthrows the priests of Baal and has their patron Jezebel stoned to death. Renewed Syrian aggression

797–82 Jehoash

Death of Elisha. Syrians expelled from Israel. Jehoash besieges Jerusalem

782–47 Jeroboam II

871–48 Jehoshaphat

848–41 Joram

Baal cult in Judah. Joram joins forces with Jehoram of Israel against Syrians. Jehu kills Joram of Judah after battle of Ramoth-gilead

841–35 Queen Athaliah
834–796 Jehoash

As the dead king's son Jehoash is only a child, his grandmother Athaliah becomes queen. She is eventually assassinated in a palace coup and Jehoash becomes king

796–67 Amaziah

Jerusalem besieged by Israel. Amaziah pays heavy tribute to Jehoash. Temple plundered

767–34 Uzziah

Jeroboam captures Syrian capital of Damascus. Israel prospers. The prophet Amos preaches against Beth-el and foretells its destruction

After Amaziah has plundered the temple to pay tribute to Israel, his son Uzziah overthrows him and seizes power

Following the assassination of Jeroboam's successor, Zechariah, by his commander Shallum, there follows a series of military dictatorships

747 Zechariah
747 Shallum
747–42 Menahem
742–40 Pekahiah
740–31 Pekah

734–28 Ahaz

Pekah, the last of the military dictators, marches on Judah and besieges Jerusalem. When Assyrians come to Judah's aid, the king of Israel is forced to retreat. Pekah deposed in mass uprising and replaced by Hoshea

Ahaz is advised by the prophet Isaiah to stand firm against Israel. Instead, he appeals to the king of Assyria. The Assyrian Tiglath-pileser III agrees to assist in return for allegiance from the kingdom in effect making the country an Assyrian vassal state

731–22 Hoshea

728–698 Hezekiah

Hoshea offers allegiance and pays tribute to the new Assyrian king Shalmaneser V. When Hoshea eventually rebels against Assyrian authority, Samaria is besieged. The city holds out for three years until it falls to king Sargon II. Israel absorbed into Assyrian empire and much of its population are deported into slavery. The kingdom of Israel ceases to exist

Religious reforms under the direction of Isaiah. The serpent staff of Moses destroyed by Hezekiah. Expansion of Judah into land of the Philistines. The prophet Micah preaches against the expansion. Anti-Assyrian alliance with Egypt. Jerusalem survives Assyrian siege but Judah loses much of its territory

698–43 Manasseh

642–41 Amon

Religious decline in Jerusalem

640–609 Josiah

Rapid decline of Assyrian empire.
Expansion of Judah into territory
once belonging to the kingdom of
Israel. The destruction of Beth-el.
Far-reaching religious reforms.
Torah discovered in the Jerusalem
Temple. Josiah killed in battle
against the Egyptians

609–598 Jehoiakim

Jehoiakim, puppet king appointed
by king Necho of Egypt

THE BABYLONIAN AND PERSIAN PERIODS

605 Babylonian prince Nebuchadnezzar defeats the Egyptians at the
battle of Carchemish and Jehoiakim transfers his allegiance to
Babylon. The prophet Jeremiah foretells that Nebuchadnezzar will
destroy Judah.

597 After the Babylonians fail decisively to defeat the Egyptian army,
Jehoiakim rebels against Babylon. In reprisal, Nebuchadnezzar,
now king of Babylonia, invades Judah and captures Jerusalem.
Temple is plundered and its treasures taken to Babylon. Seventeen
thousand leading citizens of Judah taken into slavery in Babylon.
Puppet king Zedekiah placed on the throne of Judah.

587 Zedekiah leads abortive rebellion against Babylon. In reprisal, the
Jerusalem Temple is sacked and razed to the ground. More Jews
taken into slavery.

587–39 The Jews in exile in Babylon. The prophets Ezekiel and Daniel in Babylon.

539 Babylonian Empire conquered by the Persians. Persian king Cyrus allows the Jews to return to Jerusalem and appoints a Jewish governor, Sheshbazzar, to run the city.

525 Under the governorship of Sheshbazzar's successor, Zerubbabel, the Jerusalem Temple is rebuilt. Radical reforms in Judaism. Under the direction of prophets such as Haggai and Zechariah the Hebrew Bible is committed to writing in its present form.

APPENDIX THREE

General Chronology
BCE/BEFORE THE COMMON ERA

2000 The birth of the Mari kingdom at Tell Hariri in Syria

1820 Mari king Zimri-Lim records the Habiru as one of his peoples

1800 The Mari kingdom is invaded by the Babylonians. The Hyksos migrate south into Canaan

1750 The Hyksos establish a powerful presence in Canaan

1745–1700 Increasing numbers of Hyksos continue to settle the Nile delta as Egypt's power declines. Israelites settle in Canaan. Edomites settle in Shara mountains

1700 The whole of northern Egypt falls to the Hyksos

1700–1550 The Hyksos kings govern northern Egypt, establishing their capital at Avaris. Southern Egypt remains in the hands of the Egyptian kings with their capital at Thebes. Hebrews first settle in Egypt

1550 The Egyptian king Ahmose reconquers northern Egypt. Some Hyksos are enslaved while others retreat into Canaan

1500–1450 Reign of Tuthmosis III

1500 Tuthmosis III conquers the Hyksos in Canaan and returns with many new slaves. The oldest reference to the Habiru slaves in Egypt. Israelites enslaved

1500 The oldest reference to the Habiru, on a scene from the tomb of Tuthmosis III's great herald Antef, which lists them among the prisoners of war captured during the pharaoh's campaigns

1494 Termut arrives in Egypt

1490 Kamose adopted by Termut

1471 Kamose recorded as priest of Heliopolis

1466 Kamose appointed chief steward to Tuthmosis III

1475 Habiru recorded in Goshen in the north-east Nile delta

1450 First reference to Atenism in Egypt

1430 An inscribed stela at Memphis refers to 3600 Habiru

1385–60 Reign of Amonhotep III. Rebuilding of Avaris

1362 Last record of Prince Tuthmose in Egypt

1360 Eruption of Thera. Plagues of the Exodus. Israelites leave Egypt

1360–43 Reign of Akhenaten. The Aten is installed as chief deity

1360–20 Israelites in the wilderness

1320 Conquest of Jericho

1300–1287 Reign of Set I

1287–20 Reign of Ramesses II. Rebuilding of Avaris as Pi-Ramesses

1290 Egyptians fight the Habiru at Beisham in Canaan

1250 The burning of Hazor

1200 Israel Stela mentions the Israelites having some kind of kingdom in Palestine

1180 Philistines first recorded by Egyptians in eastern Mediterranean

1000–972 David unifies the tribes of Israel. City of Jerusalem captured from the Jesubites and made the capital of the kingdom of Israel

972 Solomon king of Israel and the building of the Jerusalem Temple

932 Tribe of Judah splits from Israel and founds an independent kingdom around Jerusalem

932–10 Jeroboam I (Israel). New altar erected at Beth-el

931–14 Rehoboam I (Judah). Egypt besieges Jerusalem. Temple riches plundered

914–11 Abijam (Judah)

909–885 A series of military dictatorships in Israel

910–871 Asa (Judah)

885–74 Omri (Israel). Samaria, new capital of Israel. Pact between Asa of Judah and Omri of Israel

873–53 Ahab (Israel). Baal cult in Samaria. The cult opposed by the prophet Elijah

871–48 Jehoshaphat (Judah)

853 Ahaziah (Israel). Ahaziah continues to sanction the Baal cult. Elisha replaces Elijah as chief prophet to oppose the Baal cult

848–41 Joram (Judah). Baal cult in Judah. Joram joins forces with Jehoram of Israel against Syrians

853–41 Jehoram (Israel). Erosion of Israel's territory by Syria

841–13 Jehu (Israel). Battle of Ramoth-gilead. Jehu defeats Joram of Judah. Under the influence of Elisha, Jehu overthrows the priests of Baal and has their patron Jezebel stoned to death. Renewed Syrian aggression

841–35 Queen Athaliah (Judah)

834–796 Jehoash (Judah)

813–797 Jehoahaz (Israel)

797–82 Jehoash (Israel). Death of Elisha. Syrians expelled from Israel

796–67 Amaziah (Judah). Jerusalem besieged by Israel. Amaziah pays heavy tribute to Jehoash. Temple plundered

782–47 Jeroboam II (Israel). Jeroboam captures Syrian capital of Damascus. Amos preaches against Beth-el

767–34 Uzziah (Judah)

747–40 Military dictatorships in Israel

740–31 Pekah (Israel)

734–28 Ahaz (Judah). Jerusalem besieged by Pekah. Ahaz appeals for help from Assyria. Israel forced to retreat by the Assyrians

731–22 Hoshea (Israel). Israel defeated by Assyria. Much of its population deported into slavery. Israel ceases to exist

728–698 Hezekiah (Judah). Religious reforms under the direction of Isaiah. The serpent staff of Moses destroyed by Hezekiah

698–43 Manasseh (Judah)

650 Oldest known form of coinage used by the Lydians

642–41 Amon (Judah)

640–609 Josiah (Judah). Rapid decline of Assyrian empire. Expansion of Judah into territory once belonging to the kingdom of Israel. The sacking of Beth-el. Far-reaching religious reforms. Torah discovered in the Jerusalem Temple. Josiah killed in battle against the Egyptians

609–598 Jehoiakim, puppet king of Judah appointed by king Necho of Egypt

605 Nebuchadnezzar defeats the Egyptians at the battle of Carchemish and Jehoiakim transfers his allegiance to Babylon

597 Nebuchadnezzar invades Judah and captures Jerusalem. Temple is plundered and its treasures taken to Babylon. Seventeen thousand leading citizens of Judah taken into slavery in Babylon. Puppet king Zedekiah placed on the throne of Judah

587 Zedekiah leads abortive rebellion against Babylon. In reprisal, the

Jerusalem Temple is sacked and razed to the ground. More Jews taken into slavery

587–39 The Jews in exile in Babylon. The prophets Ezekiel and Daniel in Babylon

539 Babylonian Empire conquered by the Persians. Persian king Cyrus allows the Jews to return to Jerusalem and appoints a Jewish governor, Sheshbazzar, to run the city

525 Under the governorship of Sheshbazzar's successor, Zerubbabel, the Jerusalem Temple is rebuilt. Radical reforms in Judaism. Under the direction of prophets such as Haggai and Zechariah the Hebrew Bible is committed to writing in its present form

333 Alexander the Great annexes Egypt. The works of Manetho are written

169 Antiochus IV plunders Jerusalem Temple

167 Revolt led by Judas Maccabaeus

130 Qumran monastery built

63 Romans annex Palestine

37 Herod installed as king of Palestine

27 Augustus, emperor

19 Work begins on Herod's temple

4 Death of Herod

CE/COMMON ERA

6 Direct Roman rule in Judea

14 Tiberius, emperor

26 Pontius Pilate, governor of Judea

30 Jesus preaches in Palestine

54 Nero, emperor. Paul preaches throughout Roman empire

66 Jewish revolt

70 Romans sack Jerusalem and destroy Temple

90 Josephus writes his histories of the Jews

131 Second Jewish revolt

135 Bar Kokhba defeated at the fortress of Bethther

References

All Bible quotations are from the James I English translation.

One

9 Krakatau aftermath: Symons, G. J. (ed.), *The Eruption of Krakatau and Subsequent Phenomena*, London, 1988.

10 Mount St Helens fallout: Weintraub, B., 'Fire & Ash: Darkness at Noon', *National Geographic*, 162, 1982, pp. 660–70, 676–84.

11 Ecosystems and volcanoes: Sheets, D. P. & Grayson, D. K. (eds), *Volcanic Activity and Human Ecology*, New York, 1979.

12 Mount Pelee eruption: Kennan, G., *The Tragedy of Pelee*, New York, 1902. Perret, F. A., *The Eruption of Mount Pelee*, Washington DC, 1932. Wilson, *The Exodus Enigma*, pp. 123–6.

15 *Albatross* and *Vema* surveys: Ninkovich, D. & Heezen, B. C., 'Submarine Geology and Geophysics', *Colston Papers*, vol. 17, Bristol, 1965, pp. 413–52.

16 Mount St Helens eruption: *Mount St Helens Holocaust*, Columbian Inc., Lubbock, 1980. Lipman, P. W. & Mullineaux, D. R., *The 1980 Eruptions of Mount St Helens, Washington*, US Geological Survey, Washington DC, 1981.
Mount St Helens aftermath: Findley, R., 'Mount St Helens', *National Geographic*, 159, 1981, pp. 3–65. Findley, R., 'Mount St Helens aftermath: the mountain that was and will be', *National Geographic*, 160, 1981, pp. 713–33.

17 Krakatau eruption: Simkin, T. & Fiske, R. S., *Krakatau 1883: The*

Volcanic Eruption and its Effects, Washington DC, 1983. Fureaux, R., *Krakatau*, London, 1965.

Thera eruption: Page, D. L., *The Santorini Volcano and the Desolation of Minoan Crete*, London, 1970. Bullard, F. M., *Volcanoes in History, in Theory, in Eruption*, London, 1962.

Thera eruption: Bullard, F. M., *Volcanoes in History*, Sparks, R. S. J., *The Santorini Eruption and its Consequences*, *Endeavour 3*, 1979, pp. 27–31.

Two

21 Roman Palestine: Freyne, S., *Galilee from Alexander the Great to Hadrian*, Wilmington, 1980.
Ancient Israel: Shanks, H., Deser, W., Baruch, H. & McCarter, P., *The Rise of Ancient Israel*, Washington, 1992.

22 Jewish history: Aharoni, Y, Avi-Yohan, M., Rainey, A. F. & Safrai, Z., *The Macmillan Bible Atlas*, New York, 1993.

23 Ephesus: Cotchett, C., *Ephesus*, Florence, 1993.

28 Redford, D. B., *A Study of the Biblical Story of Joseph*, Leiden, 1970.

31 Hebrew alphabet: Comrie, Bernard, *The Major Languages of South Asia, The Middle East and Africa*, London, 1990.
Ahiram: Magnusson, *BC*, p. 154.

32 Benedek, David, *The Language and Dialects of Ancient Israel*, New York, 1982.

33 Babylonian conquest: Ackroyd, P. R. & Evans, C. F. (eds), *The Cambridge History of the Bible*, Cambridge, 1970.

34 Nimrud: Magnusson, *BC*, pp. 175–86.

35 Garden of Dilmun: Anderson, G. W. *The History of the Religion of Israel*, Oxford, 1966.

36 Epic of Gilgamesh: Prichard, J. B., *Ancient Near Eastern Texts Relating to the Old Testament*, Princeton, 1969.

37 Tower of Babel: Oates, J., *Babylon*, London, 1979, p. 143.

Three

History of ancient Israel:

    Shanks, H., Deser, W., Baruch, H. & McCarter, P., *The Rise of Ancient Israel*.

    Thomas, D. W. (ed.), *Documents from Old Testament Times*, London, 1958.

    Williams, D. (ed.), *New Concise Bible Dictionary*, Oxford, 1989.

    Rogerson, J., *Chronicle of the Old Testament Kings*, London, 1999.

46 Layard excavation: Magnusson, *BC*, pp. 175–86.

    Maobite Stone: Rogerson, *Chronicle*, pp. 101–2.

49 Dibon excavations: Magnusson, *BC*, pp. 161–5.

52 Reign of Solomon: *ibid.*, pp. 138–56.

53 Reign of David: *ibid.*, pp. 119–37.

54 Prichard excavation: *ibid.*, pp. 129–30.

56 Spring of Gihon: *ibid.*, pp. 131–5.

58 Israel Stela: Breasted, J. H., *Ancient Records of Egypt*, Chicago, 1976.

59 Age of judges: Bowker, J., *The Complete Bible Handbook*, London 1999.

60 Philistines first appear: Magnusson, *BC*, p. 98.

61 Philistines first in Canaan: *ibid.*, p. 104.

    Yadin excavations: Yadin, Y., *Hazor: Great Citadel of the Bible*, London, 1963.

62 Kenyon excavations: Kenyon, K. M., *Digging up Jericho*, London, 1957.

Four

69 Dating: Clayton, *Chronicle*, pp. 12–13.

72 No historical reference to Israelites in Egypt: Magnusson, *BC*, p. 43.

73 Khnumhotep tomb illustration: Albright, W. F., *The Archaeology of Palestine*, Harmondsworth, 1956, p. 208.
Mari: Magnusson, *BC*, pp. 36–8.

74 Hyksos: Aldred, *Akhenaten, Pharaoh of Egypt*, p. 117.

76 Manetho: Waddell, W. G., *Manetho*, London, 1940.
Bietak, M., *Tell–el–Daba II*, Vienna, 1975.
Yakob: Clayton, *Chronicle*, p. 95.
Hyksos military: Yadin, Y., *The Art of Warfare in Biblical Lands in the Light of Archaeological Discovery*, London, 1963.

77 Inscription from the tomb of Ahmose: Pritchard, J. B., *Ancient Near Eastern Texts Relating to the Old Testament*, Princeton, 1969.
Tuthmosis's campaigns: Clayton, *Chronicle*, pp. 109–10.
Tomb illustrations: Davies, N de G., *The Tomb of Rekhmire at Thebes*, New York, 1944.

78 Origin of the name Hebrew: *Encyclopaedic Dictionary*, Oxford, 1994, p. 37.
Snyder, M., *Ancient Israel*, Jerusalem, 1978, pp. 36–51.
Habiru in Mari texts: Magnusson, *BC*, p. 37.

80 Bucaille, M., *Moses and Pharaoh: The Hebrews in Egypt*, Tokyo, 1994, pp. 55–6.

82 Early nineteenth-dynasty history: Clayton, *Chronicle*, pp. 140–58.

84 Beisham: Bucaille, M., *Moses and Pharaoh: The Hebrews in Egypt*, Tokyo, 1994, pp. 55–6.

85 Jericho dating: Bruins, H. J. & van de Plicht, J., 'The Exodus Enigma', *Nature*, 382, 1996. pp. 213–14. Radford, T., 'Scientists Fix Date for Fall of Jericho', *Guardian*, London, 18 July 1996.

87 Manetho's account: Thackeray, H. (trans.), *Josephus: Against Apion*, London, 1926.

88 Core samples: Ninkovich, D. & Heezen, B.C., 'Submarine Geology and Geophysics', *Colston Papers*, vol. 17, Bristol 1965, pp. 413–452.

89 Harriot Boyd excavations: Hawes, H. B., *Gournia, Vasiliki and other Prehistorical Sites on the Isthmus of Hierapetra, Crete*, American Exploration Society, Philadelphia, 1908.

90 Seager excavation: Seager, R. B., 'Excavations on the Island of Mochlos, Crete, in 1908', *American Journal of Archaeology*, 13, 1909, pp. 273–303.

Xanthoudidis excavation: Wilson, *The Exodus Enigma*, London, 1985, p. 89.

91 Platon excavations: Platon, N., *Zakros: The Discovery of a Lost Palace of Ancient Crete*, New York, 1971.

Marinatos excavations: Marinatos, S., *Excavations at Thera*, 7 vols, Athens, 1967–73.

93 Kristos Vlachos interviewed on *The Secrets of Atlantis, Puzzles in History*, Aagean Productions, 1999.

Sekhmet statues: Aldred, *Akhenaten*, pp. 148–49 and 283.

British Museum statues: James, T. G. H. & Davies, W. K., *Egyptian Sculpture*, London, 1984.

94 Amonhotep at the height of power: Clayton, *Chronicle*, pp. 115–19. Aldred, *Akhenaten*, ch. 15.

Legend of Sekhmet: Lurker, *The Gods and Symbols of Ancient Egypt*, p. 106. Ions, *Egyptian Mythology*, p. 104.

Unrivalled numbers of Sekhmet statues: Masters, R., *The Goddess Sekhmet*, New York, 1988, p. 48.

95 *Yam Suph*: Anderson, *The History and Religion of Israel*, pp. 23–24. Magnusson, *BC*, pp. 64–5.

96 Thera *tsunami*: Galanopoulos, A. G., 'Tsunamis Observed on the Coasts of Greece from Antiquity to the Present Time', *Annali di Geofisica*, 13, 1960, pp. 369–86.

Sea withdrawal: Simkin & Fiske, *Krakatau 1883: The Volcanic Eruption and its Effects*. Wilson, *The Exodus Enigma*, pp. 132–5.

Five

102 Yonah, I., *Biblical Schechem*, Jerusalem, 1993, pp. 31–43.
106 Books of the Old Testament: Bowker, *Complete Bible Handbook*.
107 Moses name: Osman, A., *Moses: Pharaoh of Egypt*, London, 1990, pp. 66–7.

108 Ullian, D., *History of Israel*, New York, 1995.
The Sargon myth: Magnusson, *BC*, p. 58.

109 Prince Tuthmosis: Aldred, *Akhenaten*, p. 259.
Whip: Clayton, *Chronicle*, p. 120.

110 'King's true son . . .': Redford, *Akhenaten*, p. 59.

112 Prince Tuthmosis tomb: Aldred, *Akhenaten*, p. 298.

113 Illustrations from tombs: Davies, *The Rock Tombs of El Amarna*,
London, 1908.
Petrie, W. M. F., *Tell el–Amarna*, London, 1894.

114 History of the Atenism: Aldred, *Akhenaten*.

115 Noble's tombs: Davies, *The Rock Tombs*.
Names of God: Beebe, H. K., *The Old Testament*, London, 1970.

116 Hymn to the Aten: Aldred, *Akhenaten*, pp. 241–3. Samson,
Nefertiti and Cleopatra, pp. 29–32.
Egyptian religion: Frankfort, H., *Kingship and the Gods*, Chicago
1948. Daniels, C., *Ancient Egyptian Religion*, New York, 1961.

117 Inscriptions: 'The Amarna Boundary Stelae Project', *University
of Chicago Oriental Institute Annual Report, 1983*. Aldred, *Akhenaten*, ch. 4.

118 Bronze bull: Amihay Mazor interviewed on *Time Travellers: The
Mystery of the Israelites*, Akios Productions, 1992.

119 Tomb of Aper–el: Zivie, A., *The Treasury of Aper-El*, *Egyptian
Archaeology*, Summer 1991, pp. 26–9.

123 Josephus, Flavius, *Jewish Antiquities II, IX, V* (trans. Feldman,
L.), London, 1981.

124 Tomb of Turmut: Gerard, D., 'Excavations at Deir-el-Behari',
Proceedings of the American Society of Archaeology, 14, 1921.

125 Tuthmosis Kamose: Deller, B. J., *Ancient Egypt*, New York, 1923,
pp. 78–84.

126 Reign of Tuthmosis III: David, R. & David, A. E., *A Biographical
Dictionary of Ancient Egypt*, London, 1992.

Six

132 Dan excavation: Magnusson, *BC*, pp. 159–61

136 Traditional interpretation of Baal: Williams, D., (ed.) *New Concise Bible Dictionary*, Oxford, 1989, p. 47

137 Baal: Brown, F., *Hebrew and the English Lexicon of the Old Testament*, Oxford, 1906.

138 Samaria excavation: Simkiss, D., *Archaeological Review*, III, 1984.

140 Maobite Stone: Rogerson, *Chronicle*, pp. 101–2.

143 *Quaran*: Soferman, J., *The Jewish Dictionary*, New York, 1984.

144 Benedek theory: Benedek, David, *The Language and Dialects*, pp. 119–24

149 Herod's temple: Millard, A., *Discoveries from the Time of Jesus*, Oxford, 1990, pp. 88–95.

157 Benedek, David, *The Language and Dialects*, p. 26.

Seven

161 Justinian: Lloyd, P., *Documents of the Eastern Church*, London, 1953, p. 67.

162 Anati theory: *Biblical Archaeological Society Review*, July/August 1985, pp. 42–57.

164 Williams and Cornuke theory: Williams, Cornuke & Kerkeslager, *Biblical Archeological Society Review*, April 2000, pp. 38–45.

166 Hor and Horeb: Kopp., C., *The Holy Places of the Gospels*, London, 1963.

171 Tell–el–Kheleifeh excavation: Magnusson, *BC*, pp. 145–7.
Rothenberg: *ibid.*, p. 151.

172 Kenyon map: *ibid.*, p. 136.

176 Bennett excavations: *ibid.*, p. 73.
Lachish excavation: *ibid.*, p. 187.

183 Snyder: interview with the author 18 January 2000.
Mason: letter to author 6 February 2000.

185 Martin, Michael: *The Book of Jasher*, Philadelphia, 1995.

Eight

195 Ruins of Petra: Browning, *Petra*, London, 1989.
Nabateans: *ibid.*

196 City of Teman: *ibid.*, pp. 20–61.

198 Burckhardt: *ibid.*, pp. 62–79.

200 Burckhardt, John, *Travels in Syria and the Holy Land*, London, 1822.
Numairi manuscript: now in Bibliotheque Nationale, Paris.

203 Atuff Ridge site: Browning, *Petra* and Levy, Udi, *The Lost Civilization of Petra*, Edinburgh, 1996.

204 Colby: letter to author 18 February 2000.
British School of Archaeology: author interview with team member Carole Levinson, 4 December 1999.

205 Dan excavation: Magnusson, *BC*, pp. 159–61

206 Colby: letter to author, 18 February 2000.

209 Lion monument: Browning, *Petra*, pp. 210–11.
Lion and kingship: Bowker, *The Complete*, pp. 122–3. Williams, D. (ed.), *New Concise Bible Dictionary*, Oxford, 1989.

210 The terrace: Browning, *Petra* and Levy, *The Lost*.
Colby: letter to author, 18 February 2000.

212 Attuf Ridge shrine: Levy, *The Lost*, pp. 65–9. Browning, *Petra*, pp. 211– 16.

214 Krakatau eruption: Simkin, T. & Fiske, R. S., *Krakatau 1883: The Volcanic Eruption and its Effects*, Washington DC, 1983.

Nine

218 Martin, Michael: *The Book of Jasher*, Philadelphia, 1995.

219 Josephus, Flavius, *Jewish Antiquities* (trans. Feldman, L.), London, 1981.

224 Southern Graves: Browning, *Petra*, pp. 188–98.

Akkadian: Comrie, *The Major Languages of South Asia, the Middle East and Africa*.

Snake Monument: Browning, *Petra*, pp. 111–12.

225 Mangles: Irby, C. & Mangles, J., *Travels in Egypt and Nubia, Syria and the Holy Land*, London, 1823.

Pike, Henry, *The Monuments of Ancient Petra*, New York, 1924.

John Murrow interviewed by the author, 21 April 2000.

226 Roberts, David, *The Holy Land, Syria, Idumea, Arabia, Egypt and Nubia*, London, 1842.

227 Kinnear, John, *Cairo, Petra and Damascus*, London, 1841.

230 Martin, *The Book of Jasher*.

231 Wilson quoted in: Ballantine & James, *Idumea and Arabia*, Edinburgh, 1865, p. 81.

Ten

242 Nabateans: Browning, *Petra*.

243 Diodorus Siculus, *The Library of History*, Oxford, 1987.

Athenodorus quoted by Diodorus, *ibid*.

246 Sabean Stone: Levy, *The Lost*, pp. 63–5.

250 Akhenaten: Aldred, C., *Akhenaten and Nefertiti*, Brooklyn, 1973 and *Akhenaten, Pharaoh of Egypt*, London, 1968.

252 The Kabbalah: Hartley, Brian, *The Kabbalah*, London, 1971.

253 Akhenaten: Aldred, *Akhenaten*.

258 Diodorus: *The Library of History*.

Carter, W., *The Essenes*, New York, 1996, pp. 57–64.

259 The Dead Sea Scrolls: Hershel, S. (ed.), *Understanding the Dead Sea Scrolls*, New York, 1992.

260 Strabo, *Geographica*, trans. Jones, H., London, 1932.

Eleven

266 The brooch: Browning, *Petra*, p. 104–8.
Bennett, C. M., *Quarterly Proceedings of the British Institute for Archaeology and History in Amman*, Spring 1982.

267 Sabean Stone: Levy, *The Lost*, pp. 63–5
Menorah: Rogerson, *Chronicle*, p. 198.

268 Attuf Ridge site: Browning, *Petra*, pp. 212–16

269 Paul, a gentile: Brandon, S., 'Saint Paul, the Problem Figure of Christianity', *History Today*, October, 1961.

271 Stephen of Byzantium, *Ethnica*, London, 1925.
Amarna: Aldred, *Akhenaten*, ch. 1. Redford, *Akhenaten:The Heretic King*, ch. 8. Samson, J., *Amarna: City of Akhenaten and Nefertiti*, London 1972.

276 Diodorus: *The Library of History*.
Karen Varbles interview with author, 8 November 2000.

279 Hartley, *The Kabbalah*.

SELECT BIBLIOGRAPHY

Ackroyd, P. R. & Evans, C. F. (eds.), *The Cambridge History of the Bible*, Cambridge, 1970.

Aharoni, Y., *The Land of the Bible: A Historical Geography*, London, 1967.

Aharoni, Y., Avi-Yonah, M., Rainey, A. F. & Safrai, Z., *The Macmillan Bible Atlas*, New York, 1993.

Albright, W. F., *The Archaeology of Palestine*, Harmondsworth, 1956.
Yahweh and the Gods of Canaan, London, 1968.
Archaeology and the Religion of Israel, New York, 1969.

Aldred, C., *Akhenaten, Pharaoh of Egypt*, London, 1968.
Akhenaten, King of Egypt, London, 1986.

Anati, E., *Palestine Before the Hebrews*, London, 1963.

Anderson, G. W., *The History of the Religion of Israel*, Oxford, 1966.

Aune, D., *The New Testament in Its Literary Environment*, Philadelphia, 1987.

Avi-Yonah, M. (ed.), *Encyclopaedia of Archaeological Excavations in the Holy Land*, Oxford, 1976.

Bacon, E. (ed.), *The Great Archaeologists*, London, 1976.

Bagnall, R. S., *Egypt in Later Antiquity*, Princeton, 1993.

Bahat, D., *The Illustrated Atlas of Jerusalem*, New York, 1990.

Baikie, J., *The Amarna Age*, London, 1926.
Egyptian Antiquities in the Nile Valley, London, 1932.

Baines, J. & Malek, J., *Atlas of Ancient Egypt*, Oxford, 1980.

Barnes, J., *The Celts and Christianity*, London, 1968.

Bartlett, J., *The Bible: Faith and Evidence*, London, 1990.

Bartlett, W. H., *Forty Days in the Desert*, London, 1849.

Barnett, R., *Illustrations of Old Testament History*, London, 1977.

SELECT BIBLIOGRAPHY

Barrett, C. K., *The New Testament Background: Selected Documents*, New York, 1961.

Bean, G., *Aegean Turkey: An Archaeological Guide*, London, 1966.

Beebe, H. K., *The Old Testament*, London, 1970.

Ben-Dov, M., *In the Shadow of the Temple: The Discovery of Ancient Jerusalem*, London, 1985.

Bierbrier, M. L., *The Late New Kingdom in Egypt*, Warminster, 1975.

Biran, A., *Biblical Dan*, Jerusalem, 1994.

Boardman, J., *The Greeks Overseas*, Harmondsworth, 1964.

Bowker, J. (ed.), *The Complete Bible Handbook*, London, 1998.

Brammel, E. & Moule, C., *Jesus and the Politics of His Day*, Cambridge, 1984.

Brandon, S., *The Fall of Jerusalem and the Christian Church*, London, 1951.

Creation Legends of the Ancient Near East, London, 1963.

Breasted, J. H., *Ancient Records of Egypt*, Chicago, 1906.

Bright, J. A., *History of Israel*, London, 1972.

Brooke, R., *Popular Religion in Middle Ages*, London, 1984.

Brotherstone, G., *World Archaeoastronomy*, Cambridge, 1989.

Brown, F., *Hebrew and the English Lexicon of the Old Testament*, Oxford, 1906.

Bryant, A. E., *Natural Disasters*, Cambridge, 1991.

Buber, M., *Moses*, Oxford, 1946.

Bucaille, M., *Moses and Pharaoh: The Hebrews in Egypt*, Tokyo, 1994.

Burckhardt, J. L., *Travels in Syria and the Holy Land*, London, 1822.

Butlmann, R., *Jesus and the Word*, New York, 1958.

The History of the Synoptic Tradition, Oxford, 1963.

Carlson, J. & Ludwig, R., *Jesus and Faith*, New York, 1984.

Carter, W., *The Essenes*, New York, 1996.

Casson, L. & Hettich, E. L., *Excavations at Nessana*, Princeton, 1950.

Cassuto, U., *A Commentary on the Book of Exodus*, Jerusalem, 1961.

Castledon, R., *Minoans: Life in Bronze Age Crete*, London, 1990.

Cerny, J., *Hieratic Inscriptions from the Tomb of Tutankhamun*, Oxford, 1965.

Chester, D., *Volcanoes and Society*, London, 1993.

Childs, B., *Myth and Reality in the Old Testament*, London, 1959.

Clark, R., *Myth and Symbol in Ancient Egypt*, London, 1978.

Clayton, P., *Chronicle of the Pharaohs*, London, 1994.

Coburn, B., *Early Christianity in the Greek World*, New York, 1991.

Comay, J., *Who's Who in the Old Testament*, London, 1993.

Comrie, B. (ed.), *The Major Languages of South Asia, the Middle East and Africa*, London, 1990.

Cooney, J. D., *Amarna Reliefs from Hermopolis in American Collections*, Brooklyn, 1965.

Court, A., *Israel*, New York, 1985.

Curtis, A., *Ugarit: Ras Shamra*, Cambridge, 1985.

Daiches, D., *Moses, Man in the Wilderness*, London, 1975.

David, R., *Discovering Ancient Egypt*, London, 1993.

David, R. & David, A. E., *A Biographical Dictionary of Ancient Egypt*, London, 1992.

Davidson, H. E., *Gods and Myths in Northern Europe*, Harmondsworth, 1964.

Davidson, R. & Leaney, A. R. C., *The Penguin Guide to Modern Theology*, Harmondsworth, 1970.

Davies, G. I. (ed.), *Ancient Hebrew Inscriptions, Corpus and Concordance*, Cambridge, 1991.

Davies, N., *The Tomb of the Two Sculptors at Thebes*, New York, 1927. *The Tomb of the Vizier Ramose*, London, 1941.

Davies, P., *In Search of Ancient Israel*, Sheffield, 1992.

Dawson, W. R. & Uphill, E., *Who Was Who in Egyptology*, London, 1972.

Deissmann, A., *St Paul: A Study in Social and Religious History*, London, 1912.

Dickinson, O., *The Aegean Bronze Age*, Cambridge, 1994.

Diodorus Siculus, *The Library of History*, Oxford, 1987.

Dodson, A., *The Canopic Equipment of the Kings of Egypt*, London, 1994.

Dothan, T., *The Philistines and Their Material Culture*, London, 1982.

Doumas, C., *Thera, Pompeii of the Ancient Aegean*, London, 1983.

Downing, G., *Cynics and Christian Origins*, Edinburgh, 1992.

Driver, G., *Canaanite Myths and Legends*, Edinburgh, 1959.

Emery, W. B., *Archaic Egypt*, Harmondsworth, 1961.

Eusebius, *The History of the Church from Christ to Constantine*, tr. G. A. Williamson, Harmondsworth, 1965.

Evans, A., *The Palace of Minos*, London, 1935.

Evenari, M., Shanan, L. & Tadmore, N., *The Negev – Challenge of a Desert*, Harvard, 1982.

Faulkner, R. O., *The Ancient Egyptian Coffin Texts*, Warminster, 1977.

Finegan, J., *The Archaeology of the New Testament*, Princeton, 1969.

Fishbane, M., *Text and Texture, Close Readings of Selected Biblical Texts*, New York, 1979.

Fox, R. L., *Pagans and Christians*, New York, 1968.

Frankfort, H., *Kingship and the Gods*, Chicago, 1948.
Ancient Egyptian Religion, New York, 1961.

Frankfort, H. & Pendlebury, J., *The City of Akhenaten*, London, 1933.

Freedman, D. (ed.), *The Anchor Bible Dictionary*, New York, 1992.

Freud, S., *Moses and Monotheism*, London, 1939.

Freyne, S., *Galilee from Alexander the Great to Hadrian*,Wilmington, 1980.

Gardiner, A., *Egyptian Grammar*, Oxford, 1957.
Egypt of the Pharaohs, Oxford, 1961.

Glueck, N., *Rivers in the Desert: A History of the Negev*, New York, 1968.

Goldstein, M., *Jesus in the Jewish Tradition*, New York, 1950.

Grabar, A., *Christian Iconography*, London, 1969.

Grabbe, L., *Judaism from Cyrus to Hadrian*, Minneapolis, 1992.

Grant, M. (tr.), *Annals of Imperial Rome*, Harmondsworth, 1956.

Graves, R. (tr.), *The Twelve Caesars*, Harmondsworth, 1957.
The Greek Myths, Harmondsworth, 1960.

Graves, R. & Podro, J., *The Nazarene Gospel Restored*, London, 1953.

Gray, J., *The Canaanites*, London, 1964.

Greenberg, M., *The Hab/piru*, New Haven, 1955.

Hammond, P. C., *The Nabateans: Their History, Culture and Archaeology*, Gothenburg, 1973.

Harker, R., *Digging Up the Bible Lands*, London, 1972.

Harris, R., *Exploring the World of the Bible Lands*, London, 1995.

Hawkes, J., *Man and the Sun*, London, 1962.

Hayes, W. C., *Royal Sarcophagi of the Eighteenth Dynasty*, Princeton, 1935.

Hepper, N., *Illustrated Encyclopedia of Bible Plants*, Leicester, 1992.

Hershel, S. (ed.), *Understanding the Dead Sea Scrolls*, New York, 1992.

Herzog, C. & Gichon, M., *Battles of the Bible*, London, 1978.

Heschel, A., *The Prophets*, New York, 1962.

Hooke, S., *Babylonian and Assyrian Religion*, London, 1962.
Middle Eastern Mythology: From the Assyrians to the Hebrews, London, 1963.

Hooker, J. T., *Mycenaean Greece*, London, 1976.

Hopkins, D., *The Highlands of Canaan. Agricultural Life in the Early Iron Age*, Sheffield, 1985.

Hornung, E., *Conceptions of God in Ancient Egypt*, London, 1983.
The Valley of the Kings: Horizon of Eternity, New York, 1990.

Hutchison, R. W., *Prehistoric Crete*, Harmondsworth, 1962.

Ions, V., *Egyptian Mythology*, London, 1982.

Irby, C. & Mangles, J., *Travels in Egypt and Nubia, Syria and the Holy Land*, London, 1823.

James, E. O., *The Ancient Gods*, London, 1960.

Jones, A., *The Herods of Judea*, Oxford, 1938.

Jones, A. M. H., *The Decline of the Ancient World*, London, 1966.

Josephus, Flavius, *Against Apion*, tr. H. Thackeray, London, 1926.
Jewish Antiquities, tr. L. Feldman, London, 1981.
The Jewish War, tr. G. Williamson, Harmondsworth, 1981.

Kasher, A., *Edom, Arabia and Israel*, Jerusalem, 1988.

Kaufmann, Y., *The Religion of Israel, From its Beginnings to the Babylonian Exile*, Chicago, 1961.

Kedar, Y., *The Ancient Agriculture in the Negev Mountains*, Jerusalem, 1967.

Keller, W., *The Bible as History*, London, 1956.

Kemp, B. J., *Ancient Egypt: Anatomy of a Civilisation*, London, 1989.

Kennedy, A., *Petra, Its History and Monuments*, London, 1925.

Kenyon, K. M., *Digging Up Jericho*, London, 1957.
Archaeology in the Holy Land, London, 1965.

Excavations at Jericho, London, 1965.

The Bible and Recent Archaeology, London, 1978.

Khouly, A. el- & Martin G. T., *Excavations in the Royal Necropolis at El-Amarna*, Cairo, 1987.

Kidd, B., *Documents Illustrative of the History of the Church*, Oxford, 1920.

Knight, D. & Tucker, G. (eds.), *The Hebrew Bible and Its Modern Interpreters*, Philadelphia, 1985.

Kochav, S., *Israel: Splendours of the Holy Land*, London, 1995.

Kopp, C., *The Holy Places of the Gospels*, London, 1963.

Layard, A. H., *Early Adventures in Persia, Susiana and Babylonia*, London, 1840.

Levy, U., *The Lost Civilisation of Petra*, Edinburgh, 1999.

Lichtheim, M., *Ancient Egyptian Literature*, Berkeley, 1980.

Lloyd, S., *The Art of the Ancient Near East*, London, 1963.

Lucas, A. & Harriss, J. R., *Ancient Egyptian Materials and Industries*, London, 1989.

Maccoby, H., *Revolution in Judea: Jesus and the Jewish Resistance*, London, 1973.

Magnusson, M., *BC: The Archaeology of the Bible Lands*, London, 1977.

Marinatos, S., *Excavations at Thera*, Athens, 1973.

Martin, G. T., *The Royal Tomb at Amarna*, London, 1989.

The Hidden Tombs of Memphis, London, 1990.

May, H. G. (ed.), *Oxford Bible Atlas*, Oxford, 1974.

Mazar, A., *Archaeology of the Land of the Bible, 10,000–586 BCE*, New York, 1990.

Menzies, A. (tr.), *Origen*, London, 1897.

Mercer, S. A. B., *The Religion of Ancient Egypt*, London, 1949.

Meshorer, Y., *Nabatean Coins*, Jerusalem, 1975.

Metzger, B. & Coogan, M. (eds.), *The Oxford Companion to the Bible*, London, 1993.

Meyers, E., *The Oxford Encyclopedia of Archaeology in the Near East*, New York, 1995.

Millard, A., *Discoveries from the Time of Jesus*, Oxford, 1990.

Mitchell, T., *The Bible in the British Museum: Interpreting the Evidence*, London, 1998.

Moorey, P. R. S., *Biblical Lands*, London, 1975.

Moule, C., *The Birth of the New Testament*, London, 1962.

Murray, M., *Petra, The Rock City of Edom*, London, 1939.

Myers, B., *Galilee at the Time of Christ*, New York, 1998.

Negev, A. (ed.), *Archaeological Encyclopaedia of the Holy Land*, London, 1973.
Nabatean Archaeology Today, London, 1986.

Nims, C. F., *Thebes of the Pharaohs*, London, 1965.

Noth, M., *The History of Israel*, London, 1960.

Oats, J., *Babylon*, London, 1978.

Page, D. L., *The Santorini Volcano and the Desolation of Minoan Crete*, London, 1970.

Pattie, T. S., *Manuscripts of the Bible*, London, 1979.

Peet, T. E., *The City of Akhenaten*, London, 1951.

Petrie, W. M. F., *Tell el-Amarna*, London, 1894.
Researches in Sinai, London, 1906.

Phillips, G., *Act of God*, London, 1998.
The Marian Conspiracy, London, 2000.

Plankoff, A., *Egyptian Religious Texts and Representations*, Princeton, 1968.

Playton, N., *Zakros: The Discovery of a Lost Palace of Ancient Crete*, New York, 1971.

Polano, H., *The Talmud: Selections*, London, 1876.

Porter, B. & Moss, R. L. B., *Topographical Bibliography of Ancient Egyptian Hieroglyphic Texts, Reliefs and Paintings. I: The Theban Necropolis*, Oxford, 1960.

Posener, G., *A Dictionary of Egyptian Civilisation*, London, 1962.

Prichard, J. B. (ed.), *Ancient Near Eastern Texts Relating to the Old Testament*, Princeton, 1969.

Redford, D. B., *A Study of the Biblical Story of Joseph*, Leiden, 1970.
History and Chronology in the 18th Dynasty of Egypt, Toronto, 1977.
Akhenaten: The Heretic King, Princeton, 1984.

Pharaonic King-Lists, Annals and Day-Books, Ontario, 1986.

Egypt, Canaan and Israel in Ancient Times, Princeton, 1992.

Renfrew, A. C., *Archaeology and Language*, London, 1987.

Rogerson, J., *Old Testament Criticism in the Nineteenth Century*, London, 1984.

Chronicle of the Old Testament Kings, London, 1999.

Rogerson, J. & Davies, P., *The Old Testament World*, Cambridge, 1989.

Romer, J., *Valley of the Kings*, London, 1981.

Rowley, H. H., *From Joseph to Joshua*, London, 1950.

Rubin, R., *The Negev as a Settled Land*, Jerusalem, 1990.

Sandars, N., *The Sea Peoples: Warriors of the Ancient Mediterranean*, New York, 1985.

Schmidt, J. D., *Ramesses II*, London, 1973.

Scholem, G., *The Messianic Idea in Judaism*, New York, 1971.

Schreiber, J., *The Laws of the Jews*, New York, 1956.

Schurer, E., *The History of the Jewish People in the Age of Jesus Christ: 175 BC–AD 135*, 4 vols, London, 1987.

Shanks, H., *Understanding the Dead Sea Scrolls*, New York, 1992.

Shanks, H., Deser, W., Baruch, H. & McCarter, P., *The Rise of Ancient Israel*, Washington, 1992.

Sherwin-White, A. N., *Roman Society and Roman Law in the New Testament*, Oxford, 1963.

Simkin, T. & Fiske, R. S., *Krakatau 1883: The Volcanic Eruption and Its Effects*, Washington, 1983.

Smallwood, E. M., *The Jews Under Roman Rule*, London, 1976.

Smith, E. G., *The Royal Mummies*, Cairo, 1912.

Smith, G. A., *The Historical Geography of the Holy Land*, London, 1935.

Smith, G. D., *The Teachings of the Catholic Church*, London, 1948.

Smith, M., *The Early History of God; Yahweh and Other Deities in Ancient Israel*, San Francisco, 1990.

Smith, R. W. & Redford, D. B., *The Akhenaten Temple Project*, Toronto, 1988.

Soferman, J., *The Jewish Dictionary*, New York, 1984.

Spencer, A. J., *Early Egypt: The Rise of Civilisation in the Nile Valley*, London, 1993.

Stambaugh, J. & Balch, D., *The Social World of the First Christians*, London, 1986.

Stephen of Byzantium, *Ethnica*, London, 1925.

Strabo, *Geographica*, tr. H. Jones, London, 1932.

Strauss, D. F., *The Life of Jesus Critically Examined*, London, 1846.

Strong, J., *The New Strong's Exhaustive Concordance of the Bible*, Nashville, 1990.

Tacitus, *The Annals of Imperial Rome*, tr. M. Grant, Harmondsworth, 1956.

Taylor, J., *Petra*, London, 1993.

Thomas, C., *Britain and Ireland in Early Christian Times*, London, 1971.

Thomas, D. W. (ed.), *Documents from Old Testament Times*, London, 1958.

Unterman, A., *A Dictionary of Jewish Lore and Legend*, New York, 1997.

VanderKam, J., *The Dead Sea Scrolls Today*, London, 1994.

Van Seters, J., *The Hyksos*, London, 1966.

Vermes, G., *The Dead Sea Scrolls in English*, Harmondsworth, 1962.
Jesus the Jew, Philadelphia, 1973.

Waddell, W. G. (tr.), *Manetho*, London, 1940.

Wainwright, G. A., *The Sky Religion in Egypt*, Cambridge, 1938.

Weigall, A., *The Life and Times of Akhenaten*, London, 1922.

Wilkinson, A., *Pharaonic Egypt: The Bible and Christianity*, Jerusalem, 1985.

Wilkinson, J., *Jerusalem as Jesus Knew It: Archaeology as Evidence*, London, 1982.

Williams, D. (ed.), *New Concise Bible Dictionary*, Leicester, 1989.

Williamson, G. (tr.), *The History of the Church from Christ to Constantine*, Harmondsworth, 1965.

Wilson, E., *The Scrolls from the Dead Sea*, New York, 1955.

Wilson, I., *Jesus: The Evidence*, London, 1984.
The Exodus Enigma, London, 1985.

Winckler, H., *Tell el-Amarna Letters*, London, 1896.

Winlock, H. E., *The Rise and Fall of the Middle Kingdom in Thebes*, New York, 1947.

Wiseman, D. (ed.), *Peoples of the Old Testament*, Oxford, 1973.

Wortham, J. D., *British Egyptology 1549–1906*, Newton Abbot, 1972.

Yadin, Y., *The Art of War in Biblical Lands*, London, 1963.
  Hazor: Great Citadel of the Bible, London, 1975.

INDEX